CRACKING THE SHORT STORY MARKET

IAIN PATTISON

WB

First Published in Great Britain in 1999 by
The Writers Bureau Limited of
Sevendale House,
7 Dale Street,
Manchester, M1 1JB

2nd Edition published 2002

Tel: 0161-228-2362. Fax: 0161-228-3533.
Email: books@writersbureau.com

A catalogue record for this book is available from the British Library.

ISBN 1 903119 00 6

Cover design by: Essential Design
Printed and bound in Great Britain by:
Status Design & Print, Pelham Street, Bolton, BL3 3JB.

CONTENTS

What They Said About Cracking the Short Story Market

"Crammed full of goodies and written with an infectious enthusiasm. This is a must have handbook for beginners which will save them much anguish and error, and will give even the more experienced writer something to think about." *Quality Women's Fiction.*

"Thanks for such a marvellous book ... My knowledge of the writing industry has moved forward in leaps and bounds. I intend to keep my copy close at hand." *Gordon Lander*

"Lively and entertaining. I spent most of the weekend reading it!" *Miv Knight*

"Probably the most comprehensive and up-to-date guide available to writing for the UK short story market ... an essential buy for any aspiring short story writer." *Nick Daws*

"Iain Pattison writes about all aspects of writing and selling in a humorous way ... I would really recommend this book to all of you who wish to write and sell short stories, but don't exactly know how and where to start."
Review Section - Amazon Books Website

"At Swanwick Summer School book fair there was a queue the length of the main hall for Iain's best-selling book Cracking the Short Story Market."
Pamela Payne in The Woman Writer, the Journal of the Society of Women Writers and Journalists

"This is an excellent book for anyone wanting to know more about the craft of short story writing. For the beginner Iain makes success seem possible, and his tips will prove thought provoking for the more experienced writer ... If you only buy one How To book this year, make it "Cracking the Short Story Market." *Acorn Magazine*

A GOLDEN AGE

It's an amazing time to be a short story writer – arguably the most exciting time there has ever been. The world of short fiction has burst into dynamic new life, creating an explosion of thrilling opportunities. It's a new Golden Age.

Everywhere you look there are magazines bulging with exciting new fiction, competitions popping up with huge cash prizes, and cutting-edge cyberspace e-zines crying out for work from fresh, undiscovered talent.

And with a flood of new small press publications being launched every month, the possibilities just keep growing and growing. Story-tellers have never had it so good – have never had a better chance of seeing their work appear in print.

What's more, the advent of the Internet and electronic submissions now means that you can sell stories to editors on the other side of the globe just as easily as you can back home. Suddenly a whole world is open, ready and waiting.

With top women's magazines paying more than £250 a script and top competitions offering up to £5,000 in prizes, the attractions are too lucrative to ignore. So I don't blame you if you're wondering how **you** can get in on the action. How can you write entertaining and profitable short stories? And if you are already selling some of your work, how can you sell even more?

Well, this book aims to show you how to make your mark in this most stimulating, sparkling and lively branch of writing.

I regularly judge national short story competitions and I'm a fiction contributor to BBC Radio 4 and magazines such as *Acclaim*, *Woman's Own*, *Woman*, *Woman's Weekly*, *Chat*, *Take A Break* and *My Weekly*. I teach creative writing at night school and at university workshops. I also tutor for one of the country's leading writing schools.

In the course of the next 23 chapters I'm going to share some of my short story secrets, showing you how you can break into this mushrooming literary market.

I'll take you from finding an original story idea and shaping it into an entertaining tale, to deciding which magazine is the most likely market for you. I'll show you how to submit your script in the most attractive way possible. I'll even tell you how to get an agent.

Together we'll target the most lucrative publications – women's magazines. We'll study what they look for, who they're aimed at and work out how you can sell your work to them. Imagine having your name, as a contributor, in a magazine that's on the coffee tables of thousands of homes throughout the country.

We'll also look at writing for children, getting your work published on the Internet, how to win competitions, writing for radio and how to break into the world of small press magazines with chapters on erotica, science fiction and horror.

As well as useful hints on story-telling technique, we will examine some of the most common stylistic faults made by newcomers and I'll offer advice on how to make your work pacier, more polished, more focused and attention-grabbing.

I can't promise you fame and riches, but if you follow the techniques and tips in this book, I can guarantee that your stories will be head and shoulders above the vast majority on the fiction editor's desk.

Writing is fun so this book aims to entertain as well as inform. I've kept the technical language and concepts simple and, hopefully, easy to understand. Unlike some other books on the market that are packed with baffling waffle and "rocket science" explanations I've concentrated on the main points you need to know.

Okay, so there may be 15 different ways to plot a story but you only want to know the most effective techniques. The rest belong in an encyclopedia.

Treat this book as a working tool and underline passages that particularly appeal to you or make notes in the margin if it helps. I'm sure you'll want to dip back into the book time and time again as you experiment with new markets and new types of writing so I've included a handy summary section at the end of each chapter with all the main information presented in "bullet" points.

This means you can revise a certain section in a few minutes. But please actually read the chapters in full at least once. I know it's tempting if you lead a busy life just to skim through the summaries, but you'll only derive the maximum benefit if you take a little time to read and digest all the information.

There are also exercises for you to try at the end of each chapter, designed to reinforce the techniques you've learnt and let you hone your writing skills. They aren't compulsory. No-one is going to mark them out of ten or tell you off if you don't attempt them but I think you'll find them very enjoyable – so please have a go. You may find it useful to go back after a few months and have a second attempt at an early exercise to see how much your writing has improved and your style developed.

Now, I want to make two apologies right at the start. Firstly, I'd like to be able to give you specific magazine names and details but it's just not practical. Magazines come and go so quickly – and change editors and requirements so rapidly – that any "target markets" style information would probably be out of date in no time.

For that reason, I'll talk about the general principles of writing and selling great short stories. You'll have to do your own up-to-date market research when the time comes. (Don't worry – I'll show you how in chapter two.)

My second apology is about political correctness – or my lack of it. I don't know about you, but I find it distracting to read any text where the author has made his writing stilted and ugly by scrupulously trying to keep a balance between the sexes.

I'd rather refer to editors and writers as the masculine *he* as much as possible rather than have to keep repeating *he/she* and *his/her* and *him/her*. I know some people won't like this, so I'll say a pre-emptive *sorry* to them.

If this male bias irritates or offends you please feel free to mentally replace every *he* with a *she* as you read it. I won't mind, honestly!

Okay, that's enough introductory spiel from me. I know you're keen to dive in, so let's get cracking ...

1

COOKING UP A WINNER

Writing good short stories isn't difficult. In fact, it's within everyone's grasp – if you know the right techniques.

Basically, fiction writing is a mechanical process that anyone can master. True, you need that spark of creativity – the gem of a quirky idea – to get you started. But after that, actually turning the idea into a saleable piece of prose is merely a question of following basic rules. Stick to them and you can't go far wrong.

I always draw a parallel with cookery. Finished dishes can look amazing – especially if a top chef has lavished time and effort on them. But although the colours, tastes, textures and shapes all blend together to provide a treat for the senses, the chef hasn't used sorcery or paranormal skills to create the feast. All he's done is use ordinary ingredients plus a little experience and easily copied cooking techniques.

Given a recipe and access to the same ingredients, most competent cooks could re-create the same dish. It may not look quite as appealing the first time you make it – but after a few attempts most cooks would have a passable version that tasted and smelt great.

The same is true for short story writing. You may not be able to re-create every nuance of the haunting prose of highly experienced writers – that only comes with years of practice – but there's no reason why you can't write short stories that are technically competent, containing all the right ingredients in the correct amounts and in the correct order.

In later chapters I shall be looking at all the individual ingredients and techniques in some detail, but for now – by way of introduction – let's look briefly at the necessary facets of a gripping yarn.

Using this quick and easy recipe you should be able to rustle up a tasty short story. Even if you are already turning out acceptable tales, this 13-point checklist will enable you to polish and improve your prose.

So let's get cooking ...

A good short story has:

- *A single narrative thread.* Because the space in a short story is so limited – perhaps as little as 850 words – there isn't time to explore the stories of several different characters or look at how your main character reacts in a series of different environments.

  Stick to one storyline and don't deviate from it: Helen plots revenge against the woman who stole her job; Cynthia decides whether to keep the purse she found in the street; Gary faces up to his arch rival in a motorbike race to the death.

  If you find yourself widening your plotline – maybe looking at the lives of all the competitors in Gary's bike race – then you're starting to write a novel. Anything over 4,000 words is difficult to sell. Anything over 6,000 words is really a novella.

- *A short timescale.* A short story is like a snapshot – it's a moment frozen in time. It examines how a character deals with events at a particularly trying or traumatic period of his life. It isn't his life story, or a character study, or a chronicle of his various adventures.

  All the best short stories are tightly focused – one storyline covering no more than a few days. The most gripping yarns recount events happening to your hero in a few crucial hours.

- *Only one mood, pace and style.* A short story should have the same feel throughout. It shouldn't start as an emotionally packed tale of grief then suddenly switch to knockabout comedy.

  It shouldn't speed up and slow down erratically or switch from a tightly written story with short, punchy sentences and simple vocabulary to a flowing, languorous piece of prose oozing baroque expressions and overblown imagery. The moment you change gear or the voice you use, you give the reader a jolt.

- *Brief descriptions.* A short story isn't the place to show off your descriptive skills. Long descriptions kill the pace and divert the reader's attention from the plot.

You should always aim to get the maximum effect with the minimum number of words. You may want to spend a page describing every aspect of an old woman's appearance but the only useful information you'll have given the reader is that the woman was elderly. You could achieve the same effect in six words: *Ethel had salt and pepper curls.*

● *Minimum background information.* We're only going to spend five minutes or so with the characters of a short story – not marry them or let them invest our life savings – so it's not necessary to know everything about them.

Only give the background information that is relevant to the plot. If the story is about how John copes with the break-up of his marriage, the fact that he took six attempts to get his 100-metres swimming badge or that he is allergic to bananas is of no importance.

The trick is to maintain a good balance between keeping information tight and giving enough *relevant* facts about a character so that the reader can visualise him. In chapter five we'll look at some techniques for making characters come across as real, living, three-dimensional individuals and not just stereotypes.

● *Four characters or less.* There just isn't the time or space in a short story to meet an army of new faces and memorise just who each person is and their relationship to other characters. Think how difficult it is to remember all the names of people you are introduced to at a party. That's the problem the reader has if you populate your stories with a huge cast of players.

Two is an ideal number of characters for a magazine short story – that allows you to use dialogue as they talk and react to each other. Three is great for eternal triangle tales, but four is really the limit.

● *No sub-plots, hidden morals or sub-text.* Keep it simple. Tell the tale in the most direct form possible and don't try to be too clever or erudite. The plot is of paramount importance so don't allow anything to interfere with the swift and smooth telling of the narrative.

It may be that your writing speaks on several different levels and reveals all sorts of truths to the reader. If that happens, then great. But don't aim for it deliberately. Let it happen naturally. Don't give your work a message. Don't use symbolism. Don't set out to be all meaningful and deep – the chances are you'll end up with a significant tale that no-one wants to read.

● *No lengthy run-up or wind-down.* The most common reason why short stories fail to grab the reader is that writers waste those precious first few sentences in setting the scene.

Instead of getting the story off and running, they hold everything up by having an unnecessary description of the weather, or the town where the story is taking place, or the main character's mood, or his appearance, or his family history. Get into the plot right from the first sentence.

Also, know when your story is over. End it as swiftly as possible after the main character's crisis is resolved. Don't let it drift on aimlessly for several extra sentences until it runs out of puff. Just like a good joke, a short story should have a punchline.

● *Taut and punchy dialogue.* There's little point having an enticing title and an attention-grabbing intro if every time your main character speaks he sends your reader to sleep. Dialogue has to be fast-paced, exciting and dramatic.

Dialogue is a great way to inject emotion into a story. It helps build mood and tension. Aim for *sound-bite* snatches of speech which really bring your characters to life – not mundane chit-chat.

Don't even consider having a story that doesn't contain dialogue. It'll be a guaranteed turn-off.

● *As few points of view as possible.* A short story tells what happens when the main character faces a certain set of events. We should view those events through his eyes – and his eyes only.

Don't start viewing the action from another character's perspective. As well as being potentially confusing, it distances the reader from the hero – breaking the empathy link. When a story works well, it usually has a single viewpoint, with the reader imagining himself as the hero. Only switch viewpoints when it is absolutely vital to the plot and never have more than one viewpoint switch per story.

● *A main character facing up to a conflict.* Conflict is anything that upsets the smooth running of the main character's life. Maybe a bill arrives out of the blue that he can't pay. Maybe he doesn't get the promotion he was counting on. Maybe his fling with his secretary has been discovered by a blackmailer.

Whatever the conflict is – low-key or highly dramatic – it must put your main character on the spot. It must worry him. Dealing with the conflict should force him into acting in extreme or unusual ways and should pose a moral or physical dilemma. He is faced with hard decisions.

● *The plot starting at the point of conflict.* As this conflict is the basis of the story, the plot should begin when the main character faces his dilemma – should he tell his wife about the affair or lure the blackmailer into a trap?

It should end when the decision has been taken and the threat has been neutralized. For example, the blackmailer is dead or has been bought off. Or, the affair is made public and the main character resolves to face his wife's wrath. When the crisis is over, so is the story.

● *The character resolving his own conflicts.* Good fiction is about how human beings react to challenge – about ordinary people in extraordinary circumstances.

Make your main character solve his own problems – especially if it forces him to be ingenious and overcome some of his fears. Don't let him off the hook by having a lucky twist of fate rescue him from his impending doom.

Exercises

Pick three different types of short stories and read through them taking note of all the "ingredients". (You could look at a typical romance story in a women's magazine, a twist-in-the-tail story, a horror story, an erotic story ... just try to look at three *different* types.) Study how the writers constructed their tales.

Have they used *all* the ingredients listed in this chapter? See if they've broken these rules. If so, ask yourself if you think they got away with it. If not, try to say why they failed and suggest what would improve the stories. Have a go at rewriting the tales with your improvements.

Summary

✓ Writing good short stories is within everyone's grasp – if you know the right techniques.

✓ It is a mechanical process that anyone can master if you follow simple basic rules and use the right "ingredients".

A good short story has:

✓ *A single narrative thread.* It tells what happens to one main character, dealing with one crisis or dilemma in his life.

✓ *A short timescale.* All the best short stories are tightly focused – one storyline covering no more than a few days.

✓ *Only one mood, pace and style.* Try to keep the same feel, atmosphere and speed throughout.

✓ *Brief descriptions.* Long descriptions kill the pace and divert the reader's attention from the plot.

✓ *Minimum background information.* Only give facts that are relevant to the plot or which allow readers to visualise the characters.

✓ *Four characters or less.* The fewer the people, the more we care about them.

✓ *No sub-plots, hidden morals or sub-text.* Keep it simple and direct. Don't set out to be meaningful.

✓ *No lengthy run-up or wind-down.* Start crisply at the moment the action kicks off and end the second the crisis is resolved.

✓ *Taut and punchy dialogue.* Speech injects tension and emotion. Aim for exciting *sound-bite* snatches of dialogue.

- ✓ *As few points of view as possible.* See events through the main character's eyes. Only switch viewpoint when it is vital.

- ✓ *The main character facing up to a conflict.* Put your hero on the spot – he should be faced with hard decisions.

- ✓ *The plot starting at the point of conflict.* Begin when the main character faces his dilemma. That's when the drama begins.

- ✓ *The character resolving his own conflicts.* Make your hero solve his own problems. Don't have a lucky twist of fate rescue him from his doom.

2

MARKET RESEARCH

Now I know what you're thinking – isn't there some mistake here? Surely a chapter on market research should come at the end of the book. What's the point of researching outlets for your stories before you've even written them?

Well, I can understand you thinking that. It's a common attitude among new writers – usually unsuccessful new writers. They think that all the effort should go into crafting a beautifully moving piece of prose, and that artistry, creativity and emotional depth is all that matters. Grubby, mundane, concerns about actually selling the work can be left until later.

It's easy, they argue, just bung the finished story in an envelope and post it off. If the first magazine doesn't like it, try another ... and another ... and another, eventually someone, somewhere will like it. It's a great story, after all. It can't fail. Right?

Wrong! It *can* fail and it *will* fail. Just because your story is a good read doesn't mean it is right for publication. Great stories are rejected by magazines every day of the week.

To be commercially successful, yarns must conform to a number of editorial requirements – on length, tone, character type and content. And unless you tailor your work to fit what fiction editors really want, they will quite simply post it back unread.

All that artistic effort, emotional soul-searching and creativity will be a complete waste of time if your story ends up dumped at the back of a drawer instead of printed on a magazine page. Trust me on this one. The easier, and more likely, way to succeed in writing is to do your market research first – before you even so much as turn your computer on. Find out what editors want and then write it.

Do your homework so you can avoid upsetting the editor of a small press sci-fi monthly who hates stories on killer robots or the horror mag publisher who goes mad every time he sees a reworking of Dracula. Save yourself the embarrassment of sending a tale of a young couple renovating a haunted house to a magazine which only prints stories about old age pensioners overcoming adversity. And don't trip up by sending a story which breaks the magazine's taboos and is twice the length of fiction it normally prints.

It sounds ridiculously simple but it's a lesson that many budding scribes have to learn the hard way – as they paper their front rooms with rejection slips. I'm trying to save you that heartbreak. That's why this chapter comes at the front of the book.

Market research without tears

Step One: Look at the magazines.
So how do you go about market research? Well, it depends on the market you want to aim at.

E-zines are easy – everything you need is there on the web site. Chances are there will be a section telling you what type of fiction the editor wants, who the readers are and what the e-zine's "ethos" is. But with print magazines you need to do some detective work. Your first step is to browse through the magazines on the newsagents' shelf, familiarising yourself with them. You won't be able to read each magazine from cover to cover but you will be able to get a general feel for what each publishes. Look at both the features and the short stories.

When you've selected a particular title that prints the type of stories you like – mystery, ghost yarns, sting-in-the-tail, humour, romance, horror, science fiction, relationship stories – buy the magazine and take it home. Failing that, sharpen your elbows and refuse to budge from the shelf until you've read it from cover to cover.

You may also want to try the local reference library. Some keep a reasonably comprehensive and up-to-date selection of magazines which you can study for free.

But please, please, please don't use magazines you find in dentists' surgeries and doctors' waiting rooms unless they are the current issue. A dog-eared copy from twelve months before won't give the current, accurate information you need on what the magazine is publishing now. There may have been a total editorial revamp in that year. The magazine may have stopped carrying fiction or even have ceased publication altogether.

If literary magazines or small press science fiction, horror or comedy titles are more to your liking, your first step in market research is to sit down at your typewriter and compose a few letters. I'm afraid that there's no *free* way to research subscription-only magazines so you'll have to write off for back issues. Fortunately, most editors of small press magazines offer back copies at a discount. Usually these cost only a few pounds.

The addresses of small press mags are relatively easy to find. Writing magazines often carry adverts for small press publications, you can find a huge number by trawling through the Internet, and reference books like the *Writers' and Artists' Yearbook* and *The Writer's Handbook* have details of the better known small magazines.

You can save a lot of time and effort by buying *The Small Press Guide* – a detailed look at small press magazines – published by *Writers' Bookshop* and available through most bookstores. This is updated annually.

Step Two: See what makes it tick.
Read at least four consecutive copies of the magazine you've selected. Get a feel for the type of stories it publishes, paying particular attention to the mood, setting, style, plot and the type of characters which usually appear. See if you can spot similarities or trends which run through the stories.

Sometimes these similarities will be obvious (the main characters are always young housewives or middle-aged businessmen) but even if all the stories appear totally different at first glance, you'll find they have connecting features which only become apparent when you analyse them at length.

Stories may be set in varying locations or in different eras, but still all feature underdogs who have to fight against injustice to triumph. They may all predict a nightmare future for mankind if pollution and technology are not kept in check. Tales may show that even the most bitter family rift can be healed with patience and understanding, or that everyone is capable of redemption, no matter how terrible a life they've led.

These recurring themes may be deliberate, or the editor may not even be aware of them. If you can spot the *narrative trend* of a magazine you'll have a good idea of what appeals to a particular editor and be able to write something to suit.

Don't stop after you've studied the fiction. Analyse *all* the content of the magazine – articles, reader's letters, reviews and competitions all give you important background information about your audience. Try to get a mental picture of the average reader. Ask yourself: who buys this?

In mainstream publications, especially, look carefully at the advertisements. They offer vital clues to the target readership. Advertising agencies spend a small fortune making sure their messages reach the right audience. Use their expertise to your advantage.

Are the adverts for luxury goods like sports cars or basics like cornflakes? This tells you the income of the average reader. Are holiday ads for ordinary destinations like Spain or for exotic locations such as Peru? This tells you whether the readers are home-based or more outgoing and adventurous.

Disneyland Paris will obviously advertise in magazines read by parents of small children while Saga holidays will advertise in publications read by their grandparents.

Step Three: Home in on your target.
Having identified exactly who reads the magazine, think what topics would interest them. What life do they lead? What problems do they face? What are their dreams and ambitions? What are their fears?

Create your stories around these elements – involving people of the same age, sex, background and careers. Set your stories in the typical household of that average reader. Make the hero or heroine of your story someone who would read the magazine.

You know what they eat and what they drive and where they go on holiday. The advertisers have told you. You know what health and work issues worry them – it's in the articles.

Pretend you are an actor studying to play the role of that reader. Once you've got inside his or her head, you're three-quarters of the way to writing a short story that will click with them.

Be methodical in your market research

Jot down various key points you've learnt about the magazine you're analysing. You'll be surprised at how much you've deduced about your target audience just from looking at the contents.

You may find it useful to devise a market research form like the one printed here. It's a great way of concentrating your thoughts. As you fill in each category you'll soon discover what information is still missing and pinpoint vital areas that you might have overlooked in your read-through.

MARKET RESEARCH FORM

Name of publication:
Address:
Editor/fiction editor's name: his/her full name.
Frequency and type: glossy woman's weekly, colour, well produced.
Length: 80 pages.
Apparent readership: working class and middle class women over 30.
Type of advertising: list what products are advertised and what these items tell you about the readers.
Does the magazine accept unsolicited scripts? Check in a reference book, or ring up the editorial department and ask.
Type of stories: sting in the tail, romance, horror, ghost, family relationship, etc.
Style: are the stories humorous or serious? Are they realistic or more cartoon-like?
Number of stories per issue: three.
Story length: 1,500 words maximum.
Are the stories by celebrities or ordinary writers? If the stories are by famous novelists or TV personalities this may suggest the magazine won't be interested in submissions from newcomers.
Language/vocabulary level: direct simple language – no long words. A tendency towards short sentences and short paragraphs.
Any running themes? Yes, family is more important than work. True happiness comes through love, not wealth or belongings.
Articles: if the publication also carries articles, what subjects do they cover? Can these topics suggest ideas to you for short stories?
Other contents: do the reader's letters, health pages, problem pages, competitions or advice columns tell you anything about

the background and concerns of the average reader? Do they give you plot ideas?

Do you want to write for this magazine? Yes – the style of fiction appeals to me because ...

What story ideas do you have that would be suitable? A woman is apprehensive about going back to work after having children, she struggles to cope at first, but finds her child-discipline skills come in handy in the quarrelsome boardroom.

Having got a feel for the magazine it's a good idea to look more closely at the stories and study the individual elements. Pay special attention to:

- How many characters the story features.
- What the main character is like – age/gender/class/job/personality, etc.
- Are the characters realistic or larger than life?
- Even if they are larger than life, do they still act and talk in a way that's believable?
- Is the story set in the present day, future or in the past?
- Is the setting exotic and glamorous or down to earth?
- Is the plot complicated or straightforward?
- How much conflict does the story contain?
- How quickly is the central dilemma or problem introduced?
- How much dialogue is used? Is it dramatic and does it push forward the plot?
- Is the opening attention-grabbing?
- Does the ending satisfy?

We'll be looking at all these elements in more detail in later chapters so don't worry if you aren't already an expert in dialogue, plotting or characterisation. The point of the exercise at the moment is to help you study a story and see more than you'd normally spot as a casual reader.

It's a good idea to read any tale twice – the first time to take in the plot and enjoy the experience. The second time you can look at the author's techniques and see what ingredients he used to create the story. Some people call this *deconstructing* a story. I prefer to think of it merely as finding out what makes the story tick!

You might find it useful to think: what was it about this story that made the editor want to buy it? What attracted him?

Don't let yourself off the hook with the glib reply: *it obviously fitted what he was looking for*! Why did it fit? When you know that, you'll be well on your way to writing stories that sell.

Empathy is everything

Certain magazines, who want to attract a younger readership, tinker with reader's letters. They remove any references that suggest the author is over thirty five. Letters that begin: *My four-year-old grand-daughter said something hilarious the other day* become *My four-year-old daughter said something hilarious the other day.*

These editors know how important it is to make the content of the magazine speak to its readers. Readers must be able to identify with every word printed. They must think: *everyone else who reads this is just like me.*

This is especially true of the short stories. There should be nothing in the tale that jars with the readers' image of the world or that suggests it was written for a different audience.

Fiction editors even go to the lengths of scrutinising and changing the names of characters. They know that the names must be right – must conjure up the image of a person who is similar to the average reader.

Hence a young, female, upwardly mobile, city dweller who works in an office and has power lunches is unlikely to feel much empathy for a main character called Doris (apologies to all Dorises everywhere).

In the same way, a rural grandmother who is into crafts and cookery, is unlikely to take to a mobile-phone-clutching, shoulder-padded Nikki.

Study guidelines

At the same time as you are studying a magazine, send off for its guideline sheets for potential fiction contributors. Always remember to enclose a sae. Also check on the Internet. Sometimes larger magazines have their guidelines on their web sites for you to download.

Guidelines take some of the graft and guesswork out of market research. They set out just what sort of fiction the editor is looking for, and more importantly, what type of fiction he or she *doesn't* want to see.

The information they contain (see example below) usually covers such topics as:

- Story length
- Preferred style of presentation
- The genre of story required
- The preferred age/background of main characters
- Hackneyed plots to avoid
- Taboo subjects to avoid (see chapter twelve)*
- The ideal ingredients a story should have to appeal to that particular magazine
- Details on payment/serial rights
- Preferred times of submission
- Fiction editor's name
- Other useful background information

Guideline Example

Wow-Wee!!! Magazine Fiction Guidelines

Wow-Wee!!! is a bright, lively monthly magazine read by fun-loving women in their late teens and early twenties. Our readers are more concerned with having a good time and being fashionable than saving the planet or worrying about burning social issues.

This doesn't, however, mean that writers should assume that Wow-Wee!!! readers are empty headed or uncaring. Stories should never talk down to them or be too frivolous.

We like our stories to be witty, exciting and have a large dash of humour. The reader should be gripped from the first sentence. Romance is always popular, and thrillers, sci-fi, and ghost stories are acceptable – as long as the accent is on fun. No depressing tales or angst-ridden characters please.

Sting-in-the-tail, coffee-break stories are a particular favourite but don't send stories written in the first person or tales packed with technical detail or lengthy descriptions. Stories must be fast-paced and intriguing.

Avoid the old, tired plots of the conman who is himself conned or the murderer who is killed first by his potential victim. These have been done to death.

Preferred story lengths are 1,000-1,200 words for sting-in-the-tail scripts and a maximum of 3,000 words for romances and all other categories. Payment, upon publication, is £200 per 1,000 words.

All work should be double spaced and submitted with a covering letter and stamped, addressed, return envelope.

Abi Rhode
Fiction Editor

Don't rely solely on guidelines

Fiction guidelines are an invaluable aid to writers and can prevent you from making the most basic mistakes when tailoring your work to appeal to a certain publication. But please don't think that you can use guidelines as a way of avoiding the slog of market research. You still have to study the magazines and get a feel for them.

No guideline, no matter how detailed, will tell you if the tone of your fiction is right. You must see what is already being printed and compare your work to the successful stories.

As one literary magazine urges: *The clearest guide to what we are looking for is the stories that we publish in each issue. Study what we print – that's what we want.*

Reference books

Books such as *The Writer's Handbook* and the *Writers' and Artists' Yearbook* are useful as a starting point for market research but they are limited in the information they contain on any one magazine. Their most important role is in telling you which magazines don't accept fiction or only accept fiction from writers with agents.

As such books come out only once a year and have to be compiled well ahead of publication time, they are often out of date when it comes to fine details like the names of fiction editors. So don't think you can use one of these books as an alternative to doing proper, thorough market research. You'll never get a feel for a magazine by reading five lines of reference book entry. Remember, you can always phone the editorial desk of a magazine and check the name of the editor if you are unsure. It's better to do this than get it wrong.

Still think you don't need to do your homework?

It's a matter of great regret and annoyance to all writing tutors that no matter how many times people are told not to fire off material blind there are always a hard-core who ignore the advice. People still send off unsuitable stories to magazines they've never seen. It's the biggest bug-bear of editors and the one thing guaranteed to make them furious.

Don't take my word for it. Get it straight from the horse's mouth. These comments from two small press publishers are fairly typical:

"I'd say that 90 per cent of all the manuscripts I receive miss the target because they are simply not appropriate. People haven't looked at the magazine, or have read the magazine and the guidelines and not taken any notice."

"You must research your market. It's astonishing how often I get phonecalls or letters from people who say 'I haven't seen your magazine but I've got this wonderful story here'. Maybe they should study what we're printing to see if their wonderful story really fits before they waste our time and theirs."

I know I'm labouring the point – but it's worth repeating. Time spent on market research is invested, not wasted. It's the golden key to success. Know your market and you'll beat the odds to win through. Neglect your market research and you risk ending up lumped together with those poor misguided souls who regularly send war stories, horror yarns and shoot-em-up westerns to romance publishers Mills and Boon.

Exercises

Pick a selection of magazines which publish short stories. (It doesn't matter for these exercises if you use old copies.) First, analyse the publications as outlined in the chapter. Make out an *information form* for each. If you are looking at several issues of the same publication see if you can spot any trends or themes in the fiction.

Try to work out the target audience for each magazine, then go one step further. Imagine the *average* reader and write a 350-word piece for each magazine describing what that person's typical day would be like. In a second piece, of 250 words, say what each magazine's average reader's hopes and fears are.

Now pick one magazine and devise a single storyline for it which has that reader as the central character.

Summary

- ✓ Great stories are rejected by magazines every day of the week because writers haven't done their market research.
- ✓ The time to do market research is *before* you put pen to paper. Study your target publication and tailor your work to fit.
- ✓ Have a browse through the shelves of major newsagents. See which magazines publish the type of story you want to write.
- ✓ Get a feel for each type of magazine. Do this by looking at both the features and the short stories.
- ✓ Some reference libraries keep a comprehensive selection of magazines you can study for free.
- ✓ Don't use old magazines. They won't tell you what the editor is looking for **now**.
- ✓ If you want to write for the small press market send off for recent back issues.
- ✓ The *Small Press Guide* published by *Writers' Bookshop* gives details about a number of specialist, subscription-only magazines.
- ✓ Read four consecutive copies of the magazine you have selected. Pay attention to the mood, setting, style, plot and characters.
- ✓ Look for similarities or trends which run through the stories. These point to the subjects and styles which appeal to the editor.
- ✓ Analyse **all** the content of the magazine. Try to get a mental picture of the average reader. Advertisements offer vital clues.

- ✓ Think: what are the hopes and dreams of these readers? Then create stories involving people of the same age, sex, background and careers.
- ✓ When studying a story, ask yourself what it was about the tale that convinced the editor to buy it.
- ✓ Make sure that there's nothing in your stories that jars with the readers' image of the world or suggests it was written for a different audience.
- ✓ Send off for guidelines for potential fiction contributors. These set out what sort of fiction the editor is looking for.
- ✓ They also highlight taboo subjects; details on payment; serial rights; preferred times of submission; the fiction editor's name etc.
- ✓ Guidelines are useful, and reference books offer important tips, but they are no substitute for studying the magazines and getting a feel for them yourself.

3

FINDING STORY IDEAS

The question successful writers are always asked is: where do you get the ideas for your stories? It's the one thing *everyone* wants to know.

I'm sure no two authors give the same reply. We all have our own ways of sparking ideas – of kick-starting our creative motors – and what works for one writer may not generate even a glimmer of interest for another.

Some writers won't admit to the silly, sad, quirky and downright worrying things that suddenly appeal to their imaginations and make them rush to put down a story on paper. They're scared that men in white coats will come and take them away if they admit what weirdness goes on inside their heads.

Others jealously guard their story-devising techniques from rivals. If they can think up six good story ideas a day, then they're as likely to share that solid-gold secret as a guaranteed system for winning the lottery.

I always find the question a bit amusing. By asking **where** do you get your story ideas rather than **how** do you think up story ideas, the person quizzing you is implying that there is a shop somewhere – known only to professional writers – where you go to get storylines.

Maybe there should be a chain of such shops spread across the country – a sort of *Plots-R-Us*. Just whizz round with your trolley and pay for them at the checkout. (That might not be such a bad idea – I want ten per cent commission if you open the shops and make a million.)

The truth is that good short story writers don't need a storyline shop. They are constantly churning over snippets of ideas in their heads, slotting together random thoughts, seeing what gels into the beginnings of a plot.

And they keep their eyes and ears open. They'll spot the hearse that's been wheelclamped or the AA Rescue van that has broken down. They'll spot the remarkable and file it away for future use. Observation is the key. Don't let yourself become so hassled that you don't have time to look around. Story ideas are all around you. You just need to stop and watch.

Carry a notebook and pen around with you at all times. Take notes of anything you see that amuses you or captures your imagination. Listen in to conversations going on around you and take down any unusual or humorous snippets. You'll be surprised how useful these notes become when you sit down to write and need a little inspiration.

Even if the notes don't immediately spark an idea, the mere fact that you've been recording things around you, really improves your observational skills. A successful writer keeps his ears and eyes open.

See the unusual

While you're observing life, try to look at ordinary events in new and exciting ways. You never know what story ideas might occur to you.

For example, I was on holiday sitting in a small restaurant in the Canary Islands, busily flicking through the menu when a story idea hit me. I was unsuccessfully trying to find the section where the meals were listed in English. Each page I turned over was in Spanish or French or German or Swedish.

Eventually, I got my meal but I also came away with the feeling that it was silly to have so many different languages in the world. It didn't take long for that thought to move on to: what if there was someone who *could* speak all languages? How would it happen that someone could learn so many different tongues? What would that person's life be like? The result was *The Babel Fable* – a mix-up means that a coma victim is played language tapes instead of music for three years and wakes up as a one-man United Nations.

Now, I'm sure millions of British tourists have struggled with similar menus the world over, but how many would have made the mental link necessary to turn it into a short story idea? Thankfully, not many or I'd be out of a job.

So stop and think. Are you passing over similar plotting opportunities because you don't recognise them?

Top ten tips

Still stumped for story ideas? Then try these ten plot-creating devices for size. They might just spark your imagination.

1. What If?

Simply imagine a world where everything we know gets turned on its head. What if there was a place where: children hated ice cream but loved vegetables; MPs were brainwashed to always tell the truth; people were born as old age pensioners and grew younger year by year.

What if: Kennedy hadn't died; Germany had won the Second World War; animals could talk; aliens really existed. The possibilities are endless, especially for sci-fi writers.

2. Talking Pictures

Grab a bundle of old magazines. Cut out any pictures that take your fancy. Stick them in a drawer. When you look at them months later – out of context – you'll be astounded by the story ideas they spark.

I often try this one with my night school classes. I have a photograph which appeared in one of the national newspapers of the Prime Minister snapped standing in front of a bright light. It looks as though his head is surrounded by a halo. (I'm sure the newspaper intended this.) I tell my students: imagine that the PM *does* have a halo. Maybe he wakes up with it one morning. How would he explain it? What would it mean? How would religious leaders react? What problems would it cause him?

The resulting story ideas are often hilarious, quirky and downright weird in equal measures. But although they all come from the same source of inspiration, each story is unique.

3. Holy Smoke

People have been raiding the Bible for story ideas for 2,000 years – why stop now? Cain and Abel, Adam and Eve, Noah's Ark. There isn't any copyright on it.

Try giving the loaves and fishes story a modern setting or writing a tale from the viewpoint of the poor disciples who had to gather up all those crumbs!

4. Once Upon a Time

There's no copyright on fairy tales either. Imagine the fun you can have sticking Snow White and the Seven Dwarfs into a science fiction setting – maybe she's an astronaut and the dwarfs are aliens – or by having Cinderella as a downtrodden office clerk determined to make it onto the board of directors.

I used this technique when I wrote a satirical tale based around the anti-road row over the building of a new bypass. The three pigs were protestors high up in their treehouse and the wolf was a road contractor determined to bulldoze them out of the way.

5. *Read All About It*

The newspapers are packed with story ideas – hidden away in the quirky fillers at the bottom of the page. A quick scan of one day's papers should provide you with enough ideas to write half a dozen stories.

For example, a few years ago I was amused by a short item which described the misadventures of a group of Russians who hired a minibus and visited Germany on a three-day shopping spree. During the trip one of the group died from natural causes. Rather than cut short the trip, the others hid the body in the minibus and kept on shopping.

Just imagine what a great story that would make if you applied the "what if" principle to it. What if the bus was stolen? How would they tell the police about the dead shopper? What would the crooks do when they discovered they'd stolen a corpse? The title would have to be *Shop Till You Drop*!

6. *Scribbles*

I've already suggested jotting down a line or two when you see or hear something that tickles your imagination while you're out and about. Then when you need to write a story, you'll have a fund of potential plots.

But don't just leave the notebook in your jacket. Keep it by you at all times, wherever you are. Be especially sure to keep it by the bed. All the really good story ideas occur just as you're about to doze off.

7. *Funny Titles*

I often think up the title first – then dream up a story to fit. Well-known expressions make great story titles. *Political Asylum* – maybe in the future we'll lock up all our mad people in Westminster. (Some would argue we already do.) *Caught in the Act* – actor bumps off his rivals during a play.

I did this with a women's magazine sting-in-the-tail story entitled *Taken to the Cleaners*. I imagined how a Mrs Mop could get one over on a city whizzkid.

8. Bard Luck

Shakespeare can be another great source of plots. The film *Forbidden Planet* was just a reworking of *The Tempest. West Side Story* was an updated version of *Romeo and Juliet. Julius Caesar* would make a great *House of Cards*-style political thriller. The machinations and knife wielding of Ancient Rome could easily be carried out by modern media-manipulating spin doctors.

9. All The Pun Of The Fair

It's amazing how you can get a quirky new story idea from playing about with puns. *Quiche of Death* – a sinister restaurant? *Son and Hair* – a row over who is going to inherit the family barber shop?

Here are a couple to get you going. What can you devise from *Pane in The Neck* and *One Hoarse Town*? Perhaps a pushy double glazing salesman getting his come-uppance and a nasty rivalry between two competing choirs in the finals of a major singing contest? I'm sure you can think of many more.

10. Nick, Nick

Now, I'm not advocating plagiarism. I don't suggest you go round stealing other people's stories, but you can come up with fresh ideas using published works as inspiration. Read something that was okay – but you didn't like the ending or the main character? Write your own version of it, and change a few of the details. There's no such thing as a new story idea – only new settings and reworking.

The film *Outland* was merely a remake of *High Noon* – this time with the sheriff single-handedly facing baddies on a mining planet. *The Magnificent Seven* was a remake of *The Seven Samurai.*

You could give *Robinson Crusoe* a futuristic setting, or make a pirate story into a tale of corporate raiders.

Why not borrow from yourself? If you're lucky enough to have several published stories under your belt, go back and look at them. Could you take the basic elements of one of these yarns and twist them around to make a completely new story? Try telling it from the viewpoint of a man instead of a woman or a child instead of an adult. You'd be amazed how different a story can become with only a little tinkering.

The random elements approach

Now I nick-nicked this idea from fellow writer Barbara Jacobs so I hope she'll forgive me. (If you're annoyed, Barbara, I'll buy you a pint. If you aren't, I'll make it a half.)

Simply take a piece of paper and divide it into four equal vertical panels. Starting from the left, label panel one **Main Characters**, panel two **Minor Characters**, panel three **Objects** and panel four **Settings**.

Under each heading list six entries – the first things that pop up in your head. In column one, for instance, we could put the main characters: milkman, wizard, pilot, grandfather, grave robber, beauty queen.

In column two we could have the minor characters: mother, station announcer, newspaper reporter, supermarket checkout operator, vicar, dustman.

In column three we could have the objects: baseball bat, balloon, cup of tea, bicycle, stuffed parrot, train set.

In the final column, the settings could be: seaside pier, hospital ward, jumble sale, cruise liner, greasy spoon café, farm yard.

Main Characters	**Minor Characters**	**Objects**	**Settings**
Milkman	Mother	Baseball Bat	Seaside Pier
Wizard	Station Announcer	Balloon	Hospital Ward
Pilot	Newspaper Reporter	Cup of Tea	Jumble Sale
Grandfather	Checkout Asst.	Bicycle	Cruise Liner
Grave Robber	Vicar	Stuffed Parrot	Greasy Spoon Café
Beauty Queen	Dustman	Train Set	Farmyard

So how does this give us a plot? Easy – without giving yourself time to think, pick one entry from each column. These are the four elements that your story *must* include.

So if you have selected beauty queen, newspaper reporter, stuffed parrot and cruise liner – the challenge is to devise a story set on a ship that includes these two characters, and which centres on a stuffed parrot.

Perhaps the parrot is stuffed with stolen cash. Maybe the beauty queen hoped to slip out of the country unnoticed among the wealthy cruise passengers. Maybe the parrot is a toy, containing a secret microphone and the reporter has given it to the beauty queen in the hope that she'll leave it close-by when her mystery VIP lover visits her cabin.

Give it a whirl. What storyline can you think up around this parrot and these two intriguing individuals?

Sounds crazy? Well, it is a bit unusual but it can be tremendous fun and is an excellent way of jolting you out of any plotting rut. The technique works on the principle that what gives most people trouble devising storylines is the bewilderingly infinite number of possibilities of characters, places and events to choose from. Where do you start? Which do you pick? The grid takes away the element of choice – simplifying everything. Like a poker player, you must work with the cards you're dealt – even if you have to bluff like mad.

Still stuck for ideas?

Boy, you're difficult to please. Here's my final idea for finding story ideas. Turn to the problems page in your newspaper or favourite magazine. There in black and white are all you need. Every problem page is a mine of potential plots – tear-filled tales of lust, jealousy, betrayal, self-doubt and despair. Every imaginable aspect of human life is there. True Life Confession magazines and articles are just as juicy.

Change the names and a few of the details to protect the innocent (and stop you being punched in the face) and away you go. You have a never-ending source of relationship-based stories.

And remember, there are a limited number of basic ideas for plots, it's your originality in working them that counts.

Exercises

Devise six storylines and, if you have time, write them up into full length short stories.

Use something unusual you've spotted or heard as the basis for the first. Use the *What If?* principle for the second and the *Random Elements* approach for the third. Rework a well-known nursery rhyme or fairy story to give it a contemporary setting for the fourth. See what story idea you can dream up from the pun title *Singing in the Reign* for the fifth. And for the final one, get hold of an old photograph where you don't know who is in it or where it was taken. See what plotline you can find in the image on the print.

Summary

✓ People are always worried about how to think up story ideas, but it's simple if you know how.

✓ Good writers get ideas from being observant. They keep their eyes and ears open. They spot the remarkable and file it away for future use.

✓ Carry a notebook and pen around with you. Take notes of anything you see that amuses you or captures your imagination.

✓ Listen in to conversations going on around you and take down any unusual or humorous snippets.

✓ Condition yourself to look at ordinary events in new and exciting ways.

✓ There are a number of well-tried methods for jump-starting the imagination. See if any of the following ten inspire you.

1. **What If?** Imagine a world where everything gets turned on its head.

2. **Talking Pictures**. Cut out any pictures from newspapers that take your fancy and stick them in a drawer. When you look at them months later you'll be astounded by the ideas they spark.

3. **Holy Smoke**. People have been raiding the bible for story ideas for 2,000 years – why stop now?

4. **Once Upon a Time**. There's no copyright on fairy tales. Try reworking them by sticking the familiar characters into new and unusual settings.

5. **Read All About It.** Newspapers are packed with story ideas – hidden away in the quirky fillers at the bottom of the page.

6. **Scribbles**. Keep your notepad by you at all times. All the really good story ideas occur just as you're about to doze off.

7. **Funny Titles**. Proverbs and well-known expressions are great for suggesting storylines. *A Fool and His Money are Soon Parted* – that expression alone could give you several different plots. Who is the fool? How did he get the money? How will he lose it? Answer the questions and you've got the storyline.

8. **Bard Luck**. Shakespeare is another great source of plots. You can rework *Hamlet* or *Macbeth* by giving it a new, contemporary setting.

9. **All the Pun of the Fair**. You can get quirky ideas from playing about with puns. *Only Here For The Bier* – an alcoholic undertaker?

10. **Nick, Nick**. Don't plagiarise but you can use published works as inspiration. Rework a story you liked to give yourself a new version. Look back at your own stories – can they be re-angled or given a new setting?

✓ Try the *Random Elements* approach. Fill in a grid with major characters, minor characters, objects and settings. Pick one element from each column and build a story round them.

✓ The problem pages of newspapers and magazines are a mine of human hard-luck stories. Just change the names and a few of the details.

4

PLOTTING YOUR STORY

Some writers will tell you, straight faced, that they are visited by a mysterious muse who blows creativity dust in their ears. In an instant they are inspired and rush to pen a dazzlingly brilliant short story.

Well, as a cynical Glaswegian I have to say right away that I don't have a lot of truck with that rather fey notion. Figures from Greek mythology are all very well on holiday souvenirs but I don't want them traipsing round my house. And I can't rely on the vagaries of supernatural intervention when I have bills to pay and groceries to buy. As a professional I need to be able to produce short stories quickly, regularly and in bulk – so that means being a plot factory, churning out storyline after storyline after storyline.

There's no magic to the process – it's purely mechanical (just like the *Random Elements* approach outlined in the last chapter). I follow my own simple system – a few basic plot-creating techniques – which gives me countless stories.

In this chapter I'll explain how I go about conjuring up plotlines and I'll look at some of the most popular and road-tested methods for creating saleable stories.

Not all these approaches will work for you. It's very much a question of personal taste and experimentation, but I hope you'll find some techniques that are appealing and which get the creative juices flowing.

I'll look at the vital ingredients of suspense, jeopardy and conflict which make a plot gripping, and I'll even reveal how to use tension and suspense to create hilarious comedy tales.

What is a plot?

Over the years I've read thousands of short stories by new writers and found that the majority failed because they didn't have enough plot or a plot that just wasn't strong enough to sustain my interest.

Often it was because the story wasn't really a story, but an anecdote, personal recollection, character study or comedy sketch. Frequently the material was spun out to a wafer-thin 1,200 words when it really deserved just four pithy sentences.

It was usually a great pity because the pieces were lyrical, charming, clever passages of human observation which in any other context I'd have found amusing or poignant. But they failed as drama because basically nothing happened. There were no incidents. There was no chain of events. There was no crisis to be resolved or action to be followed. There was no plot.

The writers either stuck to describing a person or place in huge detail or featured a single, brief, moment in time. They failed to make that single incident into a dynamic adventure or take that well-described character and put him in a tense and unsettling setting where he'd be tested by events and have to "come through".

Occasionally, writers would have the beginnings of a plot. A main character would face a problem or upset in his life but it would be trivial and quickly overcome. The hero would resolve the mundane snag in a predictable and effortless way. Once again there was no drama. There was no *real* plot.

It was very rare that a new writer would create a dramatic situation where an intriguing main character found himself coping with unusual events in a tense and suspense-filled way. It was rare that they gave their character that most thrilling of elements to cope with – a dilemma.

I wished I was able to ring them up and say: *Hey, you need a magic formula to make your story work*, but obviously I couldn't. So here for everyone who should have got that call is a recipe that will give you the basic rudiments of plotting. You won't go far wrong if you construct a story where:

- Something of importance happens to a sympathetic and interesting main character.
- That event demands his immediate and full attention.
- It creates a dilemma or problem that has to be resolved.
- Overcoming it is tricky or awkward. Not overcoming it will have serious repercussions.
- Facing the problem makes the main character re-evaluate himself, or his life, or his attitudes, or the friendship, love and trust of those around him.
- There is a strong likelihood he'll fail to solve the problem.
- The solution is unexpected and ingenious.

Now this isn't a *one-size-fits-all* plotting formula. I admit that it has its limitations and wouldn't necessarily be suitable for a small press magazine where plots can be more free-wheeling, experimental and quirky. It won't automatically work either for a literary publication where plot is seen as less important and more emphasis is placed on mood, atmosphere and ambience.

But it's a handy starter formula that will get you swiftly producing good, workmanlike storylines with a recognisable start, middle and end ... and that will put you miles ahead of most people who enter competitions or whose stories end up on the fiction editor's slush pile.

Only the beginning

Perhaps the most common storylining error that newcomers make is to confuse the basic "set-up" of the story for the plot. The set-up is the opening situation – the crisis that starts the action. The plot is what happens from there.

Just imagine you've had a cracking idea for a story – two men are madly in love with the same girl. Both are equally determined to win her, no matter how underhand and devious they have to be. Both will stop at nothing. One day they are locked in a lift together. And guess what? The girl is locked in there with them.

You think – what a brilliant storyline. I'm home and dry. But in fact you're only just at the beginning. Sticking the trio together in the lift is an explosive situation, a marvellous set-up but it isn't the plot. The plot is the sequence of events that happens next.

Do they resolve their differences? Does one man win the girl? Is the girl so disgusted with them that she scorns both? Is it an erotic story and we end up with a steamy menage-a-trois? Perhaps it's a horror story and the lift falls, plunging them to their death. How this suspense-filled situation is brought to a resolution, in whatever manner you decide, is the real plot.

Always know the difference between a plot and a set-up. Some writers are great at thinking up basic dramatic situations but then struggle to turn them into credible stories because they don't go that step further. The story remains stuck where it started.

I find it helpful to think of a story as a journey – it goes somewhere – and the plot is the route it takes to get to its destination. If you want your story to be exciting, make the journey eventful, hassled and full of unexpected diversions and twists.

Turning that nippy idea into a plot

It's important to realise that there's no right or wrong way to plot a story – just different ways. As long as your tale holds the reader's attention, entertains and delights, then the method you use to achieve this end is as valid and effective as anyone else's.

Some people do all the hard work in their heads, mulling over ideas, developing them, trying out different permutations until they come up with a workable storyline and then rush to the typewriter as swiftly as possible. Others like to plan the storyline in instalments, jotting down notes and creating a rough skeleton. They'll think in scenes and episodes. They may jiggle the dramatic components around on the page until they have a plotline that seems to gel.

Both are fine, so go for the approach that suits you. I find that very organised, methodical people with set routines and timetables like to sketch out components, devising a mini-synopsis.

If, like me, you have a butterfly mind and are constantly daydreaming and having wildly random thoughts then you'll probably prefer to let your brain subconsciously juggle the various elements until the storyline is ready to pop up in front of your eyes (usually when you least expect it). I find devising plotlines is a productive way to spend otherwise boring rail journeys.

But whichever technique you use, the mental processes involved will be the same. You'll start off with a set-up (that initial bright idea) and probably come up with the resolution/ denouement fairly soon after that – and it will be the middle of the story that comes to you last.

For instance, you could think of a story set on a sinking ocean liner. There's only one seat left in the lifeboat and your main character is determined to get it – but he's one of twelve men all pleading to be rescued. The end of the story will be him getting that life-saving seat – but how? Does he bribe his way on? Trick his way on? Plead so pathetically that the others take pity on him? Does he know a secret about the other eleven that is so terrible that they allow him to take the last place in the boat rather than have him reveal it – even though it means certain death for them? When you've worked out the method he uses, you've got your plot.

Remember that the narrative begins at the moment the problem arises and finishes the moment the conflict is resolved. This leads to a basic structure which looks like this:

A. ***Introduction – the main character faces a worrying conflict/problem/dilemma***

B. ***Middle – in flashback we learn of the background and events that led up to the conflict***

C. ***Ending – the conflict is satisfactorily resolved***

If you are writing a longish story and have, say, three thousand words or more to play with, you can introduce a few extra complications and false solutions along the way to make the journey more eventful. But be careful not to end up writing a mini-novel.

Another equally workable structure is to have a hero who has a goal – something he desperately needs to achieve – and then put lots of obstacles in his way. He struggles to overcome these impediments but he has rivals and opponents out to stop him. Maybe it's just fate that seems to be against him. Winning through takes all his courage, ingenuity and effort.

He could be an Indiana Jones-style treasure hunter out to find the gold of a lost jungle city or an executive in a busy corporation out to secure the managing director's job in a cut-throat contest. But the setting doesn't necessarily have to be high-powered or exotic.

Characters in domestic settings have their own battles to fight. What about the grandmother who is scared of flying but desperately wants to visit Australia to see her new granddaughter? How she overcomes her fears is a smashing plotline. Then there's the poorly educated man struggling to learn to read and write so that he can read a bedtime story to his young son and feel like a real father. His mates on the darts team want him to play in a run of vital league games but it means him having to skip his adult literacy classes. What does he do? His conflicting loyalty is a gripping human story.

The permutations are limitless – the clever pupil whose parents want him to go to university and get a respectable job but he wants to see life and be a rock star; the young woman who nurses her elderly father and finds herself torn when her boyfriend asks her to marry him and put the old man into a home; the wife who knows accepting a glamorous, well paid job will make her husband feel inferior and threaten an already rocky marriage ...

They all have cherished goals but all will hurt loved ones if they pursue them. They face dilemmas and have hard decisions to make. All are placed in conflict. It's the stuff of drama – the very substance of plotting.

What is conflict?

At this stage, I think it's useful to define exactly what is meant by conflict.

There's a misconception that conflict is only about hate, confrontation, aggression and destruction. The word conjures up pictures of people yelling at each other and fighting, guns, tanks and explosions. Now, while all these things show conflict in action, they are only the most violent and extreme examples.

Conflict – especially in fiction-writing terms – is a much broader concept. It is anything that upsets the smooth-running of your main character's life.

It doesn't have to be loud and aggressive – in the right circumstances not having the right change in his pocket can be a source of conflict. It becomes a crisis for him, an urgent, worrying problem, when he is late for an interview and hasn't the right coins to put in the ticket machine at a railway station.

As that example shows, it doesn't have to involve other people. Points of conflict can be caused by inanimate objects, even the weather. Think how hassled your hero will be if he has to walk because he can't buy a rail ticket and ends up getting drenched.

Conflict comes when anyone or anything opposes what your character wants to do. When a husband and wife argue over where to go on holiday, the shouting and door slamming isn't the real conflict. The conflict is their inability to agree on a holiday destination.

The threat to your main character's domestic harmony and general well-being doesn't have to come from another person or any outside force. It may be an internal threat – a crisis of faith, a fear to be overcome, or a problem created by a flaw in the character's own personality like an addiction to drink, drugs or gambling.

Upset the status quo

Another way of looking at it is that a story deals with the events that upset the normality – the status quo – of your hero's life. He will only be happy when the equilibrium of his life has been restored and a new state of calm exists.

His upset can be quite domestic and low-key, but it doesn't have to be boring just because it has an ordinary setting. If he buys a chocolate bar from the vending machine in work every morning and one morning the machine has run out, his life has been affected.

Now, that doesn't sound like much of a plot. But what if he is collecting the wrappers to enter a competition to win a dream car and only needs one more wrapper? What if the competition closes that day? What if he has only an hour to send in his entry form?

That missing chocolate bar is now a major cause of upset for him and he won't be happy until he's found another one. Just think of the misadventures he could have dashing from sweet shop to sweet shop.

Exploit the unusual

Good drama looks at what happens when the extraordinary occurs. It shows how people react to unusual and unexpected circumstances. Your short story should do the same. We're not interested in the 364 days when George Williams gets off the bus outside his factory and clocks in; we want to know what happens on the one day that he decides to stay on the bus to see where it leads him.

Your plot should deal with the times when things go wrong, when circumstances change, when characters are thrown out of their cosy ruts. Not the days when it's business as usual.

Real drama is about the late-night knock at the door, the unexpected letter, the phone call the hero never wanted to get. Shake your characters out of their routines, dump them in unfamiliar territory, give them a challenge to cope with.

Make your hero work for his money

When your main character is faced with his conflict, don't make the problem so insignificant that it doesn't worry him or can be rectified with a swift phone call. The crisis should make your hero drop everything to deal with it. It must be important to him. It must have urgency.

He must struggle to meet the challenge. It should test him to the limit. He must have to work hard for it. There must be suspense. It should be unclear until the very last moment if he's going to succeed.

Think of every film you've ever seen. The cavalry comes to the rescue just as the Indians are about to overpower the wagon-train. The scientist finishes the weapon to kill the monster just as it smashes down the door to his lab. The gambler wins the roulette jackpot with his very last chip. Hollywood knows the emotion-wringing impact of a nail-biting finish. Make your story do the same. Keep the reader holding his breath until the last word.

The more you place your hero in jeopardy the stronger the tension will be. Tension builds suspense, and that suspense – the tingling anticipation and dread – is what holds readers glued to the page. So make your hero's failure a very real possibility. Make it so important that it will forever shatter his life. The more he has to lose, the more jeopardy he is in, the more we'll root for him.

Just think about Bill the bank clerk. He's stolen money from his employers to pay for a hip replacement operation for his elderly mother who's crippled with pain. As he drives home he has second thoughts and decides to put the money back before anyone notices. But as he stops outside the bank he realises there's someone there. The auditors have arrived on an unscheduled inspection.

How will he get the money back without anyone seeing? Will he be caught? Can he talk his way out of it if the auditors notice the cash has gone? Bill risks prison, ruin, shame. His whole future hangs in the balance. He's in extreme jeopardy. If you keep readers guessing Bill's fate to the last sentence you'll guarantee they'll be hooked.

Secrets revealed

Now, in a classic example of keeping the reader in suspense, I promised you ages ago that I'd reveal how I plot my short stories. Well, I admit I've been holding off for a while because you're going to think my methods a little unorthodox (not to mention weird) and may doubt my sanity after you've read them. All I can say is, these techniques work for me – no matter how odd they may seem – so please hear me out. You never know – your brain may work in the same bizarre way as mine.

Basically, I devise plots in two main ways – both quite mechanical. I either think of a title then dream up a story to fit it, or I think of an ending then work backwards.

Let's take the title method first. Usually I'll take a famous saying or expression and see what it suggests to me. *Dead Men's Shoes* is a good example.

In crude terms the expression means you having to wait until someone dies or retires to get his job. So this got me thinking about a main character – Tony – who wants someone else's job. Well, if he waited patiently I wouldn't have a story. It would be dull, dull, dull ... So I assumed that he wasn't prepared to wait and was scheming to bump off his rival. The expression uses the word *dead* so it seemed logical that Tony would actually kill off his rival.

Murder stories are ten a penny, so I reckoned it needed a few extra ingredients to spice it up. What if the person who was going to be killed was Tony's more successful brother? Great, sibling rivalry – now we're starting to get somewhere.

The expression also features the word *shoes* so I thought footwear had to come into it somehow. Ah – yes, what about a family business, a family shoe-making business.

Derek is the managing director with the beautiful wife, the big house and the fancy car. Tony is the idle waster forced to live on hand-outs from the family. He's eaten up with jealousy, thinking he should be the boss, not Derek.

Now we've got a brilliant set-up – but it ain't a plot. Not yet, anyway.

Next problem, how can Tony kill Derek and get away with it? Surely he'd be caught straight away? A little more lateral thinking, and the solution becomes obvious. Tony and Derek are identical twins. Tony not only wants to get Derek's job, he wants to take over Derek's life. He's going to kill Derek and then pretend to be him. There's the added bonus that Tony has always lusted after Derek's gorgeous wife, Mary. Hey, now we've even got sex in the story!

It's coming together but the plot still needs an ending – a twist ending. Tony rushes to his dead brother's house to get unsuspecting Mary into bed. But as he arrives he realises there's something wrong. Mary is acting strangely ...

At first Tony's guilty conscience makes him think she's spotted the "switch" but it's more complicated than that. Derek had been having an affair and Mary has found out. All Tony's plans are destroyed.

Believing that she's still talking to her husband, Mary announces that the marriage is over and she's throwing him out. To cap it all, Derek had put the business in her name for tax purposes and she is going to hang on to it all. Just to rub in that last piece of delicious irony, Mary says: *I could have loved you, you know – really loved you, but you were always too perfect, too self-centred. If only you'd been more caring, more human, more fun. More like Tony ...*

See how effective a story we've got – just from taking a hackneyed expression and investigating what associations it sparks? There are thousands of famous sayings – and even if you got only one idea from each there'd still be enough plotlines to last you a lifetime.

I hope this example proves that you don't have to think of a complete storyline at one go. Grab a basic idea and let it develop over time. Let the plot build up in instalments.

If it doesn't come of its own accord, sit down and force it. Ask yourself: where does the story go from here? What's the next logical step? Play about with different ideas until one clicks. And most importantly, ask yourself: how is this tale going to end? How can I finish it off neatly – yet unexpectedly?

As I said earlier, sometimes when I sit down to plot, all I have ready in my mind is a comic punchline or a dramatic denouement and I have to work backwards to find a storyline that brings me up to that "climactic" point. It's a bit like turning on TV and catching the last five minutes of a film and having no real idea who the characters are, what's going on or how they got into the tangle they're in.

A good example of this was *Postman's Knack*. I had this vision of a postman – fed up with being bitten by angry dogs – smearing his legs with some noxious-smelling substance. When a German Shepherd tries to take a chunk out of his ankle, it gets one whiff and runs away howling.

A good ending but what's the story? Well, the first step had to be working out *what* it could be that the postie put on his legs. I already knew *why* he did it. It had to be something smelly but not caustic – after all, I didn't want him burning himself. The answer came to me in a flash – chutney, apple chutney.

I know what you're thinking. Quick, sedate him. But there is a logical explanation. My friend's wife regularly made apple chutney (which tasted delicious, by the way) but the smell of the ingredients boiling away on the stove was unbelievably stomach-churning.

So I used the *What if?* principle. What if the postie's wife made apple chutney – chutney that not only smelt bad when it was being cooked, but smelt even worse when she put it on his sandwiches? He loved her too much to tell her, and had been racking his brains for years to think of a way to solve the problem.

Great, now the story is clear. A postie has a dilemma: how can he tell his wife her apple chutney is disgusting? He also has another problem: how can he stop dogs biting him on his rounds?

The answer – smear the chutney on his legs! The dogs won't go near him because of the nasty niff and the tale ends with all the other posties demanding their own supplies of the noxious paste. Suddenly, instead of wondering how to get rid of all the chutney, our hero can't get his hands on enough of the stuff.

Okay, so perhaps this idea is a little too bizarre for most people but always try to keep your mind open to silly thoughts. Take what people say literally. The next time someone says to you: *I made my boss eat his words*, let yourself picture your pal forcing a letter down his boss' throat. If you own a dishwasher and have to buy Rinse-Aid, don't stop the thought that says: *Shouldn't that be the name of a charity*?

Remember, good plotting can come from linking lots of silly and unrelated ideas.

All my life's a circle

The popular linear format

Conflict – Flashback – Conflict Resolved

is a great way to start you off on plotting, but it isn't the only way to structure a story. In fact, many yarns you'll see in literary publications and small press magazines don't use this format at all.

A particular favourite of mine – and editors – is what I'd call the *circular* or *return ticket* plotline. This is a story which brings you round in a circle (more or less) to the point at which the narrative started.

It sounds crazy but the device works brilliantly in science fiction stories and in ghost and horror yarns.

- A fossilised glove is found on a dinosaur dig. A research team is sent back to the Jurassic Era to investigate. While there, one of the team loses ... you've guessed it ... a glove!

- A general is in charge of a demoralised army. They are

fighting a foe so ruthless and savage that they have to resort to unthinkably inhuman tactics to survive. At the end of a decisive battle the general tours his troops and realises they have become the monsters they fought so hard to defeat.

- A four-man university parapsychology team is carrying out research at a haunted house. They're puzzled when there are no spooky goings-on despite the fact that the instruments say the place is awash with psychic energy. After a frustrating night, they bicker. While driving away, a fight breaks out and their van crashes, killing them all.

  Next thing we're back with the team inside the house. They're puzzled that they can't see any spooks despite the instruments telling them the place has "multiple haunting". The readings say there are ... four ghosts!

- A scientist sets off to meet his wife who has something momentous to tell him. As she rushes across the road, she is hit and killed by a lorry. Distraught with grief, and plagued by curiosity about what she had to tell him, the scientist vows to invent a time machine so that he can go back and save her.

  Ridiculed by colleagues he works on for twenty years, helped only by his friend and fellow scientist Tom. They do it. They build a working time machine and the scientist goes back to the fateful day. He stops his wife stepping out into the road, and she tells him the news he has waited two decades to hear ... she's been having an affair with Tom and they're going to run off to start a new life together.

  Feeling cheated and abused by fate, the scientist grabs his wife, furiously pushing her under a passing lorry.

This quirky format is enormous fun, generating countless plotting possibilities. I think you'll get a real buzz from it, but beware the danger that you'll lead readers round in a circle for no good reason and they'll end up feeling conned. There has to be a reason for a journey – even a circular journey.

Have a look at the storylines I've just described. They are all quite different but have one thing in common – an *ironic* punchline. The irony is what makes the stories work. We may be back at the start, but now we have to view the opening events differently; our perceptions have changed.

The last plot oozes irony on every level. The wife dies in the same way on both occasions ...the scientist labours on unaware that he'd be happier not knowing the news his wife had to tell him ... he thinks Tom is the solution to his problems but his colleague is actually the cause of them ...Tom is helping him in the hope that the time machine will work and he can run off with the hero's wife a second time ...

This storyline uses a well-loved maxim in science fiction. You can't go back in time to change history. It has a stubborn way of following its set path – no matter how hard you try to interfere.

By the way, the last two plotlines I actually wrote up into competition entries entitled *Ghost Image* and *Second Time Around.* Both won prizes so you can see the *circular* plotline format is a hit with judges too.

A hair of the dog

Another great favourite plotting technique is the shaggy dog story. The writer builds up the conflict, piling on the suspense, bringing readers to the point where they're so tense they think they'll explode then he unexpectedly hits them with a silly, comic and ironic punchline.

The release of tension is like a balloon popping and, done well, is hilarious. The readers know they've been conned but don't mind. They admire the writer's skill in creating a nail-biting atmosphere – and his cheek.

A lot of fine comedy short stories use this approach, but it requires great skill, comic timing and self-control. You have to be disciplined with yourself and not litter the text with jokes, throwaway lines, comic descriptions or characters with silly names or actions. The humour has to come at the end – purely from the release of tension. The silliness can't appear anywhere before. The reader must think he's reading a serious story. He can't be given any inkling of what's to come.

So how does this tricky magic work? How do you weave the spell? Let's see if we can construct a shaggy dog story right here in stages.

Stage One: A giant metal sphere plunges through the

atmosphere and crashes into Central Park in New York.

Stage Two: A team of top scientists is flown by military jet to examine it and find it's made of an alloy not found on earth.

Stage Three: Military leaders urge the President of the United States to blow it up. It must be an alien weapon, they claim.

Stage Four: The President's scientific advisor pleads to save it. Think what we could learn from studying it, he begs. A loud shouting match ensues with the generals.

Stage Five: At that moment a transmission comes in from a deep space satellite. It's in a language no-one can understand.

Stage Six: "It's a greeting", says the science chief. "It's a declaration of war", say the generals. The President doesn't know what to do...

Stage Seven: A hundred blips appear on the radar screen. Space ships from another galaxy are on their way here. "It's an invasion force," the generals scream, "send up the missiles".

Stage Eight: The science chief argues desperately, but the President sides with the military. "I'm sorry, but we can't afford to take the risk. I must save the planet," he says. "Launch the rockets. Nuke them!"

Stage Nine: The missiles fly from their silos, a hundred needles of instant death racing up through the atmosphere. They are locked on to their targets ...

Stage Ten: Just then a computer buff rushes into the White House briefing room frantically waving a piece of paper. "We've cracked it, we've translated the alien message," he yells.

Stage Eleven: "What does it say, man," the President demands, "the future of mankind depends on it."
Stage Twelve: The computer man looks sheepish as he reads

out the message ... "Can we have our ball back, please?"

Ouch!

Not bad for a few moment's thought. Comedy, a nail-biting story and a stinging commentary on man's fear, stupidity and violent streak. Who says funny stories can't be deep?

Don't get bogged down in detail

The plot is the most important element in a short story and nothing – but nothing – should hold it up or challenge it for the reader's attention.

Be careful when you set a story on a rocket ship to Mars that you don't spend half the time explaining how the rocket propulsion system works. The real story is about the crew – the people facing danger in the unknown.

Likewise, don't let a tale about a housewife get swamped by mundane details of her housework chores and daily routine. It is how she breaks out of the boredom that counts – not an item by item account of the groceries in her supermarket trolley.

Escapism

Women's magazines, especially, see their role as providing an interlude of tranquillity and escapism in an otherwise hectic day. That's why short story slots have names like *Coffee Break Read* or *Five-Minute Fiction*.

Readers want to be taken out of themselves for a few minutes, whisked off to a world where exciting and intriguing things happen. They want their fiction to be different – more technicolour – than real life. They read to escape drudgery and dullness, so always try for settings and plots that break away from the commonplace and mundane.

Readers can get enough depression at home with red bills, ringing phones, noisy neighbours, demanding kids and grumpy spouses. They don't need or want to read a depressing tale, so make your stories light, positive and up-beat.

Don't get me wrong. It doesn't mean that you have to put on

a flashing bow-tie and throw custard pies in your fiction. You can deal with serious and often harrowing issues, but do so in a way that leaves the reader feeling uplifted and full of hope.

The one thing we all feel these days is powerless, overwhelmed by redundancies, closures and scandals. Have storylines that show characters taking charge of their own destiny and standing up for themselves. Give readers reassurance – they look for that as much as they look to be entertained.

Rework the mixture

They say there's nothing new under the sun and it's certainly true when it comes to story-telling. Most of the storylines we use today are the same mixture of greed, jealousy, love, hate, ambition and betrayal that the Romans used in their stories. They knew all about the eternal triangle 2,000 years ago!

So it's important that a writer finds new and exciting ways to combine these basic story-telling ingredients in order to devise fresh and lively plots. It's all been done before – in broad terms – but you can find a new treatment that will make a storyline suddenly crackle with originality.

Sci-fi writers do it all the time. The film *Electric Dreams* was an eternal triangle story – a girl and two rival suitors. The modern twist was that one of her admirers was a computer.

Romance stories are all basically the same storyline – boy meets girl, loses girl, wins girl back – yet it's astounding how writers conjure up a million different variations. By varying characters and their backgrounds, period, setting and genre, they make each story vitally different from the others.

That's what you have to do when you plot your tale. Think what subtle changes in the mixture you can make to help you mint an original. Don't go for the obvious. Be daring.

See how you can give a modern spin to these age-old dramatic situations. Each of these ideas could give you several short stories.

- Falling in love with an enemy or rival.
- Forbidden love.
- Adultery and its consequences.
- Murderous adultery (eg the wife and her lover plotting to

kill the husband).

- ✧ An act of vengeance and its consequences.
- ✧ An act of vengeance mistakenly taken against the wrong person.
- ✧ An act of betrayal.
- ✧ Problems caused by sudden wealth.
- ✧ Someone wrongly accused of a crime fighting to clear his name.
- ✧ Someone taking the blame for a crime he didn't commit in order to protect a relative, friend or lover.
- ✧ A person's ambition alienating him from his friends and family.
- ✧ The ambition leading to his downfall.
- ✧ Blackmail and its consequences.
- ✧ Someone plotting to kill a blackmailer.
- ✧ A person sacrificing something or someone dear to him for a greater good.
- ✧ Lovers facing an obstacle to their happiness.
- ✧ A rivalry or feud getting out of hand.
- ✧ Sibling rivalry and its consequences.
- ✧ An ordinary person taking on authority to right a wrong.
- ✧ Redemption for an individual thought beyond help.
- ✧ A disgraced or unloved person regaining his self-respect through unexpected ways.
- ✧ A cynic rediscovering his idealism.
- ✧ The corruption of innocence.
- ✧ Someone starting a new life after a personal tragedy.
- ✧ A person proving to his critics that he has what it takes to win through.
- ✧ Solving a crime or puzzle.
- ✧ Someone repenting for a great wrong they've caused.
- ✧ Someone putting right a great injustice they've caused.
- ✧ Going after a long-lost dream.

There's certainly enough dramatic clay there to mould a few pots, or should it be Roman vases? Don't stop with just this list. Add any other intriguing set-ups that occur to you until you have a comprehensive list of potential plots. Then combine these with the set of suggested character motivations in the next chapter and you'll have a sea of sizzling storylines.

Hackneyed Plots

Look at things from the poor fiction editor's viewpoint. He reads thousands of short stories every year and must be bored rigid when the same old storylines, told in the same old ways, keep coming around and around.

He's not likely to grab your romance tale about two lonely people who accidentally meet while walking their dogs, if he has five others lying on his desk at the same time. He's looking for freshness, ingenuity, a touch of originality and flair. Hackneyed plots, told in routine ways, aren't going to get his pulse racing.

So please, make it your business to learn the hoary old chestnut plots and then avoid them at all costs. I list the worst offenders in the chapter on competitions, but to be going on with here are two real cliché plotlines: the Victorian horror tale where the narrator turns out to be (yawn) Jack the Ripper, and the post holocaust sci-fi story where the last two survivors are unsurprisingly called Adam and Eve.

Predictable plots

What makes a story gripping is the tension it generates. The reader thinks: what's going to happen next? How will she get out of that one? But if the reader knows what is going to happen – if the plot is predictable – there is no tension. No-one cares about the characters.

If you find your story is predictable, the chances are there aren't enough random elements in it; the narrative has gone down an easily surmised route. Characters don't have options and can't make unexpected choices.

Let the characters turn off the main road. Introduce a few detours. Keep your audience guessing.

Romance stories where boy meets girl and they live happily ever after don't grip us. Everything is preordained. But when boy meets girl, loses girl and has to win her back we have questions, uncertainty and tension. *Will* he win her back? *How* will he win her back?

Pile on the problems

The more problems you give your main character, the more choices he faces and the less predictable the storyline becomes.

A story about a struggling football team facing relegation has some tension. Will they go down or hang on, in a last brave goal surge during the play-offs? But there are only two possible out-comes – they win and stay up or they lose and are banished to a lower division.

What about introducing an extra complication? What if the manager knows he'll be fired if the club flops but has been offered a large bribe by the opposition to field an inferior team. We then have the added tension of wondering: will he take the bribe or will he stay true to his mates? Even if he has fielded an inferior team, can they still win through against the odds? Suddenly, the predictable either/or outcome has gone and we have a story that grips right up to the final whistle.

Remember: Don't give away too much too soon. Keep feeding the reader information and clues throughout the story. Make the journey exciting all the way to the final destination. Don't let up until the end. It's your job to give your main character hell. Make his life as complicated as you can.

Is a theme vital?

No, short stories don't have to be deep and meaningful, but I believe that a tale which has a theme will strike more of a chord with readers. It doesn't have to be a great truth or a telling insight into the human condition but a simple, easily recognised motif that will give your story a crafted, polished, feel.

How about: pride comes before a fall, money is the root of all evil, good will always triumph over bad, we get the friends we deserve, we never learn until it's too late, marry in haste and repent at leisure? I'm sure you can think of dozens more. Proverbs, especially, are a great source of dramatic themes.

Now, having a theme is brilliant but I'd urge you not to set out to give a story a moral – a worthy thought to take away and mull over. You'll just end up writing a sermon or a piece of propaganda. Either way it'll be a real turn-off. Let people draw their own conclusions from what you've written. If your story is realistic and deals with an interesting dilemma it will say something about life – whether you intend it or not.

Dead Men's shoes has a theme: *a criminal never benefits from his crimes.* But I'd be mortified if anyone thought I was preaching at them. Don't force-feed readers a message, or try to tell them how to behave, or what kind of lifestyle to follow or what to think about an issue. It's clumsy, it insults the reader's intelligence and it makes for bad fiction. When your characters should be busy getting into scrapes, causing problems and resolving conflicts, you'll have them making speeches and pontificating.

Leave your soapbox in the cupboard. Readers have picked up your story because they want to be entertained – not to find themselves on the receiving end of a moral diatribe.

Exercises

Think of the "average reader" you identified in your magazine analysis in the exercises at the end of chapter two. You've already identified the person's hopes and fears so use these to give you two separate plotlines.

In the first make the main character's biggest dream come true ... but show that it doesn't quite go the way he planned. In the second have his worst nightmare come true but show how he gets round it. In both use the *conflict – flashback – conflict resolved* format shown in the chapter.

Devise a shaggy dog story where you keep the surprise ending hidden until the last six words.

Write a circular storyline where the action comes back round to the beginning. A hint here: a time travel story is easiest.

Take our set-up with the threesome trapped in the lift and work out two alternative plotlines showing how the action develops and how it ends.

Summary

- ✓ The majority of stories by new writers fail because they don't have enough plot or a plot that isn't strong enough to sustain interest.

- ✓ To qualify as a story there must be incidents: a chain of events. There must be a crisis to be resolved; action to follow. There must be a plot.

- ✓ Sometimes, writers will have the beginning of a plot. Their character faces a problem but it is trivial and quickly overcome. There's no drama.

- ✓ To hold the reader's attention your hero must face a crisis or dilemma that demands his immediate and full attention.

- ✓ Overcoming it should be tricky or awkward. Not overcoming it will have serious repercussions. There is a strong likelihood he'll fail. And the solution he devises has to be unexpected and ingenious.

- ✓ A common error is to confuse the basic set-up of the story (the opening crisis or situation) with the plot. The plot is what happens from there – how events unfold.

- ✓ A good basic structure looks like this:

  A. ***Introduction – main character faces a worrying conflict/problem/dilemma.***

  B. ***Middle – in flashback we learn of the background and events that led up to the conflict.***

  C. ***Ending – the conflict is satisfactorily resolved.***

- ✓ Another workable structure is to have a hero who has a goal he desperately needs to achieve – and then put obstacles in his way.

✓ Conflict is anything or anyone that upsets the smooth-running of your main character's life.

✓ Conflict can be internal – a crisis of faith, a fear to be overcome, or a problem created by a flaw in the character's own personality.

✓ Good drama looks at what happens when the extraordinary occurs. It shows how people react to unusual and unexpected circumstances.

✓ Aim for a nail-biting finish. Keep the reader holding his breath until the last word.

✓ The more you place your hero in jeopardy the stronger the tension. Tingling anticipation and dread will hold readers glued.

✓ A good way of dreaming up plots is to look at proverbs and well known sayings and investigate what associations they spark in your mind.

✓ See if you can have a *circular* or *return ticket* plotline where the story brings you back to the point at which the narrative started.

✓ Another favourite is the *shaggy dog* story. The writer builds up conflict, piles on suspense and then unexpectedly produces a comic punchline.

✓ The plot is the most important element in a short story and nothing should hold it up or challenge it for the reader's attention.

✓ Always try to deal with topics in a way that leaves the reader feeling uplifted and full of hope.

✓ Have storylines that show characters taking charge of their own destiny and standing up for themselves.

- ✓ There is no such thing as an original plotline so it's important that you find a new treatment that will make a storyline crackle with originality.

- ✓ Make it your business to learn the hoary old chestnut plots and then avoid them at all costs.

- ✓ Keep the reader guessing. The more choices your hero has, the less predictable the storyline becomes.

- ✓ Having a simple theme to your story is great, but don't set out to give it a moral. You'll end up writing a sermon or a piece of propaganda.

5

CHARACTERISATION

We spend our lives surrounded by other people. Whether it's friends, relatives, neighbours, colleagues, lovers, enemies or just the woman who sits beside us on the bus, people encroach on our every waking moment. We even dream about them.

It's no surprise then that we are fascinated by our fellow human beings. We want to know what they are doing, thinking, hoping and fearing; hearing about the mishaps and mischief they get up to.

This fascination with other people's lives is just as strong, arguably stronger, when it comes to the fiction we devour. When we immerse ourselves in a short story or a book we want to read about the challenges and dilemmas that the characters face. We want people we can sympathise with, others we can detest. We want to imagine ourselves as the hero winning through against all odds or give thanks that we aren't the poor soul whose life is in a mess.

It's the characters, *the people*, that we care about, not the setting or the buildings or the landscape or the weather. And for this reason, a writer has to make sure his characters are strong and believable. He can't get away with vague outlines or mere symbols or stereotypes. He has to make them real.

Believability factor

Literature is full of marmalade-munching teddy bears, telepaths, magicians, caravanning toads, flying nannies and big friendly giants. These bizarre and improbable individuals all share one common feature – no-one would think for a moment that they really existed, yet they are totally believable.

Why do we believe in them? Why are we so ready to suspend our cynicism? The secret is simple. The writers who dreamt up these unusual characters believed in them – they visualised them as living, breathing individuals with hopes, fears, and all-too human foibles and quirks. By believing in their characters, the writers make us believe too. And you must truly believe in the imaginary people you create, you must know exactly how they talk, act and think.

Your characters don't have to be real or naturalistic to be believable. They can be as way-out or as alien as you choose to make them. But they do have to be fully-rounded individuals with personalities, likes and dislikes, faults and good points, motivations and goals. They must be imbued with such energy and depth of detail that they step off the page.

Characterisation made easy

There are dozens of different techniques for creating intriguing and unique characters. Writers all have their own pet ways of playing Frankenstein; making the figures they devise come to life before the reader's eyes.

But whatever ingenious tricks authors may dream up, all use the two most crucial elements of characterisation – putting over (a) how someone looks and (b) how he acts and thinks. In other words, his appearance and personality.

In this chapter we'll look at both these areas in depth, examine how to stop your characters from coming across as stereotypes or outrageous caricatures and take a look at how some famous writers have created stunning and memorable individuals.

Section one: Appearance

In a short story you haven't got the space for long, involved, descriptions of your characters – and, to be honest, there really isn't the need.

The reader is only going to be in their company for a little while – just as long as it takes for the central drama to unfold and be resolved – so you need to find shortcut ways of telling what your "cast" looks like. The most effective shortcuts are names, unusual features and mannerisms.

Names Character names are vital. Everyone needs a name. You can't expect a reader to feel empathy for the tall man in the black hat. It's too impersonal, too distant. It's only when we learn that he is called John that we start to feel any connection to him.

The choice of name is important. You can suggest a great deal about a person's age and background by the name he or she has. A pensioner probably won't be called Gary and you're unlikely to find an Albert leading a motorbike gang. Joe Higgins is most likely to be a middle-aged northerner while Jacqui Jones is young, single and works in a Home Counties office.

Even versions of the same name can suggest heaps about someone. Ted is a good bloke, popular with his mates on the allotment, while Edward is proud to be a solicitor. Elizabeth runs the local Women's Institute with military precision while Lizzy is always late for the mums' and toddlers' group.

The power of names is incredible. For this reason, editors have no hesitation in changing the monikers in the stories they buy. They know that unless a name is exactly right for the setting, era and genre, it'll seem odd and risks destroying the suspension of disbelief. It may jolt the reader out of the story, it may even be unintentionally funny.

For instance, Zardoc may be a wonderful ruler on the third planet in the Orion system but he isn't going to cut the mustard as an assistant manager in a supermarket. Conversely, the bold, ruthless leader of the savage tech-war mercenaries is unlikely to be called Kevin – unless it's in a sit-com!

Make sure you use names which create the mental image you're aiming for. You should know when a name feels right – short, strong names for powerful characters; long, fussy names for officious or pompous individuals.

Comic stories can benefit from characters having unusual sounding names but don't over-do it. Roger Clutterbuck is an amusing moniker, but Josiah Clutterbuck goes that bit too much over the top.

Be aware that girl's names, particularly, come in and out of fashion and you need to know the trendy names if you want your female characters to have a fresh and modern appeal. Read women's magazines to find out what the current vogue names are. But take care – they fall out of fashion just as quickly.

A safe bet for a name that won't date or seem out of period, is to go for Biblical names – Ruth, Rachel, Daniel, Mark, Luke etc. These are perennial favourites.

One important point: always make sure that you pick

names that are distinctive and as different as possible from each other. Don't start names with the same letter of the alphabet. If you have a Dave and a Don in a story the reader will mix them up. McArthur and McDonald appearing together will cause confusion.

If the reader blurs characters in his mind, he's likely to find the story incomprehensible. The moment he stops and goes back a few paragraphs to sort out his confusion, the magical narrative spell is broken.

Unusual features Basically, most people look the same. We have the standard issue two eyes, a nose, mouth, two ears, arms, legs, fingers, toes, hair etc. What interests readers is what makes someone look different from other people.

There's no point wasting space describing a cheerleader as beautiful, an old man as stooped and wrinkled, or a baby as smooth, small and pink. We all know what they look like. Likewise, there's no point describing a bank manager as grey, a labourer as burly or a sergeant major as bullying and loud-mouthed. It goes without saying.

Only tell the reader about unusual features; details of appearance that make the character stand out from the crowd – the punk rocker in a three-piece suit, the policeman who is five feet tall, the bald woman, the bow-legged ballet dancer.

Stick to describing the basics (age, sex, height, build etc) as swiftly as possible. Only *dwell* on appearance if it affects the way a person acts or gives us an insight into his or her personality. For example:

- The ugly man speaks to no-one at the party because he is self-conscious about his looks.

- The woman beside him has salad dressing down her blouse because she's clumsy.

- A short man is loud and aggressive to compensate for his lack of stature.

- An extremely tall girl feels lonely and unloved because men find her physically intimidating.

- The conman wears a smart suit and horn-rimmed glasses, and carries a briefcase because he thinks it makes him look more respectable.

We'll look in more detail at just how much description to use in creating character in chapter seven.

Mannerisms We all have dozens of distinctive little quirks of speech, appearance and behaviour that makes us different from other people. Often we are unaware of these mannerisms until they are pointed out to us.

Maybe you always dunk chocolate biscuits into your tea, blush whenever anyone tells a rude joke, frown when you tell lies or put on a posh voice when you use the phone. Maybe you wear brown shoes with black trousers or always say: *Hello, it's only me* every time you enter a room. These mannerisms tell people more about your personality than you'd realise.

When describing a person, you can suggest his personality and individuality through his mannerisms. You'll have created an individual that is not only easier to visualise but who will come across as being much more real.

Showing character through dialogue

Dialogue is one of the most powerful ways of suggesting someone's character. We give ourselves away the moment we open our mouths. People categorise (and judge) us by what we say and how we say it.

Every utterance provides information about an individual's background. You can tell a person's education, where he grew up, his class, his social aspirations, his profession and his politics by merely listening to how he talks. I've even heard it argued that you can tell if a man is married by the tone of his voice! Just think how differing sorts of people would take a faulty pair of shoes back to the shop.

"Oh dear ... I'm terribly sorry to trouble you. I know it's a lot of bother, and I'm probably making a bit of a fuss about nothing, but these shoes aren't right. They're faulty, I'm afraid." –

someone who is shy and nervous. Taking the shoes back is obviously an ordeal.

"Hey you. Yes, you. I want a word with you about these duff shoes you sold me. Just look at the soles. They've come right off. Bloody rubbish. I want them changed, and I'm not going to take any excuses." – someone loud and aggressive. An irate Glaswegian, perhaps?

"Hi. Can you help me. I bought these shoes here yesterday and when I got them home I found the soles aren't glued on properly. Can you give me another pair. I'd appreciate it. Thanks. I'll just wait here while you get them." – someone quietly confident. Do you notice how this person seems assertive without being aggressive?

"Can you help me? Well, as a matter of fact you can, my dear. These shoes are quite useless. Just take a look at them. The sole isn't attached properly. Quite awful. You just can't get the workmanship these days, can you? And it's certainly not the kind of thing I'd have expected from a well-known shop like this." – someone older and well-to-do. Perhaps this person is a bit lonely too. Do you notice how he or she is trying to start a conversation as well as complaining?

Hidden clues

Often it's not the information the character is providing that helps us to understand him, but the way he articulates it.

It can be as subtle as a one word clue. In the evening do you eat dinner or tea? Sit on a couch or a sofa or a settee? Watch TV in the sitting room, lounge or the parlour? Do you nip to the loo or go to the toilet?

Look at how people from different backgrounds would describe their parents.

1. Ma and pa
2. Mum and dad
3. Mother and father
4. Mater and pater
5. Mom and pop

6. Mama and papa

Just these three words tell us volumes about who is speaking – their social class, their nationality and the closeness or formality of the relationship and the era in which the story is set.

Section Two: Motivations

We all have at least one driving force that guides our actions. For some it's a love of money; for others it's the need to be appreciated and respected. You may feel that the main force in your life is a strong desire to protect and cherish your loved ones. Perhaps it's a burning hunger to put one over on your rivals. All these forces – both good and bad – are motivations. They are the needs, desires and aspirations which shape our lives; and govern our actions and relationships with others.

We've seen it in police shows hundreds of times. The detective says: *Once we find out the motive for the murder, we'll know where to look for our killer.* The same is true for writers. Once you identify what motivates your characters, you will know why they think and act as they do. You will understand what gives them complexity; what makes them different from the others.

The reader needs to understand your hero's or villain's motivations. What drives him is as important as a description of his appearance (or mannerisms, or speech patterns, or dress) in helping create a rounded picture.

Often it's the character's motivations that make readers decide whether or not they like him. You can respect a person who lies to protect others, but not someone who lies to get himself out of trouble.

Moreover, if you – the writer – know what makes your hero tick, you'll be able to predict his future actions and assess how he'd react to an unexpected change of circumstances. **This is particularly important when plotting your story**. The reader will accept a dramatic change in someone's personality and actions, if you show the motivations that have caused it – and they are believable.

In *Death Wish* we believe that Charles Bronson's mild-mannered architect can become a gun-toting vigilante because we see his wife being murdered and his daughter sexually abused by a gang. In *A Christmas Carol* we believe that the miser Scrooge can change because the ghosts show him, not the joys of Christmas, but how unhappy he really is. They make him want to be a better man.

What makes your hero tick?

Here is a sample list of over thirty motivations that might govern the actions of your characters. The list isn't definitive – there are plenty more you could add.

Guilt	Revenge
Malice	Compassion
Bravado	Bravery
Rivalry	Love
Hate	Hiding a secret
Greed	Envy
Fear	Contempt
Cowardice	Protecting something/someone
Gallantry	Thwarting others
Creativity	Desire
Need to conform	Need to be different
Being charitable	Curiosity
Pride	Need for acceptance
Self-loathing	Sense of justice
Insecurity	Bloody-mindedness

REMEMBER: don't confuse personality traits with motivations. A person may not be evil by nature, but may be motivated towards evil deeds by circumstance. He or she may act completely out of character if there is the right motivation provided.

Stereotypes

The word *stereotype* is an old printing industry term. It described a technique for making printing plates where molten metal was poured into a mould, shaped to the appearance of a finished page. The advantage was the speed at which an identical page could be moulded if the first plate became damaged.

When we use the term stereotype in writing, we're talking about a similar process. Instead of creating new, living, believable characters, we simply go to the mould and pour out another batch of bland, formula cartoon cut-outs.

Now, we know that no two people are the same – that's what makes life interesting. Everyone's personality, appearance and attitude to life is different. So it's the duty of a good writer to reflect this diversity of character in his or her writing. It's laziness to fill your stories with bumbling vicars, jolly policemen, singing Welshmen, weak-chinned aristocrats, goatee-bearded psychiatrists, Essex girls called Sharon, sweet old grannies, sadistic teachers, nosy neighbours and all the other fodder of second-rate sit-coms.

By using these empty symbols instead of characters, you insult the intelligence of the reader and reinforce prejudices. You reduce your writing to the level of the saucy seaside postcard.

If you fill stories with stereotypes so that your characters are identical to everyone else's, why should a fiction editor single your work out for publication?

Put yourself to the test

Think none of this applies to *you*? Convinced *you* don't think in stereotypes?

Try this quiz and find out. I've listed different types of people. I want you to write one word in the space provided, to describe them. Don't stop to consider – put down the very first thought that comes into your head.

Scotsmen	....
Germans	....
Women drivers	....
Nurses	....
Teenagers	....
Robbers	....

Army officers	....
MPs	....
Blondes	....
Italians	....
Train spotters	....
Convicts	....
Nuns	....
Race horse owners	....
Second-hand car salesmen	....
Chat show hosts	....

Did you fall into the stereotype trap? Shame on you if you had the words *gentlemen* or *posh* for army officers or *mean* for Scotsmen or *sleazy* for MPs or *rich* written down against race horse owners. By pigeon-holing types of people in this lazy way you are closing your mind to endless character possibilities.

What about Major Richard Sharpe, Bernard Cornwell's dashing Napoleonic hero plucked from the ranks by the Duke of Wellington? Although he is a thoroughly good sort, no-one would describe Sharpe as either posh or a gentleman.

And what about Andrew Carnegie – one of the world's great philanthropists? He was Scots.

Would you describe Winston Churchill as sleazy? And what about our race horse owners? Many horses are now owned by syndicates of ordinary punters – many from modest backgrounds – who all club together to buy a filly.

Remember that you have to look beyond the obvious to know a person's true personality. Don't stick labels on people and judge them by their job, hobbies, appearance, sex or race.

Real people are complex and multi-facetted. Take the example of Elsie who lives rough on the streets of London, surviving on charity hand-outs and occasional visits to a church-run soup kitchen. At first glance you'd see her grimy face and dirty, dishevelled clothes. Her language is coarse and slurred. But what can you really tell about her beyond her obvious tramp-like appearance?

Has she always been like that? What if I told you she could play the piano? Immediately we'd see more to her. This is a woman from a well-to-do background who has fallen on hard times. Suddenly she's a person not just another anonymous down-and-out.

So how can you put this across to the reader without giving a large dollop of boring background information? Simple, she may look like all the others at the night shelter, but Elsie is the only one who has her tatty belongings in a *Harrods*' carrier bag. Even on the street Elsie never forgets who she once was and still feels superior to the others living rough.

It's this kind of subtle detail that helps characters to exist in three dimensions; that makes them more than just a routine invention of an unimaginative writer.

Making a stereotype work for you

There's only one time when using stereotypes in a story is defensible – and that's when you are using the reader's own prejudices and lazy thinking against him.

The most effective sting-in-the-tale stories lull the reader into a false sense of familiarity by using stereotypes. Just as the reader thinks the black man being questioned by police is a mugger or that the cleaning woman is badly educated, the writer turns the tables.

The black man is a priest who was going to the victim's aid or the cleaning woman is a redundant city trader who works as a char so that she can look for stock exchange tips thrown away in the waste paper bins.

Fame game

That's enough of the theory of bringing imaginary individuals to life. Let's now see how famous writers Sue Townsend, Ian Fleming, Michael Crichton and John Le Carre skilfully use these various techniques to make their characters fascinating and vibrant. Here are a few extracts:

Jack Barker's denim shirt sleeves were rolled to the elbow. His already handsome features had been further enhanced by subtle touches of colour. His accent combined the flattened vowels of the north with the crisper intonation of the south.

He knew his smile was good; he used it often. He had

alarmed his civil servants by telling them that he intended to write his own speeches and it was his own speech that he was reading now on the autocue. Even to his own ears it sounded stilted and ridiculous.

The Yeoman of the Silver Plate scrutinised Jack Barker, the new Prime Minister.

Very nice, he thought. Smaller than he looked on the telly, but very nice. Clothes a bit Top Man and shoes a bit Freeman Hardyish, but a good, fine-boned face, adorable eyes – violet, and lavish eyelashes like spider's legs.

Sue Townsend - The Queen and I

Morris was in his late twenties, wearing a tie, and pants from a business suit. He carried a briefcase. His wing-tip shoes crunched on the rocks.

Grant was amused to see Morris gaping at Ellie. She was wearing jeans and a workshirt tied at the midriff. She was twenty-four and darkly tanned. Her blonde hair was pulled back.

Gennaro had forgotten how short Hammond was; as he sat in the chair, his feet didn't touch the carpeting; he swung his legs as he talked. There was a childlike quality to the man, even though Hammond must now be ... what? Seventy-five? Seventy-six? Something like that.

Shortly before midnight Ian Malcolm stepped on to the plane at Dallas airport, a tall, thin, balding man of thirty five, dressed entirely in black: black shirt, black trousers, black socks, black sneakers ...

He sat in one of the padded chairs. The stewardess asked him if he wanted a drink. He said: "Diet Coke, shaken not stirred."

Michael Crichton - Jurrassic Park

The door opened. A short slim man with sandy hair came in and walked over to the desk and stood beside Bond's chair. Bond looked up into his face. He hadn't often seen the man before, but he remembered the very wide-apart clear grey eyes that never seemed to flicker.

With a non-committal glance down at Bond, the man stood

relaxed, looking across at M. He said: "Good morning, sir," in a flat, unemotional voice.

Ian Fleming - Dr. No

Leamas was a short man with close, iron-grey hair, and the physique of a swimmer. He was very strong. This strength was discernible in his back and shoulders, in his neck and in the stubby formation of his hands and fingers.

He had a utilitarian approach to clothes, as he did to most things and even the spectacles he occasionally wore had steel rims.

He had an attractive face, muscular, and a stubborn line to his thin mouth. His eyes were brown and small: Irish some said.

Leamas looked like a man who could make trouble, a man who looked after his money, a man who was not quite a gentleman.

John Le Carre - The Spy Who Came In From The Cold

Did you like them? They're all very effective pieces of character creation.

Can you see the cunning way that Ian Fleming and John le Carre use the physical descriptions of the characters to suggest important clues to their personalities?

Leamas has a *stubborn* line to his mouth and looks like a man *who could make trouble*. He has a physicality to him that makes him threatening. He is someone you treat with respect.

Fleming's character is the secret service armourer in the James Bond books – a guns specialist. He is an emotionless technician, a man more used to dealing with weapons than people. Yet, although there is a lack of emotion about him, the man isn't bland. He is calm, confident, expert. His grey, wide eyes never flicker. You can imagine that looking into them is like peering down the barrel of a gun!

What do you reckon to Ian Malcolm, the mathematics whizzkid who's going to find himself being chased all over Jurassic Park by ravenous killer dinosaurs? Michael Crichton *tells* us straight away that this is a character who likes to be noticed. Malcolm wears black – not to be inconspicuous, but for just the opposite effect!

And catch that snappy line of dialogue: *Diet Coke, shaken*

not stirred. Those five words speak volumes about this man. He drinks Coke so he's young – at least he thinks he is. He drinks Diet Coke so he likes to be trendy (and why not when you're dressed entirely in black?) Perhaps he also drinks Diet Coke because he's worried about getting fat.

By parodying the famous James Bond line, Ian Malcolm shows he likes films, likes to wisecrack, has a keen sense of ironic humour and secretly fancies himself as a bit of a hero.

This is marvellous characterisation, which describes Ian Malcolm in lots of subtle and oblique ways. We've got this individual's personality quirks pinned down in just two short sentences.

Notice just how short and punchy Michael Crichton's descriptions are? It's one of his trademarks. His terse, crisp, thumbnail character sketches are well worth studying. He's one of the tightest, most economical writers in the business – a role model for anyone who wants to write slickly.

My particular favourite of this batch of extracts is Sue Townsend's Yeoman of the Silver Plate excerpt – a very clever and amusing piece of multi-layer, multi-character description.

On the surface it is telling us all about Jack Barker being unsophisticated and a bit of an innocent, but really it says much more about the Yeoman of the Silver Plate and his attitudes – not only is he camp and fancies the new Prime Minister, but he's a terrible snob as well.

This is characterisation taken to an art form. It shows just what you can do with a few well-chosen images.

You may not be able to pen word portraits as ingenious and excellent as these (certainly not at first), but you can use the same general principles to make your heroes fresh, lively and memorable. Remember, characters must be more than just faceless chessmen you move around the board of your story. Make the people who inhabit your tales believable individuals with credible motivations, goals and fears, and readers will warm to them.

They'll care what happens to your players, and then you've really hooked them.

Exercises

Imagine that you are a scriptwriter and have been given the task of devising a TV detective to be the central character in a new crime series. He or she must be believable but radically different from any other telly cop in the past.

Describe the detective in 500 words, giving details of his (or her) background, appearance and mannerisms. Show how he goes about solving crimes. Provide a suitable name and say a little about the location.

Imagine that the vicar from your local church has been caught taking money from the collection. Suggest twelve diverse motivations that might have led him to act in this way. Turn three of these into storylines and write them up as full-length stories.

Summary

✓ It's the characters in stories – the people – that we care about, not the setting, the buildings, the landscape or the weather.

✓ A writer has to make sure his characters are strong and believable. He can't get away with vague outlines.

✓ Characters don't have to be naturalistic to be believable but they have to be fully-rounded individuals.

✓ Even if they are aliens or goblins they must still have personalities, likes and dislikes, faults and good points, motivations and goals.

✓ In a short story you need to describe your characters quickly. The best shortcuts are names, mannerisms and unusual features.

✓ Character names are vital. Everyone needs a name. You can't expect a reader to feel empathy for an anonymous figure.

✓ You can suggest a great deal about a person's age and background by the name he or she has.

✓ Unless a name is exactly right for the setting, era and genre, it'll seem odd and risks destroying the suspension of disbelief.

✓ Know when a name feels right – short, strong names for powerful characters; long, fussy names for officious or pompous individuals.

✓ A safe bet for a name that won't date or seem out of period, is to go for Biblical names – Ruth, Rachel, Daniel, Mark, Luke etc.

- ✓ Pick names that are distinctive and as different as possible from each other. Don't let the reader mix up characters in his head.
- ✓ Stick to describing the basics (age, sex, height, build, etc) as swiftly as possible.
- ✓ Readers are interested in what makes someone look different from other people. Only tell the reader about unusual features.
- ✓ When describing a person, you can suggest his personality and individuality through his mannerisms.
- ✓ Dialogue is another powerful way of suggesting character. Every utterance provides information about an individual's background.
- ✓ The way people speak reveals their background, upbringing, the closeness of their relationships and the era in which the story is set.
- ✓ Once you identify what motivates your characters, you'll know why they think and act as they do.
- ✓ The reader needs to understand your hero's or villain's motivations. What drives him is as important as a good description of his appearance.
- ✓ Often it's the character's motivations that make your readers decide whether or not they like him.
- ✓ A person may not be evil but he may act in an evil way (completely out of character) if the right motivation is provided.
- ✓ Always make your characters real and different. Don't use stereotypes. They insult the intelligence of the reader and reinforce prejudices.

✓ Using stereotypes is defensible only when you are using the reader's own prejudices and lazy thinking against him.

6

DIALOGUE

Dialogue scares new writers. They'll do anything to avoid it – cross the street, move house, change their names. But you can't run away from it forever. Dialogue must be faced and mastered if you ever hope to make it into print.

Don't take my word for it – browse through any magazine. Have you ever seen a published story that didn't contain at least some dialogue? We spend our lives talking to each other and we expect the characters who inhabit the stories we read to do the same.

As we've said in the previous chapter, it's only when characters open their mouths and speak that they truly come to life. Take a look at any group at a party. The people who don't speak – the wallflowers – are ignored. Characters who don't speak create about the same impact.

So what exactly is dialogue? In its simplest form, it's just a conversation between two or more characters. It's just like the chats you hear and take part in every day. Nothing more threatening or complex than that.

Then why is it so scary?

The reason most new writers give is that, deep inside themselves, they know they just can't reproduce conversations that are real; that sound right.

So how do you make characters speak like real people? How do you pick up on each person's individual mannerisms and unique speech patterns? Surely it's impossible – unless you're a trained linguist who has the time to go round tape-recording conversations and analysing them?

The good news is that you don't have to. In fact, it doesn't matter if your dialogue isn't authentic, as long as it sounds as though it might be. Dialogue isn't an accurate representation of how people speak. It's a carefully selected series of words uttered by characters that pretends to be real speech.

The purpose of dialogue is to put over vital information – about what's happening, how people feel, the tension of the situation or the background of the main characters. It puts over information in much the same way as your descriptions do. It tells the reader important facts and snippets of information he needs to know.

Ums and Ahs

When you look at a story, you'll see that the way the characters talk isn't realistic at all. There are no *ahs* and *ums*, no woolly phrases or sentences that drift off at a tangent, no sentences left unfinished. Everything is clear, quick and clean. If only we talked like that in real life.

In real life you might say: "*How do I like my coffee? Er ... um ... well. Eh? That's a tricky one. Normally – when I say normally, I mean not absolutely all the time – I take milk, with sugar. A couple of spoonfuls. But not when I'm on a diet ...*"

The super slick character in a story will say: "*I take it hot and sweet. Just like my women.*"

Now the second version may sound like real conversation, but it isn't. It's merely a way of conveying information to the reader. The point isn't just that the character takes sugar in his coffee, but that he is a big-headed prat with a 70s medallion man mentality.

Is dialogue really necessary?

Yes, it's vital. I've lost count of the number of short stories I've had to eliminate from competitions because the writer didn't have any dialogue at all.

Characters need to speak. They need to be heard – out loud! If you don't let us hear what the character thinks and feels out of his own mouth, he'll remain forever a symbol (not a living, breathing, individual) and we won't care about him or what happens to him. Dialogue brings us closer to a character. Deny us his words and you're making sure that he'll remain distant, vague and unsympathetic.

Rob a story of dialogue and you're likely to fall into the trap of summarising events rather than letting them unfold in real time. You'll end up **telling** instead of **showing**.

When we hear the characters speak we experience the events in the story as they happen. We're there in the thick of the action. But when characters don't speak, the writer has to put over the missing dialogue in other ways – usually in long, fussy descriptive passages and clumsy, intrusive explanations. We're no longer involved in the story, at the main character's side, sharing his adventures. Instead, we're listening to a narrator recounting the adventures in a flat, static, second-hand summary. It's a poor substitute for a ring-side seat on the action.

Instant impact

To prove my point, consider which of these extracts has more impact:

A. "*I hate you*," Marie screamed, waving the knife in John's face. "*I'll make sure you never betray me again. I'll make sure you never look at another woman ... ever*!"

   Edging back, he gulped. "*L-l-look*," he stammered, "*can't we be calm and talk about this? You don't need the knife*."

B. Angrily Marie confronted John, waving a knife in his face. She told him he'd never betray her again with another woman. He backed away nervously, asking if they could talk it out. He told her that she didn't need to threaten him with the knife.

The answer is obviously A. There is life, danger, emotion when Marie screams in rage. Option B isn't dramatic – in fact it reads like the minutes of a committee meeting.

One is exciting, the other guaranteed to have you snoring into your cocoa, yet both contain the same basic information. See the difference that dialogue makes?

Dynamic dialogue

Most of what we say in an average day is boring, repetitive and commonplace. Short story dialogue can't afford to be any of these things. It's the key phrase, the vital speech, that brings tension, humour or drama to the piece. It's the writer's equivalent of the journalist's sound bite.

"*Three eggs and a pint of milk, please.*" isn't dialogue. It doesn't add anything to our understanding of the character, the setting or the events unfolding.

"*My God! It's going to blow! Run everyone*!" is dialogue. It quickens the pace and builds the tension.

Dialogue has three main functions:

1. To move on the action of the story. "*Honey, sit down. I've got a surprise for you. It wasn't indigestion after all ... I'm pregnant*!"

2. To reveal more about the characters. "*Love you? I could never love anyone poor.*"

3. To inject excitement. "*If you don't hand it over, I'll kill you – so help me*!"

In all these instances, dialogue is providing information – not just slavishly mimicking everyday speech. If your dialogue isn't telling the reader something crucial about the action, the characters or the atmosphere, it shouldn't be there.

To take the earlier example, it's far better to say: John went into the supermarket to buy eggs and milk.

"*I'm disgusted at these prices,*" he told the checkout girl, "*it's eating up my pension.*"

See how the dialogue reveals something about John and how he feels about the situation?

Don't fall into the 'Hello' trap

Beware having your characters waste their dialogue on routine greetings and pleasantries. There is no need to have them wishing each other good morning or asking: *how are you keeping these days*?

It's surprising how much space in a short story you can gobble up with people saying hello and goodbye to each other. It's amazing how much such greetings kill the pace.

Also, don't allow characters to rabbit on pointlessly just for the sake of hearing their own voices. Unless a conversation is emotion-packed and plays an important part in moving the plot forward, leave it out.

Take a look at these two exchanges. Conversation A is guaranteed to cure insomnia and hopefully would never make its way into a published short story. Conversation B is lively, information packed and vital to the development of the plot.

EXAMPLE A

"Cooee dear. Hello!"

Mary sighed and came out from behind the counter where she'd been hiding. It was just her luck. She had hoped the old busybody hadn't spotted her but now she knew she was in for an hour's ear-bashing.

"Hello, Mrs Marshall" she said wearily. "How are you?"

"Musn't grumble dear. Musn't grumble. How's yourself?"

"Fine. I'm great."

"And your husband, dear Ken?"

"He's fine too."

Mrs Marshall beamed. "I thought he was looking pleased with himself at the writer's circle," she said. "We all so enjoyed the story he read out. He's so talented."

" I like to think so," Mary agreed.

"It's a disgrace that he's never had anything published. Editors just don't know good writing when they see it. That's the trouble."

Mary smiled to herself. "Yes, that's more or less what Ken was saying. Still, maybe one day. How's your writing coming along?"

The older woman shrugged. "Not so good, if I'm honest, dear. I just can't seem to get my characters to say anything really interesting. They just stand around all day nattering about inconsequential things."

"I'm sure you're exaggerating."

"No, Mary. They haven't a dramatic word to say. They just gossip on pointlessly."

"Ah well," Mary told her sympathetically. "They're probably just being mundane and boringly realistic. We can't all live action-packed lives. How's your ankle? I hear you sprained it the other week ... "

EXAMPLE B

"Oh hello, my dear, trying to avoid me?"

Mary sighed and came out from behind the counter where she'd been hiding. It was just her luck. She'd hoped the old busybody hadn't spotted her but now she knew she was in for an hour's ear-bashing.

"Hello, Mrs Marshall" she said wearily. "I didn't see you there. How are you?"

"Musn't grumble I suppose, not that anyone really cares. But it's not me we should be talking about. How's your husband? I hope he's not too unwell."

" Unwell? No, Ken's fine."

" Are you sure? It's just with him not being at the last few meetings of the writer's circle we all thought he must have some sort of illness."

Mary frowned. "Sorry, but I think you must be mistaken. Ken never misses the circle meetings. It's the highlight of his week. He was there last night."

The old woman shook her head. "No, dear. He wasn't. In fact, he hasn't been for at least the last three meetings. It's been more than a month." She looked questioningly. "Didn't he tell you? I'd have thought you'd have known."

Mary's mind froze. What was the witch on about? Of course Ken had gone to the writer's circle. Why wouldn't he?

"In fact," Mrs Marshall continued, "neither has that young girl who writes the poetry. We thought she must be ill too. You know, Jane – the pretty one with the long legs and the ..."

The older woman stopped in mid-sentence, as though suddenly struck by the terrible implication of what she'd just said. Mary knew it was an act. The biddy had sought her out just to drop the bombshell at her feet. The old cow was enjoying every moment of it.

"Can you excuse me a moment," Mary said, images of Ken and the girl whizzing through her mind. "I need to sit down. It's a bit stuffy in here."

"Oh dear, silly old me. Putting my big foot in it again. I hope I haven't said anything out of turn. I didn't mean to cause any trouble. I wasn't suggesting ..."

"No, no. I'm sure there's a perfectly simple explanation. He's probably lost interest in writing and is embarrassed to admit it." Mary fought to smile but she felt faint, sick.

She sat down heavily. "I'm sure he's just waiting for the right moment to tell me. He's probably been going down to the pub these last few weeks."

The old woman looked her in the eye, her gaze both probing and pitying. Was there a trace of contempt too?

"Ah ... yes. That'll be it," the older woman replied without conviction. "I'm sure he's a good man, your Ken. I'm sure he wouldn't ... it's just a coincidence ..." She sniffed thoughtfully. "But they do say the wife is always the last one to know ..."

Mary found herself shaking. No wonder the bastard had always looked so happy when he went out the door. How could he!

She didn't know what was worse – that her husband was a no-good two-timer or that she had to find it out from Mrs Marshall of all people. The crone couldn't keep her trap shut for two minutes – it was probably all over town by now.

The first passage is a classic example of lots of talking but no-one saying anything – at least, nothing worth hearing. By the end of the story the characters remain exactly where they were.

The second passage, on the other hand, is the turning point in the narrative. In an instant a few *careless* words have destroyed Mary's happiness and introduced terrible conflict into her life.

Notice how the old woman turns the knife, working on Mary's fears with the words: *But they do say the wife is the last to know*. She is obviously savouring every delicious moment.

See how this exchange moves on the plot, tells us a lot about Mrs Marshall's snide, cantankerous personality and highlights the uneasy relationship between the two women. The dialogue is the key element in making this scene work. Aim to make your dialogue work like this. Every time a character opens his mouth make sure he says something of importance.

Sense of excitement

Here are a few more examples of dialogue earning its keep. Even in a few lines these short sound bites help create drama.

"At 9am tomorrow we go in for the kill. We buy every share we can lay our hands on. This takeover will be so hostile, it'll wear bovver boots!"

"You've got to be off your trolley to get taken in by all that brainless bilge. You won't catch me believing any of that superstitious horoscope claptrap."

"You want to cast another actress in the part? Someone younger! Well, thanks a bunch for the compliment. That makes me feel great. You may not have noticed, but I'm not over the hill quite yet."

"I wouldn't expect you to notice. When have you ever noticed anything I've done? When have you ever cared? I'm the invisible man. For all the love and attention I get from you I might as well not exist."

"Of course, it's obvious you think we're all morons. We may have been turning out prize-winning products for twenty years but you know that's been a fluke. Dim-wits like us should have failed ages ago. Well, thank heavens you've come to the rescue with your dazzling university know-how and your framed business management certificate."

There's only dialogue in these extracts but see how much information you're able to pick up purely from these lines? Notice how you can tell all sorts of things about the people speaking – their emotional state, their relationship to those they're addressing, whether they have the upper hand or are being defensive, whether they're being sarcastic ... even their age.

There's not a single word of description or explanation accompanying these lines. Yet they work wonderfully. That's how good dialogue should perform.

Don't dabble with dialect

Apart from the fact that regional dialect is difficult to write, it is tiring and irksome to read. By the time readers have waded their way through all the "*Oooo arghs*", "*Ee by gums*" and "*Way eye, bonnee luds*" they'll probably have lost all notion of what the plot is about.

Long screeds of dialect aren't necessary. Just write that a character speaks, for example, in a broad Scots voice and the reader will do the rest. He'll imagine he hears the dialogue being spoken with a Caledonian accent. You can help the process along by using the occasional Scots word or phrase – your hero could say "*you ken?*" instead of "*you understand?*" or call people Wully instead of Willy.

This should be enough to create the effect you want, but be careful not to overdo it – you don't want to make him sound as though he's just walked out of a Monarch of the Glen shortbread tin.

You don't have to drop in lots of "*nowts*" and "*eh-ups*" to suggest a regional accent. You only have to start a piece of dialogue with "*When I were a lad ...*" and the reader is immediately whisked off to The Dales.

The effect can be achieved just as dramatically by re-creating the word patterns associated with a particular area. For example, the statement "*Beryl is plump*" could be spoken by anyone in Britain. But when the sentence changes to "*She's very plump, is our Beryl*", then you know the person speaking it is most likely to have come from Lancashire or Yorkshire.

It even works on a trans-Atlantic level. The phrase "*It was fabulous, like*" is definitely British. (Can't you just hear the Black Country twang?) But move the word *like* to another part of the sentence and you're in California. "*It was like, fabulous!*" Gee, was it?

Keep your ear tuned for these little quirks of speech and you'll always be able to give the impression that your character has a regional accent. All right, me ducks!

Ealing Comedy syndrome

This is a nickname I have for a very common ailment that afflicts thousands of new writers. Ask them to write dialogue spoken by the type of people they're familiar with and there's no problem. But ask them to imagine how someone from a different background speaks and suddenly the Ealing Comedy symptoms appear.

For no apparent reason their characters all begin to sound like extras from those old 1940s black and white comedy films they show on TV on Sunday afternoons.

I'm not being "class-ist" about this. I've seen middle class writers who make any working class character sound like a Cockney road sweeper. "*Well, stone the crows. There's going to be a right to-do about this one, governor, and no mistake.*"

Equally, I've read working class writers who make middle class characters sound like they have just stepped onto the platform in Brief Encounter. "*I know it's terribly forward of me to ask, old girl: but do you really love me? Truly, truly love me ... with all your heart?*"

And as for the poor upper classes! Everyone mangles the speech patterns of aristocrats. They all end up squeaking like chin-less wonders. "*Oh how simply super. It's frightfully nice that you could come to Twickers for the rugger.*"

Okay, I know what you're thinking. No-one could write dialogue that bad. Well, yes they could. I've read dialogue in competition entries that has been even worse.

The ironic thing is that even back when these wonderful black and white classic comedies were being made no-one really talked like that. So please, don't write dialogue like that unless, like some famous alternative comedians, you are doing a send-up of the genre.

Keep your dialogue realistic. Stay away from hackneyed lines. No matter how well you draw your characters, and how much effort you put into making them fully rounded and unique individuals, you're back in stereotype land if your magistrate says: "*Well, what have you got to say for yourself, young feller, me lad*" and your crook declares: "*It's a fair cop. You've got me bang to rights. I'll come quietly.*"

You can indicate that a character comes from a particular class or has a certain social status in a much more restrained and subtle way.

To suggest that a character is working class have him say *me* instead of *my*. "*That's me house over there.*" Or you could have him say; "*I done it*" instead of "*I did it.*"

It's possible to convey that your hero is upper class by having him use the expression *one* instead of *I*. "*One tends to know instinctively when something is right.*"

People who are authority figures often have a more slow and ponderous way of speaking. They don't use contractions. Instead of saying something chatty like "*I don't*" and "*I won't*", they'll tend to say "*I do not*" and "*I will not.*" This gives them a rather pompous air.

As for the middle classes – if you want to put across that a character is middle class there are certain key phrases that you can use. Middle class people often start sentences, especially when they are annoyed, with "*Do you realise ...*" They also use the phrase "*Excuse me*" when actually being excused is the last thing they want; they just want to dominate the conversation.

Put the two together and you get: "*Excuse me, do you realise that you're parking in my space!*"

Another key phrase is: "*I cannot conceive of ...*" as in "*I cannot conceive of a dustman talking like this.*" A variation on this is: "*I cannot believe that ...*" Then there's: "*I cannot for the life of me see why ...*" Don't these phrases put your teeth on edge? They remind me of every school teacher I ever had to listen to.

Single words help create the same "suburbanite" feel for a character. The moment he says: *absolutely, actually, honestly, ridiculous, infuriating, fiasco, excruciating, surely, splendid or super*, we know he wears a suit, lives in a large house and drives a middle range saloon car.

I'm sure you can come up with lots of other ideas for hinting at a character's class. Listen to how people from different backgrounds use language and pick up on these little tell-tale words and speech quirks. Make a note of any phrase or verbal gimmick that seems to work well. Study how other successful writers get round the problem and then copy their techniques.

Setting out dialogue

Setting out dialogue is easy. If you follow the accepted layout conventions you'll have no trouble in making yourself and your characters understood.

Remember to identify who is talking, and to start a new line for each character each time they speak. This makes it easy to see at a glance who is talking:

"I'm hungry," Bill said.

"I don't see why," his wife answered. "You only ate an hour ago."

"But it wasn't very much."

Dialogue is normally set out like this:

1. "It is a far, far better thing I do today than I have ever done," he said. "Far better than you'll ever know."

2. "Do you remember when we used to dance here every night?" he asked. "It was June and there were a million stars in the sky."

You can also set it out like this:

3. "It is a far, far better thing I do today," he said, "than I have ever done. Far better than you'll ever know."

4. "Do you remember," he asked, "when we used to dance here every night? It was June and there were a million stars in the sky."

Notice in examples 3 and 4 that a comma is inserted after *he said* and *he asked* to tell the reader that the sentence has been broken; that more follows.

Also notice in 3 and 4 that the second section of dialogue starts with a small (lower case) letter. It doesn't matter which of the two methods you use: 1 and 2 or 3 and 4.

I often like to use the device of dropping the dialogue tag (the words that identify who is talking) into the middle of the speech. This gives the effect of a pause in the middle of what the character is saying – as though he's thinking carefully as he speaks.

"It's a device," Alan said, "that makes my dialogue seem more measured and thoughtful."

Did you notice that the closing set of inverted commas (quote marks) comes after the final punctuation in the line of dialogue. Many people seem to be confused about this point and often insert the quote marks in the wrong place. Dialogue should look like this:

"Can I have another biscuit?" he asked.
NOT "Can I have another biscuit"? he asked.

Likewise, it should be:

"And that's why I became an actress," she replied.
NOT "And that's why I became an actress", she replied.

It's the same when the line of speech stands alone with no dialogue tag attached.

"And I thought you really cared."
NOT "And I thought you really cared".

When dialogue carries over into a new paragraph, the inverted commas or quote marks are shown like this:

"It is a far, far better thing I do today," he said, "than I have ever done. Far better than you'll ever know.

"I remembered the milk and the biscuits so that everyone could have their cup of coffee."

Notice that there are no quote marks at the end of the first paragraph after the word *know*. This tells the reader that the same character is talking even though we move to a new paragraph.

If the quote marks were inserted, the reader would assume that: *"I remembered the milk and biscuits so that everyone could have their cup of coffee*," is being spoken by a second (as yet, unidentified) character.

Pauses, interruptions and unfinished sentences

If you have a character who pauses between words, set the dialogue out like this:

"*I don't really like to complain, but I thought my steak was ... horrible*," Dan said.

OR

"*Group Captain, I can assure you that we have our ... methods ... for extracting information*," he hissed.

If the character doesn't finish his sentence, the dialogue will look like this:

"*Mr Bond, if you don't co-operate, I'll have to ...*" *Goldfinger motioned to the gun. Bond didn't need the threat spelt out to him.*

If your character is interrupted, the dialogue will look like this:

"*There's no way you'll get me to talk. No wa –* "
"*Shut up,*" *Holmes interrupted,* "*we both know you'll tell me what I need to know, so spare me the stupid bravado.*"

Sometimes, two characters will talk at the same time but not really listen to each other.

"*And I wanted you to fix that dripping tap and mend that cupboard and cut the grass, and walk the dog. I'm fed-up with it. What I need is ...*"
"*A sock in your mouth?*" *Fred suggested.*
" *... a man who knows what he's doing. Not some layabout.*"

Dialogue tags

When you are letting the reader know who is talking, it isn't necessary to have long, impressive words like: he *intoned*, she *digressed*, he *ruminated*, he *pontificated*, she *opined*.

Keep it simple: he *said*, she *replied*, he *asked*, she *answered*, he *admitted*, they *agreed*, he *hissed*, she *yelled*.

The whole point of dialogue tags is that they shouldn't be consciously noticed. If the reader stops to puzzle out what a long word means you break the flow of the story. Likewise, don't overdo the use of dialogue tags. If it's obvious who is talking, don't bother with a tag. Too many tags slow down the flow of your dialogue. For example:

"I'm hungry," he said.
"I don't know why. You just ate," his wife replied.
"But it wasn't very much," he said.
"It was more than I had," she replied.
"But I'm a big man, with a healthy appetite," he said.

Better to write:

"I'm hungry," he said.
"I don't know why. You just ate," his wife replied.
"But it wasn't very much."
"It was more than I had."
"But I'm a big man, with a healthy appetite."
"Well, you should earn more and maybe I'd be able to afford more food," she snapped.

As you can see, it's crystal clear at all times who is saying what. But if you do need to insert quite a number of dialogue tags then I'd recommend sticking with plain and simple *he said* or *she said*.

It's unobtrusive and after a while the reader won't notice it. He'll take in the information on a subconscious level but won't be thinking to himself: *Oh, no, not another dialogue tag. I'm fed up with them*!

If you find yourself using extended dialogue tags – he said *angrily*, she replied *through gritted teeth*, John suggested *nervously*, Mary countered *with a triumphant sneer* – then that's a giveaway that your dialogue isn't up to scratch.

The words a character utters should, as much as possible, tell you the way the line was spoken and his frame of mind. If your dialogue is bland and ambiguous, you need to beef it up by making the characters more expressive and emotional.

Don't have a neutral line of dialogue like: "*Okay, don't nag. I don't need to be constantly reminded*" which sounds like a gentle reproach when what you really want is the character exploding with fury.

"*For God's sake, will you give it rest! That's all I ever hear. Day in and day out – well I'm sick of it. You hear? Sick of it!*" See the difference? If you want your fiction to fizz, make the dialogue emotion-packed.

Pause for thought

Quote marks should only be used around words that are actually spoken out loud. Don't put them around thoughts.

It should be:

I hope it's okay, Janice thought.
NOT "I hope it's okay", Janice thought.

Some writers put thoughts into italics – *I hope it's okay,* Janice thought. If this appeals then fine, adopt this style but beware of overusing it when you have a story involving a character musing at great length. A lot of italics can look odd and ugly on the page.

Putting it all together

We've covered a lot of ground in this chapter. So let's see how all the elements of dialogue come together in a story.

The following yarn of mine about a haunted bank appeared in a popular women's magazine. It was printed with the title *Watch Out – All She Wants Is Your Money*! The fiction editor obviously thought that this was shorter, snappier and more humorous than my suggested *Balancing The Spooks*!

See how the dialogue tells us about the background, frame of mind and attitudes of the characters, moves forward the plot and creates a comic/eerie mood.

Balancing The Spooks

Derek Chandler could contain his fury no longer. "I don't believe it," he snarled at the piece of paper in his hand. "I just don't bloody believe it."

Across the breakfast table, Samantha stopped painting her fingernails and frowned. "Oh dear. Whatever is the matter, poopsy?"

"It's this bank statement," he snapped, waving the sheet at her, "they've mucked it up again. Those cretins have only gone and paid someone else's direct debits out of my account!"

Samantha frowned and glanced down the sheet. She read slowly; lips moving silently.

"See," Derek said, stabbing a finger at the column of names and numbers, "seventy five sodding quid to Bognor Regis Spiritualist Mission and twenty five pounds to Psychic News. It's incredible. They've mixed me up with some loony!"

The girl pouted. "Derek, lovesy, are you sure it's a mistake? It's down there in black and white. You didn't make the payments, then forget? I'm always doing things like that."

Derek gave her a withering look and tried to work out what he'd ever seen in her. Sure, she had a great body, but not a single brain cell. Elaine had been right – Samantha was a bimbo.

At the thought of Elaine, he shuddered. His wife had been dead five months now, but he still hadn't got used to the idea that she wasn't going to walk back through the door. He also hadn't got used to the idea that he had got away with killing her.

Everyone thought the road accident was a terrible tragedy, but Derek had known it was the only way that he'd get his hands on his wife's fortune. Their friends had been sympathetic – even turning a blind eye to Samantha's sudden appearance in his bed – and he'd enjoyed playing the grief-striken widower.

Now, finally, he was within grasp of Elaine's million pound inheritance. The executors were freeing her estate tomorrow.

He stared again at the Churchill Investment Bank's logo – a bemused-looking dragon, perched jauntily at the top of the statement – and made up his mind. He'd go in after breakfast and give them hell. While he was there, he'd make sure that the formalities were complete for the unfreezing of Elaine's account.

"You're not the only ones who can breath fire," he muttered darkly.

"I'm so terribly sorry. I just don't know what to say. It's so embarrassing." Stuart Whitmore, the branch undermanager, looked so upset that Derek expected him to burst into tears.

"I just can't explain how these mistakes could have happened," Whitmore whined. "We've been having problems ... in our computer room."

Derek's eyebrows rose, suddenly worried about the million tucked away. "Problems? What sort of problems?"

The banker licked his lips. "Nothing ... em ... serious. Just a few gremlins. Electrical fluctuations, temperature drops, that sort of thing."

Derek demanded more details. "Personally, I think it's a practical joker," Whitmore said, running his finger around the inside of his collar, "but it's got the girls a bit rattled. Someone has been switching the lights on and off, moving things about, leaving messages on the screen. They think it's a ghost. Ridiculous, of course, but we can't explain why the heating won't work in there ... "

Whitmore talked on, but Derek wasn't listening. He'd just remembered who the bogus – or was it, phantom? – payments on his statement had been made to.

"I'm sure it's all a big prank," Whitmore told him, "but funnily, yours seems to be the only account affected."

As he walked to his car, Derek felt cold. Trembling, he looked back at the bank. At one of the upper windows, a woman's face stared back at him. She looked chillingly familiar ...

Derek slept badly that night, sucked into a terrifying dream. He was remembering Elaine's death. He was with her, walking side by side along the pavement.

He'd just told her about Samantha but instead of being upset, Elaine had smiled pityingly.

"Run off with some common little tart," she'd sneered. "What's wrong? Old age catching up with you? Want to prove you've still got what it takes in bed?"

"I happen to love Samantha and she loves me," he'd replied stiffly; colouring.

Elaine's smile widened. "No, my poor deluded dear. All you love is her nauseating schoolgirl giggle and the way she wiggles about in her tight jeans. That's not love – it's plain old lust."

She shrugged. "As for that stupid bitch – all she wants is to get her hands on your bank balance. Any fool can see that."

Derek had argued, but Elaine was adamant. "I don't need to remind you that all the money is mine. If you leave me, I'll make sure you're cut off without a penny."

There was an icy triumph in her voice. "We'll see how long your brain-dead Lolita hangs around when you haven't got enough cash to keep her in lollipops."

A red mist flooded Derek's vision. As the lorry came into view, he found his hands grabbing Elaine's shoulders, clasping them tight, pushing, pushing ...

In reality, Elaine had screamed – her wail mingling with the angry hiss of the lorry's hydraulic brakes – but in the dream she laughed. "You fool. You won't get rid of me this easily," she cried as the lorry's wheels ran over her. "I'll get my revenge!"

Derek woke wrapped in sweat-soaked sheets. He gasped, fighting the urge to scream. Samantha slept on; her features blank, untroubled.

He thought about waking her, telling her about the nightmare, but he knew she wouldn't understand. Instead, shaking, he staggered to the bathroom and splashed cold water on his face. After a while, the panic subsided.

He dressed hurriedly. At least, he reflected, he'd be on time for the bank opening. Gradually, he relaxed.

He savoured the delicious anticipation as he drove along the motorway. It was going to be the greatest pleasure in his life – waltzing into the bank, removing Elaine's money and disappearing off to a new life.

It would be a life packed with excitement. It wouldn't feature Samantha, of course. She was too much of a liability to take along, he realised that now, but the world was full of young willing women easily bedazzled by the lures of a millionaire ...

Derek whistled as he walked into the bank. Whitmore was behind the counter; features pinched.

"I believe you're expecting me," Derek grinned, "I've come about my wife's account."

Whitmore sighed. "Ah ... I'm glad that you've called in Mr Chandler, because the manager is keen to have a word."

Derek nodded. He'd been expecting this. The old buzzard probably knew he was going to close Elaine's account and wanted to talk him into keeping it open. Let him try, Derek thought happily, it won't do him any good.

Charles Duggan, the grey-haired manager, didn't rise when Derek was ushered into his panel-lined office. He didn't offer his hand or the customary glass of sickeningly sweet sherry.

Instead, he sat motionless behind his large desk, regarding Derek with an unblinking stare.

"Frankly, Mr Chandler, I must say that I'm a bit disappointed," he began. "You are, of course, perfectly entitled to do whatever you like with your wife's money but I'd have hoped you'd have taken time to think things through."

Derek frowned. Disappointed? Think things through? What was Duggan blabbering on about?

"I'd have at least expected you to discuss it with us before doing something as rash as this," the manager continued, producing a sheet of computer print-out.

Derek's mouth fell open. "As rash as what?"

"Giving away all your late wife's estate," Duggan answered, "giving away every penny."

Giving away the money? Derek felt the world tilt. It couldn't be true!

"I don't know what you're talking about," he hissed, "I came here to collect my million pounds. Now will someone please tell me what the hell is going on."

Duggan looked at Derek in bafflement. "But our computer records clearly show you requested the transfer of all the funds in the account."

Cursing, Derek snatched the print-out. It was true! A long list of charities had suddenly become richer at the press of a button. Cat's homes, dog's homes, Save the Hedgehog, The Red Indian Fellowship Trust!

He tried to yell, but the words caught in his throat. It all became clear. The last two entries screamed out at him. Eastbourne Home for Distressed Mediums and the Scunthorpe and District Psychic Research Institute.

He'd been metaphysically mugged, robbed from beyond the grave. Elaine had got her revenge.

He sat, stunned, as a chilly breeze ruffled his hair and a woman's laugh echoed in his ear.

"There's no chance we can get the money back? Tell everyone that it was all a big mistake?" he asked, trying to ignore the water glass moving unaided across the table.

Duggan shook his head. "No, Mr Chandler. I'm sorry. Not the ghost of a chance."

Exercises

Write a 350-word descriptive passage where two people in a car are lost and disagreeing about what route they should have taken. Don't have any dialogue in it.

Next, rewrite the passage so that the two characters are actually speaking. Compare how much more exciting and emotive the second version is.

Write four short passages where each of the following characters gives a best man's speech at a wedding: (a) a pushy salesman; (b) a nervous person; (c) a pompous solicitor; and (d) an American. Be careful with (d) not to make your American a caricature.

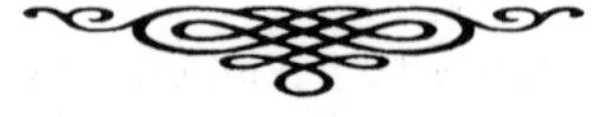

Summary

- ✓ Dialogue scares new writers but it must be faced and mastered. Magazines won't publish stories unless they contain dialogue.
- ✓ It's only when characters open their mouths and speak that they truly come to life.
- ✓ Rob a story of dialogue and you'll end up telling instead of showing.
- ✓ Don't worry about not being able to recreate 100 per cent authentic speech patterns. Dialogue isn't an accurate summary of how people really speak – it only pretends to be.
- ✓ Like description, it is another method of putting over vital information – about what's happening, how people feel, the tension of the situation or the background of the main characters.
- ✓ The way characters talk isn't like real-life speech. There are no 'ahs' and 'ums', no woolly phrases or sentences that drift off at a tangent, no sentences left unfinished. Every-thing is clear, quick and clean.
- ✓ Most of what we say in an average day is dull, boring, repetitive and commonplace. Short story dialogue can't afford to be – it has to zing.
- ✓ It's the key phrase – the vital speech – that brings tension, humour or drama to the piece. It's the equivalent of the journalist's sound bite.
- ✓ Dialogue has three main functions – to move on the action of the story, to reveal more about the characters and to inject excitement.

- ✓ If your dialogue isn't telling the reader something crucial about the action, the characters or the atmosphere, it shouldn't be there.
- ✓ Beware of having your characters waste their dialogue on routine greetings and pleasantries.
- ✓ Don't allow them to rabbit on pointlessly. Every time a character opens his mouth make sure he says something of importance.
- ✓ Avoid writing in dialect. It is tiring and irksome to read and detracts from the action.
- ✓ Suggest a character comes from a particular part of the country by using a key word or two. Re-create the speech patterns of the region.
- ✓ Resist the temptation to make your characters talk as though they've stepped out of a 1940s comedy film. Keep your dialogue modern and realistic.
- ✓ Keep your dialogue tags simple – *he said, she replied, he asked, she answered, they agreed, he hissed, she yelled*, etc.
- ✓ Don't have overlong dialogue tags. The words a character utters should tell you the way the line was spoken and his frame of mind. It shouldn't need to be explained.
- ✓ If it isn't obvious how a character is feeling then your dialogue needs to be more expressive and emotionally charged.

7

DESCRIPTIONS

As readers, we all need descriptions. They are a vital part of prose. Without knowing how the characters and settings look, we can't visualise them – tales become populated with vague, fuzzy people living in an indistinct land. It's difficult to see them clearly.

If all we're told is that the story's main character is a man then we can begin to build a mental image of the hero. We know he isn't a woman or a child or an animal or a machine. But beyond that we're stuck – left to guess.

Is he tall or short, fat or thin, young or old? Is he black or white, well-dressed or scruffy, well-educated or ignorant? We don't know. And until the writer tells us, giving us the vital information we require, the hero will remain a stranger. We can't feel any real attachment or sympathy for a stranger – especially one who is nothing more than a blurred shape in the distance.

It's only when we learn more about our hero – starting off with his name – that he becomes a person instead of a symbol. Only then do we move closer and start to care about what happens to him.

The same is true of settings. It's not enough to tell us that he lives in a house. We need to know what kind of house. Small and cramped, large and roomy, a country cottage or a modern town terrace? They alter our mental picture of how he lives and who he really is.

Descriptions of people, era and locations paint in the fine detail that helps to bring the story alive. They provide colour, shape, texture and tone. They make the scene real. So if you are the kind of writer who skips over description as an unnecessary chore, you are robbing your work of its subtlety and depth. You are inviting the reader to spend time in a stark, unfurnished room.

More than just pretty pictures

It's easy to dismiss description as just showy window dressing, but good, expressive writing does more than just produce pleasing word pictures and sharper mental images. It's a powerful tool for adding atmosphere and excitement.

Think how many horror tales you've read where your flesh begins to crawl even before the monster has appeared on the scene. The writer uses his descriptive powers to build a mood of dread and menacing anticipation. Perhaps it's the darkness of the night or the terrified look on the faces of the villagers or the ferocity of the gathering tempest. His descriptions take us to the heart of the storm, cowering in fear ...

The lightning ripped the sky apart, like black velvet tearing in a flash of frenzy. The growling thunder boomed louder each time ... creeping nearer and nearer.

Peterson felt his chest tighten, his breath coming in gasps. This was stupid, he told himself. He knew better than those superstition-bound peasants. This was the age of reason. There were no demons hiding in the empty blackness. So why was he sweating? Why was he clutching the gun so hard that his fingers hurt? And why did the rushing wind scream into his brain like the tormented wails of lost souls ...

Nothing has happened in this scene – there's no dialogue, no character inter-action – yet it has still created a sense of apprehension. It is an overture for the terrors to come. The descriptions have worked their dark magic to fill us with foreboding.

Chilling stuff, especially the use of the expression *growling* which makes the thunder seem like a monstrous beast stalking our hero. But did you notice how the description also moved the plot forward? There's no definable action here, but it has pushed us surreptitiously towards the climax.

Even as Peterson chides himself for his unease, we know his fears are justified. Something unspeakable is about to happen. He's about to face a malevolent supernatural force.

And what about the line about his fingers gripping the gun so hard it hurt? You can be sure the gun will play an important part in the horrors to come. This is a teasing clue. See how good descriptive writing is more than just drawing pretty pictures. It works hard to suck the reader into the story, to play with his emotions, pique his curiosity and fill him with anticipation. It helps propel the plot forward and, written with skill, reveals new and sometimes unexpected facets of the character's personality and background. We now know that Peterson looks down on the villagers, thinking them foolish and child-like but realises he's no better. He, too, has fallen victim to his own superstitions.

Always ask yourself: do my descriptions work hard enough? Do they operate on different levels? Are they bringing the story to life?

A good writer should be able to capture the essence, the spirit, of what he is describing as well as just its physical appearance.

Keeping your eyes open

The real secret of creating powerful and truthful descriptions is observation. A good writer is one who **sees**, who notices small quirky details in the world around him and incorporates them into his fiction. Most people can describe people and objects in a routine and unimaginative way, but a good storyteller spots the hidden – what the others miss.

Train yourself to look for the unusual, the small tell-tale signs that there is more going on than meets the eye. It's amazing how just one careful observation can transform our perception of a character:

> *Derek is a lottery winner who has scooped several millions but still insists on wearing cheap shoes.*
>
> *Mary stares longingly at other men when she thinks her husband isn't looking.*
>
> *Grace washes her hands fifteen times a day.*

We know so much about them – the real them – just by those small points of description. Even a detail of setting can help describe a person in new and unexpected ways. Charles the third Baron of Liverstake is quite unremarkable and uninteresting in a stately home – but what if he lives in a council house? Now things start to become intriguing.

Striking a balance

Getting the right amount of description is an art form, a skill honed as you develop as a writer. Good authors instinctively know just how much background material to put in and how much to leave out.

No-one can tell you what is appropriate for any given story but it's a useful rule of thumb to think that the longer the piece, the more descriptive passages you can have and the more involved they can be.

This is particularly true of a lengthy literary magazine tale or radio story which depends very much on atmosphere and the slow build-up of tension. It may not have very much plot, but concentrates instead on creating a feeling of setting or era and in showing detailed characterisation.

In most stories under 2,000 words this kind of leisurely word painting is a luxury. Okay, so the narrative needs good, vivid descriptions but it also needs to be free of unnecessary images. It needs pace, sharpness and movement. The aim here is to keep the plot surging forward – telling you just what you need to know to make sense of the unfolding events and nothing more. There isn't time to listen to "mood music".

Keep it short

If you are writing a long description it must be because you have a lot of information to put over – not that you can find lots of different ways to say the same thing, or want to give more detail than is required.

Just because you *can* find 300 words to describe a rugged, stormy coastline doesn't mean that you *should*. The brief line "spray-lashed cliffs" conjures up the same picture. Aim to get the most striking image possible with the minimum amount of words.

For example, you could spend half a page sketching a pen portrait of a large, inhuman, graffiti-sprayed, derelict, urban sprawl where frightened people live terrible, lonely, down-trodden lives. I'm sure it would be an excellent gritty read in a novel, but unnecessary in short fiction – you could put over the same information by merely saying that your hero hated living in a "concrete-souled city".

I've used "concrete-souled city" and "spray-lashed cliffs" because these are triple-word descriptions. Such expressions are particularly powerful. Perhaps that's why so many cliché expressions are three words:

hale and hearty
old and grey
happy, go lucky
mean and moody
down and out
fit to burst
fun and games
rose-coloured spectacles
hard faced bitch
live and kicking

Always use the power of three to make your descriptions short, punchy and attention-grabbing ... but devise your own powerful prose. Please leave hackneyed expressions in the bin where they belong.

Don't get carried away

When describing a location don't feel that you have to sell the place to the reader as though you are an over-keen travel agent. You don't have to go all lyrical and gush with purple prose.

A common fault is an author getting so wound up sketching the setting that the desert island becomes the main character instead of the castaway.

Don't let descriptions bog down a story or compete for attention against the plot. If your story over-runs, the first thing that should be chopped out are unnecessary images.

Keep it simple

Descriptive passages aren't the place to show off your extensive vocabulary, your dazzlingly poetic turn of phrase or your new thesaurus. Use simple, easily understood words and direct, clear-cut images.

Tell the story in the most basic way possible. Don't have obscure or flowery phrases. Descriptions shouldn't stand out from the rest of the text or hold up the action. They should never be an exercise in self-conscious cleverness or arty word-play.

Don't have anything that jars with the reader or sends him rushing to a dictionary to look up an unfamiliar word. One florid image or fussy phrase can destroy the mood of a story.

Woolly words

Look upon **adjectives** with suspicion. Most of them are passengers, wasting space but giving little or no information.

Charming cottage – what does that mean? Is the cottage a wow at parties? Beautiful? Full of character? A bit of a rogue? Quaint? Unusual?

Charming tells us next to nothing. So do woolly adjectives like *delightful, nice, wonderful, enchanting, splendid, lovely, bewitching, superb, magnificent, excellent* and *spellbinding*. They tell us one thing only – that the writer is expressing some form of approval, but not why.

I could tell you it was an *excellent* day yesterday. But you wouldn't know what made it excellent for me. It might be that the sun shone brightly, my agent sent me a huge cheque and I had a deep and refreshing snooze in the afternoon. It might also mean that it rained heavily but my prize tulips were saved from dying of thirst. Excellent can mean anything.

There is no room in a short story for imprecise adjectives that need further explanation. Rip them out and replace them with words that pull their weight.

Only use adjectives that convey information such as: *red, large, deep, six, cold, long, sharp, wet, second, eerie, tasty*, etc.

Are you using adjectives to bolster a weak and inaccurate noun? Why bother describing an old, rambling country-house with dozens of sumptuous rooms and large, manicured grounds when either *mansion* or *stately home* creates the same picture.

Likewise, why describe someone as a dirty, dishevelled, homeless person in rags when *tramp* will do?

Too often an array of adjectives shows that the writer has picked the wrong noun and needs to give extra information to make the image clear.

The same often applies to writers who use too many **adverbs**. They've selected a verb that is vague and imprecise.

Why say: *I ran hurriedly* or *at great speed* when what you really mean is *I sprinted.*

Try the oblique approach

Sometimes the most effective descriptions can be the ones that don't seem at first glance to be descriptions at all.

You don't have to write two sentences of carefully penned prose on a downpour to let the reader know it was raining. If the hero shakes out his umbrella before he enters a building, the reader will know it was wet. If the private detective in your story always smells of mints the reader will pick up on the fact that he drinks. Don't go to the trouble of describing a teacher in great detail if the fact that his hands are covered in chalk dust tells readers all they need to know.

Be subtle – make the description an unremarkable part of the fabric of the story. Readers should be aware of the information but not how they got it.

Resist the temptation to be an intrusive narrator. Don't **tell** readers how a character feels or thinks. **Show** them. Make the character's manner, words and actions reveal what he or she is like. Let the reader pick up on all the clues. Don't tell us that Joyce is a bully. Show us Joyce acting as a bully.

Narration is always second-hand. It's never as gripping as seeing the action. A dull statement *John was sad* won't have the power and impact of a short scene where we actually experience his melancholy and despair:

John rubbed his eyes, aware they were red and puffy. He knew people would stare, but he didn't care. It didn't matter any more. None of it mattered.

The aching sense of loss came back stronger than before, sharper, more bitter, threatening to engulf him.

Use your descriptive powers to take us inside the hero's head. Help us share his feelings. Don't waste the opportunity by blandly summarising events or emotions that should be experienced in all their depth.

Be a dripping tap

The worst way to use description is to have huge dollops of information splurged down in the middle of a story. The reader won't be able to take it all in and while he struggles to memorise the information, the narrative slows right down or, worse still, comes to a dead halt.

This is known as an "expository lump". Basically, the writer is so anxious to explain a tricky concept or important background facts that he drags people away from the story's exciting conflict and dumps them in a lecture hall:

"Now I know you really want to find out what happens to the hero in the crashing plane, and we'll get to that eventually, but I want to talk to you first about the technical intricacies of aero engines. This is a truly gripping subject and if you just bear with me for a few moments ..."

Alternatively, it could be that the writer thinks it's important that you know a great deal about the main character and can't wait to tell you all about this fascinating person. Well yes, it would be nice to learn a little bit about the hero, but do we need to sit down to watch a slide show of John's friends, family, job, history and lifestyle?

If you must give the reader information, ration it. Give it a little piece at a time. Don't stop the flow of the story for it. Use the dripping tap approach. Give information in tiny drips at regular intervals, one fact at a time. Let one piece of description soak in before dripping the next.

See things through the character's eyes

All through your story we see events through the eyes of the main character so it makes sense not to break this link by the narrator luring us away to look at buildings or beaches or the weather.

It's much more effective to make your descriptions part of the vista the hero is viewing. So instead of saying: *The girl had blue eyes and a small, pert nose* say: *Bill noticed that the girl had blue eyes and the cutest small, pert nose.*

Instead of writing: *The house looked unloved and dirty – not the type of place to spend a cosy romantic evening* say: *Mary shuddered as she spotted the dust and grime covering every surface of the house. Her heart sank as she realised that she and Gary would have to spend the night there. So much for a romantic hideaway, she thought.*

This technique helps your descriptions to be an integral part of the plot, not something grafted on afterwards.

Use the five senses

Every time I hold a workshop I get my students to write a short descriptive piece about a house blaze or a walk in the park. When they read their work out loud I get the others to keep a tally of how many of the five senses were used.

Usually the answer is two – **sight** and **sound**. People describe how the fire roared and how the flames leapt up from the rooftops; or they say how beautiful the blooms were to the eye and how quiet the park was with only the gentle sway of the wind through the trees.

The other three senses – **touch**, **smell** and **taste** – are more or less ignored. Few people mention the smell of the flowers or the acrid tang of the smoke or mention the feel of ash falling on their face or the gentle texture of a petal.

When I point out that most students have used only two of their five senses, they are genuinely surprised – but I'm not. In this television age we spend much more time in front of the goggle box than we do reading. We become accustomed to receiving information from the screen and the loudspeaker. It's the only two senses the TV can stimulate. Even in the best cookery programmes we can only imagine how a dish smells and tastes. We can only guess at the food's texture.

When you write, remember this TV conditioning and make a conscious effort to include the three neglected senses in your descriptions. They add a powerful dimension.

Just think of visiting a hospital: isn't the distinct smell of disinfectant one of the most memorable experiences you come away with? Think how the aroma of newly baked bread lures you to the bakery section of the supermarket. Doesn't that show just how powerful the sense of smell can be?

Try describing sandpaper without mentioning that it is rough to the touch or tell someone about a lemon without mentioning its sour taste. It's not easy.

Using all five senses in your descriptions makes them richer, more satisfying and more realistic, but there's an added bonus for the reader. Instead of being distanced from what you describe, he'll feel that he's actually experienced what you are talking about. Make him think he's lived your story – not just read it.

Good descriptive writing should always capture sensations: the pounding of the heart, the sting of the rain, the lurch as a car plunges over a cliff, the panic of drowning, the terror of a door creaking open at midnight ...

Always ask yourself: how would that character feel at this point and put over the emotions and stimulation he would be experiencing.

Injecting excitement

The words you choose are crucial in creating a tingling sense of danger and fright, but you can enhance this sensation by giving your work a hurtling, breathless feel.

When people become agitated they talk rapidly, in short, staccato gasps. The more angry or afraid they are, the more terse their language and speech patterns become. You can re-create this tension by ensuring that your paragraphs and sentences get shorter and more clipped as the story builds to a dramatic climax.

The gun went flying. Dave dived for the floor. The lights exploded. One, two, three. Then darkness, silence. Nothing. He waited; motionless, frightened.

See how punchy this makes the text. The reader can't help but be swept along by the action.

Describing characters and places

As I mentioned in chapter five, it's important to put over as much information as you can about a character in the most economical way possible – through name, physical description, mannerisms and speech patterns.

But don't fall into the trap of being *too* economical. Ironically, it may be that you know your characters so well that you assume that the reader knows all about them too. You forget to give a vital clue. I've read stories where writers have forgotten to give the main character's age, job, background or even gender.

Don't be caught out this way. Remember that the reader and your hero are strangers – they are meeting for the first time. Make sure you've told the reader everything he needs to know about this new acquaintance. That's everything he *needs* to know, not everything you'd *like* to tell him. Don't forget that you're still strapped for space and have no room in a short story for luxuries like elaborate and flowery character studies. Keep to the basics – the police photo-fit details.

age
sex
height
build
distinguishing features
job
marital status
unusual mannerisms

If you have all these you're well on your way to making the character take form on the page.

Personality profile

If you find it a problem to describe your characters in any detail it may be because you don't know enough about them. As in real life, it's difficult to talk for long about someone who is just a casual acquaintance. You run out of facts.

If this is a problem, you may find it a useful exercise to create life histories for your main characters. Really get to know them: where they come from, what they like and why they act the way they do. Create a personality profile form similar to the one shown on the next page and fill it in, fleshing out your hero with relevant background details.

PERSONALITY PROFILE		
NAME		....
DATE OF BIRTH		....
PLACE OF BIRTH		....
MAIN CHARACTER TRAIT		....
PROFESSION/JOB		....
SIGNIFICANT EVENTS		....
....		
APPEARANCE:	Hair	....
	Eyes	....
	Complexion	....
	Clothes	....
	Height/Build	....
HOBBIES		....
HABITS		....
LIKES		....
DISLIKES		....
RELATIONSHIPS:	Family	....
	Others	....
HOUSE		....
PETS		....
CAR		....
STRENGTHS		....
....		
WEAKNESSES		....
....		
PROBLEMS		....
....		
AIM IN LIFE		....
....		

There won't be room in a short story to use more than a few of these facts, but you will find that you probably have a better understanding of the hero and can describe him with more confidence.

It's a particularly useful technique when you are devising two characters who will be rivals in a story. Give each his own CV and ensure that their backgrounds are as different as you can make them. The more stark the contrast between them the better.

Use real people as a template

Many writers find it helps if they base their characters on real people – friends, family or acquaintances. This gives them a starting point. It's much easier to describe someone you can see and study, rather than a vague, half-formed person.

Not everyone has a strong imagination – it's nothing to be ashamed of – and using real people as a starting point can take some of the mental pain and frustration out of describing characters.

You don't have to stick slavishly to what the real people are like. You might want an older person in a story to resemble your father in the way he walks and talks – and his awful dress sense! But you may also want your character to be a computer hacker and your father (bless him) has trouble getting his pocket calculator to work.

Fine. Take the elements you need from dad and graft on other personality traits and skills from other people you know – perhaps from a friend who's a keyboard whizz kid.

And hey presto – you've created an individual who is an amalgam of various people you know, but who is different in important ways from all of them. In this case we've an elderly, badly dressed man who looks as though he's ready for his pipe and slippers but who is unexpectedly an Internet surfer with the skills to crack any computer code. Interesting!

This *mix and match* approach is ideal for giving you a never-ending stream of new and exciting characters to inhabit your stories.

The danger, of course, is that your friends will recognise themselves in your creations and be offended if you've painted them in a less than flattering light. My advice is to make sure you always alter a few details – just to make sure. It's not difficult to throw in a few red herrings like changing the person's age or attitudes or even gender.

It doesn't take much to throw someone off the scent. Friends and family will often refuse to accept that you've based a character on them – even though it's glaringly obvious to you and everyone else! "*I'm nothing like that*," your victim replies indignantly. "*Your main character is awful – vain, stupid and unsympathetic. I'm adorable. Everyone knows that!*"

Lights, camera, action

For characters to work on the page, the author has to be able to picture them clearly. Different writers all have their own favourite methods for doing this. Personally, I find it useful to imagine that my short story is going to be made into a film and cast well-known actors in the main roles.

I may be unsure quite how my hero will look or sound but I find it suddenly becomes simple when I imagine how an actor like, say, Michael Caine or Sean Connery would look and sound in the part.

To a certain extent I write the part for the actor I've picked – so if you read one of my stories and can hear a particular actor's voice in your head saying the main character's dialogue, then don't be surprised. Why not have a go at this technique, it may work for your style of writing too.

Picture this

The mix and match technique also works well for describing settings. Dip into the lucky-bag of places you've visited or seen on television and blend them together.

Take a pinch of tropical island beach and a smidgen of Paris night life, work in a dash of London fashion stores and a teeny drop of Irish hospitality and you're half way to creating a dream location for your holiday romance story. Add in some dark and dangerous New York street life and the story becomes much more vibrant and packed with suspense.

This method has the advantage of giving readers familiar elements in the setting of the tale – so it's easily pictured – but mixes them in an original cocktail that is unique to your yarn.

If you haven't travelled much beyond your hometown, don't worry. Get hold of some travel brochures and describe the images you see in the photos. Don't worry that this isn't creative or real writing. Many of the brochure descriptions of hotels and resorts are more fiction than fact anyway!

Photographs can be a useful way of assisting your memory and powers of description. If you want to describe a real building but can't remember all the fine details, go out and take a picture of it. (But don't trespass or invade anyone's privacy while you do it.) When it comes time to write your description, keep the photo by your keyboard.

A couple of extra thoughts

Make a difference I've already mentioned that it's a good practice to give your characters names that are distinct and different from each other. This stops the reader confusing them in his mind – especially if he's reading quickly.

Well, for the same reasons, it's just as important to make your characters as varied as you can in their background, personality, appearance and the way they talk.

If your hero is tall, loud and fearless, make his rival short, quiet and timid. If two friends are going to see a horror film, make one girl cynical and unafraid of monsters while her friend is dreading the prospect because she's going to spend two hours hiding behind her seat.

Use your descriptions to help the reader see each character as a clearly defined – and separate – individual. This highly effective technique is used throughout fiction. There can be few sharper contrasts than that between the wildly eccentric, exciting and intuitive Sherlock Holmes and his side-kick – dull, down-to-earth and plodding Doctor Watson.

Differences in personality, age and culture can generate all sorts of emotional and juicy clashes between your characters. And, as we know, conflict is the heart of drama, it's what powers a storyline.

Imagine an otherwise routine first date between a man and woman. See how interesting it becomes when he neglects to find out that she is a vegetarian and he takes her to a steak house. The story heats up when she lights up a cigarette and he announces that he is vehemently anti-smoking. Suddenly this meal is a potential battleground. This is one true love that isn't going to run smoothly.

The more contrasting your characters are, the more likely they are to clash. The more they disagree, the more electricity is generated.

Take the *X-Files* as a classic example. We have Fox Mulder, the naive believer in the supernatural, in permanent conflict with his partner, the dispassionate, rational and methodical scientist Dana Scully. Do they ever see eye to eye on a case?

Their clashes in background and attitude are at the very centre of every episode. It also fuels the unmistakable sexual chemistry between them.

One at a time Have you ever gone to a party and been introduced to a crowd of strangers and realised just a few moments later that you can't remember anyone's name? It's terribly embarrassing and happens to me all the time. I know that I'd have no problems if I were introduced to each person one at a time and had five minutes with each to get to know something about them. It would help them register on my memory.

Exactly the same process takes place when you introduce characters into a short story. If you bring them on in a crowd, the reader has great difficulty in telling them apart. After a few paragraphs he's forgotten who anyone is. They haven't had time to register as individuals.

So give him a chance to get to know each character a little before introducing the next. Never bring in more than two at a time.

Have another look at my short story *Balancing the Spooks* in the previous chapter. See how I start off with Derek, who is having a tantrum. Then after we have learned why he's angry, I introduce his girl-friend Samantha.

A few sentences on, when the relationship between the two is well established (as is Samantha's dopey personality) I then mention Elaine – Derek's murdered wife. A few paragraphs later, when we're happy that the reader knows who Elaine is, I bring in Stuart Whitmore, the bank undermanger.

It's an easy pattern to follow if you want to keep your story clear and easily followed. Introduce a character, wait a couple of sentences until he's had time to be accepted by the reader, then move on to the next player in the drama.

Think of Yul Brynner in the film *The Magnificent Seven*. The script could have had him meet the other six gunfighters in one scene – perhaps in a chance encounter in a saloon. It would have got the action going a lot quicker certainly, but we would have known very little about the gunslingers as individuals. Hence we wouldn't have cared about them, or what they did.

Instead, the script has Brynner's character meet each of his future cowboy colleagues one at a time. By the time Brynner has assembled his team, we have a clue to each gunman's personality and a glimpse of the sometimes dire lives they'd been living.

The same technique was used in *The Untouchables* as Kevin Costner – as Chicago gangbuster Elliott Ness – gathered his team around him one at a time. (He started off by recruiting Sean Connery, which is a fairly clever way to go!)

Introduce your "party guests" one at a time. If it's a good enough story-telling technique for Hollywood, it's certainly good enough for us.

Footnote

Way back in the first chapter I said you should try to keep the number of your characters to a minimum. It's a very common mistake for new writers to overcrowd stories with too many "walk-on" parts and "bit-players".

Only include people who are going to be vital to the plot and whom you will describe in detail. There's no need to mention the milkman who happens to be putting a pinta on the doorstep at the time that your real characters are talking upstairs, or to mention the postman who delivers the blackmail letter. (Unless, of course, he wrote it!)

Only include those individuals that you will refer to by name and who'll have lines of dialogue to say. Imagine that you are casting the piece as a theatre play. You wouldn't want to pay for actors who don't do anything and whose only function is to make the stage look busier. You'd soon sack them. So do the same in your story. Sack the "extras". Only have the main players.

Exercises

Write a 200-word description of a place you've visited on holiday. Next, summarise the description down to just 10 key words. Try not to lose any of the important information ... or the atmosphere!

Devise a character by using different elements from real-life people you know. Write a 500-word profile of him or her. Make up a form like the one given in this chapter and fill it in with the character's details.

Write a 300-word description of someone drowning. Include all 5 senses and make the reader feel the sensations of panic and struggle.

Summary

- ✓ Descriptions are vital. If we don't know how the characters and settings look, we cannot visualise them.
- ✓ Descriptions provide colour, shape, texture and tone. They make the scenes real.
- ✓ Expressive writing is a powerful tool for adding atmosphere and excitement. It sucks the reader into the story, playing with his emotions.
- ✓ A good writer should have the ability to capture the essence, the spirit, of what he is describing as well as just its physical appearance.
- ✓ The secret of creating powerful and truthful descriptions is observation. Train yourself to look for the unusual. One careful observation can alter our perception of a character or a place.
- ✓ The longer the piece, the more descriptive passages you can have and the more involved they can be.
- ✓ This is particularly true of literary magazine tales or radio stories which depend very much on atmosphere and the slow build-up of tension.
- ✓ In stories under 2,000 words the narrative should be free of unnecessary images. It needs sharpness, movement and pace.
- ✓ Only use a long description if you have a lot of information to put over. Aim for striking images with the minimum amount of words.
- ✓ Three-word descriptions are particularly powerful.
- ✓ Don't get too lyrical and gush with purple prose. Don't let descriptions bog down a story or compete for attention with the plot.

- ✓ Use simple, easily understood words and direct, clear-cut images. Choose adjectives and adverbs with care. Use them sparingly.

- ✓ Be subtle – make the description an unremarkable part of the fabric of the story. Don't **tell events – show** them happening.

- ✓ Use your descriptive powers to take us inside the hero's head. Help us share his feelings.

- ✓ Don't give background information in huge dollops. This slows the story. Drip information like a leaky tap.

- ✓ Describe places, people and events as they're seen through the main character's eyes.

- ✓ Use all five senses. Make the reader feel the sensations the hero is experiencing.

- ✓ To inject excitement give your work a hurtling, breathless feel. Ensure that your sentences get shorter as the story builds to a dramatic climax.

- ✓ Don't fall into the trap of being *too* economical when describing a person. Give the reader *all* the information that's crucial.

- ✓ Ensure that character backgrounds are as different as you can make them. The more stark the contrast between them the better.

- ✓ Many writers find it helps to base their characters on real people – but change a few details to stay out of trouble.

- ✓ It's okay to use photographs of people or places as an aid to your imagination. Describe what you see.

- ✓ Give the reader a chance to get to know each character a little before introducing the next. Never bring in more than two at a time.

✓ Only include people who are going to be vital to the plot – those who have something to say for themselves.

8

VIEWPOINT

In novels you can create tension and extra depth by telling the story from different viewpoints. Each chapter or scene can be a different character's perspective of events.

However, in short stories there really isn't the space to do this so it's advisable to stick to one viewpoint throughout – that of your main character – unless it's a clever sting-in-the-tail and the viewpoint switch is crucial to the denouement.

It is far more powerful to stay with only one perspective throughout – seeing the story unfold through the eyes of the main character; describing the events as the hero, and only the hero, would see them.

Using only one viewpoint gives your story a sharp sense of direction and it helps the reader empathise much more closely with the main character.

But it does mean that you have to be absolutely certain who **is** your main character. You don't want to find that you get to the halfway point in your story and discover that it isn't the detective but his doctor friend who is the mainstay of the action.

Choosing your main character

Often the hero of your tale is obvious – the humble clerk who sets out to prove she is every bit as good as her bosses or the accused man fighting to prove his innocence.

But sometimes it is not so obvious and you have to think a little about what effect you are trying to create with the story and which of the characters will most help you achieve this.

Try this example. You are writing a story about John, a middle-aged lecturer, who is celebrating his 50th birthday. His wife, Jane, has planned a surprise party. She has invited Tina, one of John's students, unaware that John and Tina are secret lovers. During the party the truth about John and Tina's affair is revealed and Jane walks out on her husband.

Whose point of view should the story be told from? John's? Jane's? Tina's? Or maybe one of the other guests? This is an interesting choice because the tone and direction of your story will alter drastically according to whose eyes you view events through.

Are you trying to generate sympathy for John – a man caught out by his emotions? If you are, he will be most sympathetically portrayed if we let him be the central character and tell the story from his viewpoint.

Do you want the reader to sympathise with Jane, the wife? We'd feel her pain the most intensely if she was the central character.

Or do you want to portray student Tina as a sympathetic character? Was she an innocent seduced by the older man? If she was, the reader will soon forgive her if she is the story's main character.

There is the potential to have three strikingly different stories. Let's take a look at them.

A. John's viewpoint

The drunk's words seem to hang in the air – "Life's so bloody unfair. Look at John. He's got a gorgeous wife, yet he gets to screw around with some nymphet young enough to be his granddaughter. Is that fair, I ask you?"

John was aware that the party had suddenly fallen quiet, conversations ending in mid sentence. All the eyes in the room swivelled to stare at him. In the accusing silence, he knew it was finally over. He was revealed for what he was – a weak, selfish, adulterous bastard.

He felt his face flush red with shame. No wonder the guests glared at him with contempt. Fighting the urge to run, he looked frantically first at Jane then at Tina.

His wife stared back at him, open mouthed, stunned. He could see that she couldn't take in what she'd just heard. In a moment, he knew she'd break down when the full pain of his betrayal hit her.

And Tina? He looked at her for signs of anguish but she stood unfazed, her young face serene, unaffected by the awfulness of what was happening. It had been her easy-going, unruffled manner that first attracted him, but now in a telling instant he saw it for what it was – apathy. She was dead inside. She just didn't care. At that moment he realised he hated her, and that he loved Jane more than anything in the world.

B. Jane's viewpoint

It was true. It had to be. The look of trapped terror on John's face was all the confession she needed. He looked like a little boy caught stealing from the fridge, frightened and pleading. Oh please, don't hate me, his eyes said to her, I won't do it again.

Suddenly it all made sense, the late night meetings at college, the private phone calls he'd taken in the study, the mysterious extras on the credit card bill ...

She'd been such a fool, she realised. Such a blind, stupid, trusting fool. All the time he'd been sleeping with that brainless bimbo, that little slut! All that time ...

Jane knew that she should be screaming at her husband, shrieking her fury and pain at him, lashing out at him with her fists but her body was so numb. It was an effort to move, to react.

She felt her eyes drift to Tina's face. The bitch looked smug, with none of John's guilt marring her pretty little face. Was that a sneer forming on her lips, a triumphant gleam in her gaze? The little cow knew she'd won.

Well, she could have him, Jane told herself bitterly. If she wanted an overweight 50-year-old has-been, she was welcome to him. John had always been a burden to her, an obstacle to her happiness. Well, now things were going to be different ...

C. Tina's viewpoint

She did what she always did in a crisis. She froze. Tina knew that her face looked calm and untroubled but inside her stomach churned, her body searing with pain.

Suddenly the whole mess was public ... and she knew what people would say. Scheming little tart out to bed her tutor, making sure she got good grades and all that extra attention. But it wasn't true. It wasn't like that. The affair hadn't been her idea. At first she'd spurned John's advances, telling him not to be so silly.

He was married, and so much older than her ... but he hadn't let up. Everywhere she went he was there, seeking her out, joking with her, offering advice ...

Despite her reservations, she found herself thawing to him. He was persistent and charming and clever ... and she was lonely away from home, so very lonely.

Falling in love with him had just happened. She hadn't planned it, hadn't even been aware of what was going on until it was too late. Now, she could see it as just a tawdry affair. Now she could recognise John for the master manipulator he'd so obviously been.

Swallowing hard, she looked at Jane and saw hate in her expression. She couldn't blame her. At that moment Tina felt her heart go out to the older woman. How could she have hurt this decent person so much? How could she have come between this woman and the man she so obviously loved?

Tina wanted to tell her how sorry she was ... how ashamed. But she knew that right now words wouldn't make any difference. Nothing could make things better.

So, is Tina an innocent seduced or a scheming adulteress out for all she could get? Is John a ruthless seducer or a small greedy boy trapped in a man's body? And what about Jane? Is she a small flower that will be crushed by the betrayal or a woman who will use the affair as an excuse to get rid of a husband she never really loved?

It all depends on your viewpoint! All these interpretations are possible and equally valid.

See how each character can manipulate our emotions in their favour when we see events through their eyes? For this reason, it's inevitable that the reader will *always* be on the side of the main character – so think carefully about who the protaganist of your story is going to be.

First or third person?

Okay, so you've selected the main character and worked out that you'll relate the story as he would have seen it happen.

The next question is are you going to write the story in the first person or the third person?

That means: are you going to put yourself in the shoes of the main character, effectively casting yourself in the lead role? Let's look at the following example:

I looked into her staring vacant face searching for a glimmer of intelligence and singularly failed to find it.

"I've booked a room," I told her. "The name is MacIntosh."

"Booked a room?" she repeated dully. "Name of MacIntosh?"

"Yes. By phone. A double, with bathroom. Two nights, full board."

She scanned the computer screen, frowning as though it was a Mensa application form. I could swear she was moving her lips as she read.

I began to regret having chosen Cosy Nook Inn out of all the adverts in the Yellow Pages. The receptionist may have been brain-dead but I suspected I was a bigger moron for having picked her hotel in the first place.

Or are you going to stay one stage removed, telling the story from the standpoint of a detached narrator?

Kevin looked into her staring vacant face searching for a glimmer of intelligence and singularly failed to find it.

"I've booked a room," he told her. "The name is MacIntosh."

"Booked a room?" she repeated dully. "Name of MacIntosh?"

"Yes. By phone. A double, with bathroom. Two nights, full board."

She scanned the computer screen, frowning as though it was a Mensa application form. He could swear she was moving her lips as she read.

He began to regret having chosen Cosy Nook Inn out of all the adverts in the Yellow Pages. The receptionist may have been brain-dead but Kevin suspected he was a bigger moron for having picked her hotel in the first place.

There are pros and cons to both approaches and the decision whether to write in the first person – *I did this, I did that* – or the third person – *he did this, he did that* – is important. It sets the tone of a story and helps readers decide how closely they want to identify with the main character.

Here are the points for and against each style:

First person

Advantages:

1. Most people feel happier writing in the first person. They find it easier to show the personality of the main character if

they inhabit his body. The moment you use the word 'I' you've made the reader imagine himself as the hero.

2. It saves a lot of descriptive writing and carefully crafted characterisation. The barriers come down instantly. We know what makes him tick. Unless he's an out-and-out cad readers will find something to like, or forgive, in his personality.

Disadvantages:
It's often perfectly acceptable to tell a story in the first person, but there's a danger that you'll fall unwittingly into one of several potential traps.

1. The biggest danger is the likelihood that you won't actually write from the character's viewpoint at all, but merely put yourself (the real-life writer) into the action.

That's okay if the character is similar to you and would react the same way as you would in real life. But what if you are a 60-year-old, middle class woman magistrate, and the main character in your story is a working class, teenage, male gang member?

Could you write with conviction (excuse the pun) about stealing cars or getting into fights? Could you really stop your set of values impinging on to the character's?

2. You're trapped inside the body of one person. The reader can only know what that character knows, and go where that character goes. This can be extremely limiting.

Imagine your story is about a man wrongly imprisoned by corrupt police. You want to tell the story from the prisoner's viewpoint, but also you want to show the efforts being made by his friends to free him.

By using first person you are trapping the reader in a stark prison cell. The real excitement of the story is happening miles away. But the readers can't be there to see it happening. At best, they'll hear it when someone comes to visit the prisoner and report events.

3. You're saddled with that character's views and prejudices. You may feel uncomfortable looking at the world through one

blinkered pair of eyes. In reality, the main character may be rude, arrogant and hateful. But if you let that character be the narrator he's not going to run himself down. It's like asking someone to write their own job reference.

4. You may find that you need to continue the action beyond the point at which the hero dies. He lays down his life to fight for a noble cause and you want to show the benefits that derive from his sacrifice.

If you are inside the main character, it's just not possible to hang around to watch without destroying the perspective. You are him. Once he's dead, so are you.

5. You can cause confusion and irritation by writing the story from the 'I' viewpoint but not making it clear whether the hero is a man or a woman. As a result, the reader can't visualise the main character or put the hero's actions into context and soon becomes puzzled and annoyed.

The problem takes on comic overtones when the mysterious and unsexed protagonist suddenly puts on a dress and buys a lipstick. Can we assume that the 'I' character is a woman? Or is this a man with a lot of secrets to keep?

I'm not being funny here. I've lost count of the number of short story entries I've had to eliminate because I'd read all the way to the end without being able to tell what gender the story's main character is supposed to be.

Get round this potential minefield by having your hero introduce himself or herself to someone early on in the story, or have another character refer to your protagonist by name.

My heart sinks as he comes over.
"Ah, Miss Jones. How good of you to finally turn up."

Third person

Advantages:
1. As a detached narrator, you are able to distance yourself from the actions of your characters. You can make them as mean and nasty as you like, safe in the knowledge that no-one will believe that's how you think or behave in real life.

2. You can tell the reader what a character thinks of himself, then contrast this with what the world thinks of him. This can be a very effective comic device.

3. You can enter the mind of any character – giving us the potential to see a story from any viewpoint. (See "switching viewpoints" below.)

Disadvantages:

1. You may find it harder to get into the mind of the main character.

2. You may be unsure through which character's eyes to tell the story.

3. It may be more difficult to make an unsavoury character palatable to the reader.

Whichever method you finally settle on, please don't mix third person and first person in the same story. It is very irritating for your reader!

Switching viewpoints

I believe that single viewpoint short stories are strongest, but you may decide that you want to have a multiple viewpoint story – perhaps if you are writing for a more literary style of magazine.

If you do, don't fall into the trap of rushing from one character's mind to another, bouncing back and forth like a tennis ball at Wimbledon. It confuses the reader – especially if you don't adequately signpost these switches in perspective and leave the reader wondering: whose eyes am I seeing this through now? Whose thoughts am I hearing?

Keep it simple. If you *must* switch viewpoint, make it obvious to the reader. Leave a line of white space and start a new scene. Make it clear in the opening sentence of the new segment just whose eyes you're now looking through. For example:

(END OF SCENE ONE)

John knew he was right. Knew he had to protect her. She's only a child, he thought.

(START OF SCENE TWO)

Karen felt she'd explode. Why can't he treat me like an adult, she thought angrily.

And a word of warning

Don't accidentally change viewpoint. The effect of seeing events through the hero's eyes is shattered when the author describes things that the main character couldn't possibly see.

You must stay inside the character. It's no good having John saying: *I tried to hide my sorrow, but Sheila saw it in my expression.*

Just think about it for a moment. Can you see your own expression – without getting hold of a mirror? No, of course not, you're locked in behind your eyes. And that's where the main character should remain. The instant that we go from inside the hero to outside the hero, the viewpoint has been altered. You are seeing events from someone else's point of view.

Exercises

Let all your anger out. Write a 400-word piece saying why a particular individual or type of person (eg wheelclampers or tax inspectors) makes your blood boil. Get it all down on paper.

When you've done that, imagine that you are the individual you were attacking. Now write a 400-word piece **in the first person** defending yourself, putting your point of view. Show why the criticisms and jibes in the first piece were unfair. Make the reader sympathetic towards you.

[I'll tell you now, this is a tricky exercise to pull off. Putting yourself in someone else's shoes is difficult enough but it becomes twice as hard when it's someone you despise.]

For the next exercise, take the party scene which we've used in this chapter – remember John the lecturer and his romantic entanglements? Imagine you were there at the party as one of the guests. Write your version of what happened in 350 words, from your viewpoint. What are your impressions of the events? Who do you side with – John, Jane or Tina?

Summary

- ✓ In short stories it is more powerful to stay with one perspective throughout – seeing events unfold through the main character's eyes.
- ✓ Describe the events as the hero, and only the hero, can see them.
- ✓ Only change perspective if it's a clever sting-in-the-tail and the viewpoint switch is crucial to the denouement.
- ✓ Using only one viewpoint gives your story a sharp sense of direction – and it helps readers empathise more closely with the main character.
- ✓ You have to be certain who **is** your main character. The story's tone will alter drastically according to whose viewpoint you choose.
- ✓ An important choice is whether you will tell the story in first person or third person.
- ✓ In third person the narrator is outside the story, describing events from above.
- ✓ In first person the narrator is the main character, in the heart of the story, describing events happening to him.
- ✓ There are advantages and drawbacks to both approaches so it is important to know what effect you're trying to achieve.
- ✓ Most people find it easier to show the personality of the main character if they inhabit his body.
- ✓ When you use the word 'I' – *I went here, I did this* – you make the reader imagine himself as the hero. It saves a lot of descriptive writing and careful characterisation. The barriers come down instantly.

✓ There's a danger, however, that you won't write from a character's viewpoint, but merely put yourself (the real-life writer) into the action.

✓ That's okay if the character is similar to you, reacting the same way as you would in real life. But it's hopeless if he is totally different to you.

✓ Another disadvantage is that you're trapped inside the body of one person. The reader can only know what that character knows, go where that character goes. The real action might be elsewhere.

✓ You may need to continue the action beyond the point where the hero dies.

✓ You can cause confusion by writing the story from the 'I' viewpoint if you don't make it clear whether the hero is a man or a woman.

✓ Third person offers the advantage of being able to distance yourself from the actions of your characters.

✓ Another plus is being able to enter into the mind of any character – giving you the potential to see a story from any viewpoint.

✓ The drawback is that you may find it harder to get into the mind of the main character or be unsure which character should be the hero.

✓ Whichever method you settle on, don't mix third person and first person in the same story. It is irritating to read.

✓ If you opt for multiple viewpoint, don't rush from one character's mind to another in mid text, bouncing back and forth like a tennis ball.

✓ If you must switch viewpoint, make it obvious to the reader. Leave a line of white space and start a new scene.

✓ If you are writing from the hero's viewpoint don't suddenly switch position to describe how he looks to other people. That's their perspective, not his.

9

FLASHBACKS

Flashbacks are a simple but highly effective way of enriching a tale. They transport the reader back to a dramatic event or encounter that has a crucial bearing on the present. Used properly, they add an extra layer of meaning to a narrative.

Used badly, flashbacks confuse and confound the reader, dragging him away from the immediate action and leaving him baffled, unsure about where in time and space he should be.

Unfortunately, too many inexperienced writers botch flashbacks by using them at the wrong time, for the wrong reasons and giving the wrong information. Others sprinkle flashbacks through their stories like currants in a cake. Every five paragraphs the reader is zipped away to yet another time zone.

I hope that by the end of this section you'll know exactly when to venture into the past and when to stay firmly in the present.

Point of order

The easiest way to tell a story is to start at the beginning and carry on to the end, showing events unfolding in chronological order.

It may be the easiest way, but it certainly isn't the most exciting. In fact, it's a recipe for a dull, plodding, predictable tale. It's far better to start your story at the point of conflict and show in flashback, the events which led up to it.

The chronological approach is all very well in children's stories and fairy tales, but adults demand more sophisticated methods of story-telling. Few readers will stay around while you painstakingly build up a setting and a set of characters, then slowly introduce a point of conflict.

It's faster and more gripping to plunge them straight into the story and fill in the odd bits of background knowledge they need in flashbacks, as you move along.

This works particularly well in the classic short story formula outlined in chapter four. Here it is again:

A. Introduction – the main character faces a worrying conflict/problem/dilemma.

B. ***Middle – in flashback we learn of the background and events that led up to the conflict.***

C. ***Ending – the conflict is resolved.***

Flashbacks allow you to tease and manipulate the reader's emotions. You hold back information until the moment it has maximum effect.

For example, John is out for a walk by the canal. He spots a girl drowning. She calls to him for help, but he can't swim. Which do you think is more dramatic?

(a) We know from the beginning of the story that John can't swim?

(b) Only when John sees the girl floundering, do we learn, in a flashback sequence, that he can't swim and hence can't help her?

The answer is obviously (b). If I'd told you in the opening paragraphs that John couldn't swim, you'd have been alerted that there would be some incident involving water later on.

It is better that the reader should suddenly be hit with the knowledge, and the most dramatic way to put over the information is in a flashback.

As John sees the girl floundering, he thinks back to the day, years ago, when he almost drowned in the same canal.

Immediately, we are able to understand John's dilemma. We can empathise with his uncertainty. Dare he risk drowning himself to rescue her? Can he overcome his fears? We've given an extra layer of danger and uncertainty to an already tense scene.

This is one of the main points of using a flashback. It helps us understand the motivation of the main character – why he reacts as he does. It gives us vital pieces of information about what occurred in the past; about what events helped to shape his attitudes and actions in the present.

A dramatic difference

How much difference can a flashback make to the intensity of a tale? Well, just imagine you've written a gritty short story covering the clash between two world-class boxers. It'll be okay as a yarn – the fight will obviously provide a certain amount of action and suspense. We'll want to know who wins. But will it hold us breathless in an unbreakable grip? Will the tale have us desperately rooting for one boxer or the other?

This world title bout takes on a deeper significance when we learn in flashback that the two boxers grew up as rivals in the ghetto and fought each other bare-knuckled for the price of a meal. We become even more emotionally involved when we learn that the world champ stole his opponent's girlfriend and the challenger is out to win her back at all costs.

Suddenly the match is packed with sub-text. It isn't just about who will wear the sporting crown. It's a thrilling final showdown to settle old scores and wounded pride. It's the grudge match of all time.

The reader won't be able to help himself. He will take sides and will care passionately about what happens. Just imagine the tension, excitement and drama this one flashback has added to a routine story.

In the mood

As well as enhancing drama and intensity, flashbacks build mood. They can make a story feel sad or wistful by taking the main character back to a point in his life when he felt secure or optimistic. He looks back with regret as he compares the old days with his life now. Perhaps he's a divorced man who dearly wants to be reconciled with his ex-wife, or he's a man who was once at the top of his profession but is now seen as an old-fashioned has-been.

Flashbacks can just as effectively create a feeling of mirth and delight. The hero looks back at how gauche and naive he was as a student and looks forward to his meeting with his old tutor. Perhaps he remembers being slighted by his old boss and savours the fact that the boss is now coming to him to beg for a job.

The following extract is a good example of a flashback creating atmosphere – in this case a sense of bitterness and regret.

Writer Fiona Henderson has been invited back to her old school to make the prize day speech. While revisiting her home town she desperately tries to patch things up with her father whom she's let down terribly:

She glanced up, aware that the taxi driver was staring at her in the mirror.

"Don't I know you?" he asked, half shouting over the road noise. "I'm sure I've seen you around. I've not driven you before, have I?"

"No, I shouldn't think so," Fiona replied. "I live in London.This is my first time back in Glasgow for years."

The driver pursed his lips. "I could have sworn I'd seen you before." Then, after a few moments, he clicked his fingers.

"You're that writer – Fiona ... what's her name?"

"Henderson," Fiona volunteered.

"Yeah, Henderson. That's it." The man grinned, happy to have solved the riddle. "You're doing the prize day speech at St Helen's. My nippers were going on about it. And there was a big bit in the paper, with a picture."

He half turned to look at Fiona, making the vehicle swerve. "Imagine having you riding in the back of my cab. Just wait until I tell the missus. Reads all your books she does. Must be your biggest fan. When she's got her nose buried in one of them I can't get a cheep out of her." He laughed. "I reckon your books are ruining my love life!"

The driver introduced himself as Willy Johnstone, although he pronounced it as Wully.

"That business, back there?" he asked. "Trouble with your old dad?"

"Something like that," Fiona agreed.

"Yeah. Same with my dad. Wanted me to let him move in with us, but there's no room. So we had to stick him in a home. Same sort of thing for you?"

Fiona nodded, unwilling to be drawn in.

"Yeah," Willy continued, "families are murder. They'll drive you round the twist every time. My mate George had the same bother."

He chatted on, hardly pausing for breath, but Fiona wasn't listening. What was it he'd said? Families will drive you round the twist? He didn't know the half of it.

She tried to concentrate on the speech she was about to give, to imagine the strangeness of revisiting her old school, but her mind kept straying back ... back to the row.

* * * *

It had been a mistake, of course. It was five weeks into the promotional tour, and her judgement was in shreds – clouded by travel, fatigue, inadequate sleep, too many hotel meals and too many rushed interviews.

Marcia was insistent and when your publicity agent was insistent, you didn't argue. She had to do the chat show. It could make or break the book in America.

"We're all really sorry about your mother," the agent had argued, "but she's gone, and you can't bring her back. Rushing back to Britain for her funeral isn't going to do her or you any good."

Eventually, confused and exhausted, Fiona gave in. She sent flowers and a telegram to her father to explain things.

Marcia had looked relieved as she drove Fiona to the studio instead of the airport.

"Your mother pushed you hardest to succeed as a writer," she told Fiona. "This is what she'd have wanted, believe me."

Fiona almost did believe her – but it was a lie. Two months later, when she returned to Scotland, there was no one to meet her at the airport; just a short message on the answering machine from her brother, Colin.

"Congratulations, Fiona. I never really knew what a selfish person you were until now. You've broken Dad's heart. What sort of person doesn't come home for her mother's funeral?

"Dad kept saying you'd be there. Even on the way to the service he thought you'd show. He just couldn't believe you'd turn your back on us. Neither did I – but we were wrong, weren't we?

"Well, I hope your precious book makes you a fortune. Don't call us back. In fact, don't ever call again. We're finished with you."

And he meant it. Fiona tried calling, but Colin put the phone down on her. Letters were returned unopened. It was the same with her father. Eventually, sad and angry, she'd stopped trying.

She had vowed never to return to Glasgow – until the letter from St Helen's changed her mind ...

* * * *

Willy wouldn't let her out of the cab until she had signed three autographs. She watched him drive off, waving happily, before turning to go through the school gates ...

The flashback here is a crucial component of the story. It conveys mood and information, but also helps to win over the reader. Fiona has done something most of us would feel was unforgivable – missing her own mother's funeral – and this makes her a potentially unsympathetic character.

But there are mitigating circumstances and this quick glance back in time shows that she shouldn't be judged too harshly. It also helps illustrate just why her family feel so angry and betrayed.

Without this vital flashback the story would be robbed of much of its emotional charge.

Going and coming back

One thing that can wreck a story is the writer taking the narrative back to the past but not signalling clearly enough that the action has switched period or setting. The reader tries to read on but is confused about why things have suddenly changed for no reason. Why is John suddenly younger? Why is he at his parents' house in the country instead of being in his city penthouse flat?

Always alert the readers that you're about to go back in time:

John closed his eyes, and suddenly he remembered that time ten years before he'd left home ...

Likewise, always tell them that you've come back to the present:

That was then, back when things were so much easier. But John knew that things wouldn't be so easy now. Not today.

Such signposting will keep your story running smoothly and prevent any confusion. I know some new writers are a little self-conscious about putting up a huge banner that says "Hey folks, we're now back in the present" but readers don't actually mind. Many won't even be aware they've read a hidden "sign", having absorbed the message on a subliminal level.

In the story extract you've just read, I used an additional "marker". To help re-inforce the point that I was going in and out of a flashback I broke the text into separate scenes – split up by extra space.

Dividing the text into scenes in this way is optional. Some writers do it any time that there's a change in period or setting. Others don't bother. Adopt this format if it appeals to you or if it is the usual house style of the magazine you're writing for.

Personally I always feel it's better to have too much sign-posting than not enough.

Follow the rules

Flashbacks are easy to do and, when used sparingly, can be extremely effective. Just stick to the following dozen rules and you won't go far wrong.

1. Don't use flashbacks to brighten up a boring, flagging story. If the narrative is dull, it will still be dull if you drop a flashback into the middle of it. The only difference is that it will then be both dull and disjointed.

2. Don't allow the flashback to be more exciting than the main narrative. If it is, the reader will ask why you're bothering with all the boring present day stuff. Why not just write a tale around the incidents in the flashback?

3. Never have a flashback within a flashback. It will confuse the reader, muddle the narrative beyond redemption and cause you nightmares in choosing which tense to write in.

4. Always use what English teachers call the "pluperfect" or "past perfect" tense in flashbacks. That means including the word *had* in many of your sentences to constantly remind readers that events took place at a former time. For example: *reluctantly he* ***had*** *gone to meet her; "I'm fine,"* ***she'd*** *assured him;* ***she'd*** *driven home in a daze;* ***he'd*** *known he was doomed etc.* And to quote from the story ... *"Fiona* ***had*** *known that she should be with her family. But Marcia* ***hadn't*** *let up."*

5. Don't use flashbacks just for the sake of stylistic self-indulgence. Like all gimmicks they should be used for a

good reason, not just to show that you know how to write them.

6. Don't have too many flashbacks. It rapidly becomes tedious – the more flashbacks you use, the more likely the reader is to spot that you're using a literary device. The moment the reader starts to pay attention to your writing style, instead of being sucked into the story, you've failed.

7. Don't have flashbacks that are so long that the reader begins to forget what the story is about – or forgets exactly where in the action they left it.

8. Don't give every detail of a character's past in a flashback. Only show those events that have a bearing on the present day story. For example, a sister hates her brother because he embarrassed her in front of her first boyfriend – that's why she's not inviting him to her wedding.

   In the extract I showed you earlier there are many other interesting incidents in Fiona Henderson's life, but they aren't relevant to the current narrative. For that reason they aren't included.

9. Don't abandon the rules of **show** and **tell**. You may have journeyed back to the past, but don't just give the readers a dull summary. Have events unfold before their eyes. Make them think they're witnessing it all happening – even if those events are 20 years old.

   I was pushed for space in the flashback and couldn't re-enact every detail of Fiona's dilemma and her falling out with her family. But by keeping the summary short and packed with dialogue, it still has pace and impact.

10. Never use flashbacks purely to supply atmosphere. If they don't contain vital information, they've no right being there no matter how much mood they create.

11. Don't start a flashback too soon in a story. Let us get used to the main character, and the conflict he faces, before you whisk him back in time.

12. Don't use flashbacks to try to get yourself out of plotting difficulties. It's really lame near the end of a story to have a detective suddenly recall something said to him weeks before – some vital clue we hadn't heard about before.

Credibility gap

Now, you may be thinking: what's the difference between a writer having his detective suddenly remembering a vital clue and the earlier example of using a well-timed flashback to show that John almost drowned in that canal. Surely it is the same thing – holding back information from the reader until the right moment?

No, not really. Granted, you are holding back information but it's the writer's motivation that counts in whether or not this is acceptable.

In the detective example, the writer is using the technique through laziness. It's a shortcut way to get round a problem. It's changing the rules – making things unnecessarily easy for your hero and the reader feels cheated when he reads it.

In the drowning girl example, the flashback showing that John almost drowned is actually making things harder for him. He can't just dive in without a second thought. It makes the reader more involved. He doesn't feel cheated when he learns about John's previous swimming problems – he feels even more emotionally tied to the story.

It's all a matter of credibility. Readers are very perceptive and know immediately if you are using a flashback to squirm out of trouble. So don't try!

Exercises

Have a look at three short stories which feature a flashback sequence. Study how the authors signpost the switch into the past and the return to the present. Make a note of these techniques.

Now, using one of the three signposting methods you've identified write an 800-word piece where your main character remembers an event in the past which he now bitterly regrets. Take him back to that day and play out the scene before returning him to the present.

Write a passage of 1,000 words based on the example in the chapter of John finding the girl floundering in the canal. Start off with him seeing the girl in trouble then use a flashback to show John nearly drowning as a child. Bring him back to the present and have him rescue the girl – but remember to show how afraid he is because of his childhood near-miss.

Imagine you are one of the two boxers in the grudge match title bout mentioned in the chapter and write an 850-word sequence – including a flashback – showing why you hate your opponent so much.

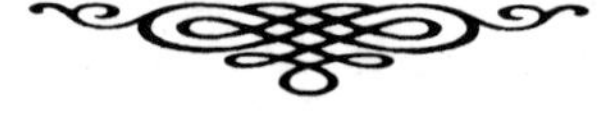

Summary

- ✓ Flashbacks transport the reader back to a dramatic event or encounter that has a crucial bearing on the story in the present.

- ✓ Used well, they can add an additional layer of meaning to a narrative.

- ✓ Used badly, they drag the reader away from the immediate action leaving him unsure where in time and space he should be.

- ✓ A short story which relates events in chronological order is a recipe for a dull, plodding, predictable read.

- ✓ Few readers will stay around while you painstakingly build up a setting and a set of characters then slowly introduce a point of conflict.

- ✓ It's far better to start your story at the point of conflict and show, in flashback, the events which led up to it.

- ✓ The classic short story formula is:

  A. Introduction – the main character faces a worrying conflict/problem/dilemma.

  B. Middle – in flashback we learn of the background and events that led up to the conflict.

  C. Ending – the conflict is resolved.

- ✓ Flashbacks allow you to tease and manipulate the reader's emotions. You hold back information until the moment it has maximum effect.

- ✓ They help the reader to understand the motivation of the main character – why he reacts as he does.

- ✓ They give vital pieces of information about what occurred in the past; what events helped to shape his attitudes and actions in the present.

- ✓ As well as enhancing drama and intensity, flashbacks build mood. They can make a story feel sad or wistful or funny by taking the main character back to the point when he felt secure or optimistic.

- ✓ One thing that wrecks a story is the writer taking the narrative back to the past but not signalling clearly that the action has switched period.

- ✓ Always "signpost". Alert readers that you're about to go back in time. Likewise, always tell them that you've come back to the present.

- ✓ Don't use flashbacks to "brighten up" a flagging story. If the narrative is dull, it will still be dull even if you drop a flashback into the middle.

- ✓ Don't allow the flashback to be more exciting than the main narrative.

- ✓ Never have a flashback within a flashback. It will muddle the narrative.

- ✓ Always use the *pluperfect* or *past perfect* tense in flashbacks.

- ✓ Never use flashbacks just for the sake of stylistic self-indulgence, and don't have too many in a story.

- ✓ Make sure you don't have flashbacks that are so long that the reader forgets what the story is about – or where in the action he left it.

- ✓ Don't give every detail of a character's past in a flashback. Only show those events that have a bearing on the present.

- ✓ Don't abandon the rules of show and tell. You may have journeyed back to the past, but don't just give the readers a dull summary.

- ✓ Don't start a flashback too soon. Let us get used to the main character, and the conflict he faces, before whisking him back in time.

- ✓ Never use flashbacks to try to get yourself out of plotting difficulties.

10

ATTENTION GRABBING INTROS

Every country in the world has ancient folk legends about blood-sucking creatures of the night – it can't be just a coincidence. Vampires must exist. They are all around us, watching us hungrily!

Well? Do vampires exist? Are they lurking behind next door's privet? I don't know and, frankly, I don't very much care. Sorry Dracula ... back in your box.

The reason I wrote the opening paragraph was to show how effectively you can hook the reader's attention – if you hit hard and swiftly with a tantalising morsel of information.

When readers buy a novel or subscribe to a specialist small press publication they're prepared to spend a little time easing into the story. They've allocated time to read, they're mentally prepared for a long slog and they'll stick with the story. After all, they've forked out several pounds and don't want to waste their money.

The opposite is true with a "coffee break" short story in a popular glossy magazine. The chances are it's being read on a whim, by someone who's sitting nervously in a dentist's waiting room. It's no wonder that he's got the attention span of a hyperactive toddler. He's got other things on his mind.

Hooking that reader is a tough challenge. Your short story is competing with racy articles, readers' letters, horoscopes, other writers' short stories and the distant whine of the drill. You have to catch his interest immediately and totally. There's no time for waffle or stylistic self-indulgence. You have to hit him like a tidal wave. He has to be sucked into the story before he realises what has happened.

All over in an instant

The average magazine reader only devotes about ten seconds to reading an intro, and deciding whether he wants to carry on through the story. That's about 30 words.

Do you hook the reader in the first 30 words of your short stories? If the answer is no – then you're sunk.

Readers aren't the only ones judging you in a hurry. A fiction editor facing a pile of 200 scripts hasn't got the time to wade through to the end of each story. He'll make up his mind by reading the first few sentences. If they're gripping, he'll read on. If not, the manuscript goes on the reject pile.

That may sound harsh but it's rare for a tale to start with a poor intro and then miraculously improve a few paragraphs on. A fiction editor, reading thousands of stories each year, has a nose for it. He can tell a stinker from reading the first two sentences.

That means that an attention-grabbing, "must-read", intro is vital. Without it, you're dead. Think of the intro as your sales pitch – it's the one crack you get at impressing an editor. You can't afford an opening that's dull, predictable or confusing.

Don't fall into the trap of wasting the opening sentences of your story on unnecessary, scene-setting descriptions. Few readers will stick with your vampire tale while you spend the first page describing how cold the night was, how creepy the castle looked against the moon, how jittery the villagers were, how loudly the owls hooted. Readers will yawn and say: *Yeah, yeah, I've seen a horror film before. I don't need all this scene-setting. Get on with the plot before I fall asleep.*

They want the action – the point of the story – to start from the first word. Better that you begin with: *"The body's drained," the doctor whispered, "there isn't a drop of blood left in her."*

That opening creates more atmosphere and more tension than any amount of gothic word-pictures – no matter how cleverly or poetically arranged.

Avoid starting with character studies. The reader is only going to be with your hero for a page or two – maybe ten minutes at most. He doesn't need to know the character's life story or be led through his family tree.

He certainly doesn't want to struggle through two pages of biographical notes before the story starts. Don't waste your introduction on your hero's CV. The reader isn't going to offer him a job.

Make your intro work hard

If you want to write short, sharp fiction your opening few paragraphs have a crucial job to do. They should be telling the reader:

WHAT the story is about

WHO the main character is

WHERE it is happening

WHEN it is happening

WHY the central conflict or crisis has come about

HOW that crisis affects the main character

Make sure that you answer as many of these questions as possible as rapidly as possible – within the first two pages or 500 words of text. Go back through your opening and check off these points.

If your intro doesn't work, it's likely that one of these key points is missing and the rest of the story won't flow logically, leaving the reader confused or irritated.

Keep 'em guessing

Aim to strike a balance between answering the necessary Who? Why? Where? What? When? and How? questions – and giving away all your secrets in the first couple of paragraphs.

It isn't necessary to cram everything into the first 50 words. Tease the reader by leaving out an intriguing piece of information from the first few sentences – as long as you do this deliberately to create suspense and not purely by mistake. In some respects the less the reader knows at first the more likely he is to be snared. His own curiosity traps him.

See how quickly you're plunged into this tale: *"I don't know why I killed her. I didn't mean to. It just sort of happened!"*

BAM! It fires the imagination, while leaving all sorts of enticing questions unanswered. And I've used only 16 words (five seconds).

The reader will hang on to find out who I am, who I killed, how I did it and why. They'll also want to know: was it a total accident or had I intended some harm to the woman and it got out of hand? Do I feel remorse?

There's just enough information so that the introduction makes sense, but not a scrap extra. If you want to find out more, then you'll have to read the story.

This shameless manipulation of the reader's curiosity is perfectly acceptable – as long as by the time he reaches the 500-word mark I've explained enough of the plot to answer his initial question. By the time he's passed this point he should be wondering: *How is this going to end?* not *What is this about?*

Now see how the following openings catch your attention:

PETER'S eight-year-old eyes were close to tears. "But why can't I go to see Granddad? I've never been to a hospital before. I promise I'll be good. Honest, mum."

Elaine shook her head slowly, hoping her son wouldn't see how much this was hurting her.

"STRIPPERS? I'll give him strippers!" Brenda fumed at the stag-night advert in the paper. "If he thinks he's nipping out with the lads to ogle naked floozies, he's got another thing coming."

DEREK Chandler could contain his fury no longer. "I don't believe it," he snarled. "They've mucked up my bank statement again – they've paid someone else's direct debit out of my account! Seventy-five pounds to some spiritualist mission."

THERE was an edge of panic in Frank Peter's voice I'd never heard before.

"Jack, we've got trouble," he gulped, "the rats are out. Some lunatic's released them."

RACHEL'S news was a bombshell. David didn't know what to say for a moment. Hurriedly, he took a gulp of his wine.

"So you got the promotion," he repeated, trying hard to smile.

A TREMENDOUS cheer went round our spotter plane – central control had found Bert Higgins! In my relief, I cheered too, yelling until my lungs ached and tears coursed down my cheeks.

Three weeks of scouring every country and nation state had paid off. We'd located the Preston bus driver who was the only man who could save the human race.

LYNDA Bryant threw in the last shovelful of earth, patted it down and surveyed her handiwork with quiet contentment. It was a good, neat job – not easy in the rain, especially by torch-light.

Gazing down at the ragged rectangle cut out of the lawn, she sighed. "Well, Fred," she muttered, "you always said you wanted to spend more time in the garden."

Setting the mood

Do you notice how the intro not only starts the action and catches the attention, but sets the mood of the story? You should be able to guess, from the opening, whether a story is going to be sad, funny, romantic, horrific or just weird.

There are two main schools of thought on intros – people who say you should always start with a snatch of dialogue, and those who say you should never start with dialogue.

Those in favour of dialogue say that it plunges the reader straight into the action. The antis say a snatch of dialogue, with little to put it into context, confuses the reader.

It's entirely a matter of personal preference and, of course, the house style of the magazine you're writing for. However, it's important to include dialogue early in the tale. It's the dynamic element that injects excitement; bringing your characters alive.

Good, crisp dialogue gives a feeling of pace and movement. An emotion-charged line of speech can launch the story out of the starting blocks like an Olympic sprinter. It surges forward, taking the reader with it. A story that begins with overblown description or needless background information sets off at a walking pace and gets slower.

Straight to the conflict

Writing an opening that screams "**read me**!" isn't merely a question of choosing some clever dialogue or baiting a hook with a teasing phrase. It must take the reader to the very second that the conflict starts, the moment your hero's life is altered – the real start of the plot.

Don't tell us about Matt Brown having breakfast with his family, catching the train into work and sitting down at his desk. Don't bore us with the details of his mundane morning, before springing the surprise that his office has blown up. Start off with the bomb. That's the interesting bit!

"You're alive," Matt's brain screamed to him as he staggered from the wreckage, "you've survived!"

He glanced at the ruins of the office and marvelled that anyone had walked away from the blast. All 17 floors of the tower block were levelled; devastated.

Whoever planted that bomb knew what they were doing, he thought as he looked at his legs and saw that they were pouring with blood.

A lot to do

You can see by now that your intro has to work harder than any other part of the story so it's worth spending a bit of time revising and polishing it until it's just right. You only get one shot to snare the reader.

Ask yourself: does my opening establish character and setting? Does it get the story off at a cracking pace and arouse the reader's curiosity? Does it suggest the mood and era of the story? Does it bring the reader in at just the right dramatic moment?

It's a tall order, but the writers of good short stories know the importance of exciting intros and will work on an opening over and over – maybe a dozen times or more. They know that first impressions count.

Exercises

Study the first six paragraphs of three short stories (a sting-in-the-tail, a romantic story and a sci-fi or horror tale).

What tricks do the authors use to get your attention? Look for the "hooks" that grab you. Make a note of each. Have a go at rewriting the intros to improve on them – see if you can make them more atmospheric.

Write an intro to a story (100-250 words long), making sure it answers all the **Who**? **What**? **When**? **Where**? **Why**? and **How**? questions. Now rewrite the intro six times leaving out one key "5Ws" element each time.

Compare the six. Which one do you think is most intriguing and likely to pique the reader's curiosity? Say why.

Write a 100-word intro for a horror story, a children's story and a radio yarn. Pose a mystery in each which will hook the audience.

Summary

- ✓ It's vital that you hook the reader's attention – by hitting him swiftly with a tantalising morsel of information.
- ✓ You have to catch his interest immediately and totally. He has to be sucked into the story before he realises what has happened.
- ✓ The average person will devote as little as ten seconds to reading an intro, and deciding whether to carry on. That's about 30 words!
- ✓ A fiction editor does the same. He'll make up his mind by reading the first few sentences. If they're gripping, he'll read on. If not, he'll reject it.
- ✓ That means you can't afford to write an opening that's dull, plodding, predictable or confusing.
- ✓ Don't waste the opening sentences on unnecessary and showy scene-setting descriptions. Don't allow it to be just mood music.
- ✓ The reader doesn't want to struggle through two pages of biographical notes before the story starts. Don't waste your intro on your hero's CV.
- ✓ Your opening should tell the reader: **what** the story is about, **who** the main character is, **where** it is happening, **when** it is happening, **why** the central conflict or crisis has come about and **how** that crisis affects the main character.
- ✓ Make sure that you answer as many of these questions as possible as rapidly as possible – within 500 words of text.
- ✓ But it isn't necessary to cram *everything* into the first 50 words. Tease the reader by leaving out an intriguing piece of information.

- ✓ Give only the facts necessary for the introduction to make sense. Keep the suspense going.

- ✓ The intro sets the mood. You should be able to guess, from the opening, whether a story is horrific, funny, romantic, or sad.

- ✓ Try to get a snatch of dialogue into your opening. It's the dynamic element that injects excitement, bringing your characters alive.

- ✓ The intro must take the reader to the very second that the conflict starts, the moment your hero's life is altered – the start of the plot.

11

EDIFYING ENDINGS

Just how you end your story is every bit as important as how you start it – arguably more important. It's the last thing people read and will be the part of your story that sticks most in their memory.

So it's worth spending a great deal of time crafting and polishing the last few sentences to make sure they really work. The reader must feel the conclusion to your tale is a logical and satisfying climax to the train of events.

The ending must fit in with the mood and pace of the story and must tie up any loose ends of the narrative that would otherwise leave readers feeling puzzled or cheated. It should never be rushed or cramped, with the last events sketchily described, or condensed as the writer runs out of space. Nor should the narrative's conclusion be an abrupt cut-off as the writer realises he can't take the storyline any further.

I often read competition entries where writers faced a rigidly set word-limit, misjudged how much room they had left and so tried to fit at least a third of the plot into just a few sentences. Sometimes they would just ditch the remaining section of the storyline, leaving the main character hanging in mid-air. These misguided authors probably hoped that I'd think they were being enigmatic and experimental. They weren't successful – the stories just felt clumsy and unresolved.

An ending should read as though you planned it. And you *should* plan your ending before putting ink on paper. After all, you're not much of a tour guide if you ask readers to accompany you on a journey when you don't even know the destination.

Give your endings impact

You don't want the reader to get to the magic words THE END and shrug indifferently. You don't want the reader to say: *So, was that it?*

The ending of your story should be a climax – a punchline. It should elicit an emotional response. It doesn't matter whether readers laugh, cry, sigh or groan – as long as they react.

Know when to stop the narrative

Ending your story swiftly is crucial. The art of good story-telling is knowing when to shut up.

Make your tale conclude the moment the plot does. Don't let it roll on for several paragraphs like a supertanker that has reversed its engines but is still carried forward by its own lumbering momentum.

If a narrative starts the moment the main character faces a crisis, then it should stop the second that crisis is resolved. Don't give us epilogues, further adventures or a moment's thought to consider the moral of the tale. Don't give the reader time to get bored.

Upbeat endings

New writers are often puzzled when fiction editors write: *I liked your story but I felt it needed a more upbeat ending.*

I've heard more than one budding story-teller say: *What does he want – jokes at the end? The story is about a woman dying of cancer. I can't make it funny. She dies – it's not a happy ending.*

This may be a natural reaction but it isn't the right way to look at the comment. The writer has misunderstood what the fiction editor is asking for. He isn't asking for a happy ending. He's asking for a positive ending – not the same thing at all. Even in the saddest story there is room for optimism and hope. Readers want to come away from a story, even a weepie one, feeling that not everything in life is depressing and morbid.

Okay, so the main character is dying of cancer – but there could be worthwhile things to come out of the tragedy. Maybe she has been estranged from her family and her illness brings them back together again. Maybe she has been someone who lived in fear, always feeling threatened by the challenges in life. Suddenly, as she faces death, she finds the courage and dignity that eluded her all those years.

These are positive outcomes, yet the storyline hasn't been fundamentally altered. There is no miracle Hollywood-ending cure discovered in time to save her but, in a way, she has triumphed.

Change for the better

The fiction that I find most satisfying is when the hero faces up to adversity and becomes a better person because of it. He doesn't have to beat his opponents or resolve the crisis to be a winner – finding inner strength or a lost innocence is a triumph in itself.

One of the most satisfying endings can be when a character realises that he was too busy making money and chasing promotion to take care of the ones he loved and resolves to make amends. Likewise, when a character has that telling moment of revelation, realising that he has turned into the kind of person he promised himself he'd never become.

Remember, you have introduced conflict into this poor person's life – introduce it for a reason. Make this conflict a catalyst for change. The reader will want the hero to emerge from his crisis a wiser, kinder and more likeable person.

Fairy Godmother endings

Readers are rooting for your main character. They identify with him – maybe even want to be him – and want him to win through against the odds. They'll find it immensely satisfying if he overcomes his difficulties by his own hard work, quick-footedness and ingenuity. They'll think: yes, that's the way I'd have tackled it. Yes, I have those same admirable qualities.

What will annoy and disappoint readers is if you give your hero a little helping hand. Just as his house is about to be repossessed, he miraculously wins the lottery or the boss has an unexpected change of heart and doesn't sack him, but gives him a promotion and wage rise instead.

I call these Fairy Godmother endings, because just when everything looks bleak, fate obligingly snatches your hero out of danger. The threat to his livelihood and well-being vanishes with the wave of a magic wand.

As well as being an insult to the reader's intelligence, such endings are a real let-down. I always feel cheated when I read one. I feel conned into caring about the character when he was never really in any trouble at all.

The worst of all Fairy Godmother endings is: *and then I woke up and realised it was all a dream.* Aghhhh!!! This cop-out ending is infuriatingly a favourite with writers who enter competitions. There are always a dozen, written by people who have created a story so implausible, so confused, so tied up in knots, so plainly ridiculous that pressing the Emergency Exit button is the only way to escape back to the real world.

Well, I'm pleased to tell you that these poor souls never win. Judges hate dream endings. By the way, so do fiction editors. Your dream is their nightmare!

Surprise endings

It would appear that everyone these days wants to write sting-in-the-tail stories and, at up to £350 for a 1,000-word Coffee Break yarn, it's no wonder.

These teasing tales are fun to read and even more fun to write. They're a great chance to show how clever you can be, combining a little bit of trickery with a big dollop of humour. And fiction editors can't get enough of them.

There's nothing so satisfying as seeing someone's face when they get to the punchline of one of your twists and realise they've been had.

The headaches

Engaging sting-in-the-tails are comparatively easy to write but inexperienced writers seem to have trouble with them. No other form of short story causes so many headaches.

That's because so few people really understand what makes a twist story work. They write tales where the ending doesn't develop naturally from the plot – it's bolted on as an obvious afterthought: *A gang pulls off the perfect bank robbery, drives to their country hideout and starts dividing up the loot ...then inexplicably there's a gas explosion which kills them all.*

Others trip up by having a climax which asks the reader to accept something that is clearly ridiculous. A good example of this is a story which has the main character, Malcolm, driving a bus all day. In the last paragraph the writer tries to have the impossible twist ending that Malcolm isn't a human – he's a dog. This is plainly silly and the reader won't wear it.

If you have Malcolm driving the bus then reveal at the end that he is only twelve years old, the reader will believe you. The twist is unusual (far-fetched even) but it isn't impossible. It could happen. Perhaps his father is a bus driver and taught him to drive around a deserted car park.

The principle

The sting-in-the-tail story works on the principle of misleading the reader – but not lying to him. In the example above, the writer didn't say that Malcolm was a grown man, but he let the reader assume it.

As readers we often make assumptions; guessing at bits of information that are missing, filling in the blanks. This is what makes us such easy prey for the twist-in-the-tail merchants.

We make assumptions often without realising it. If I say the word "granny" to you, you will probably already be using your imagination to picture an elderly woman – perhaps with grey hair and a cat. What if I then tell you the granny in my story is 33 and works as a go-go dancer in a night-club? I didn't lie to you. I didn't describe her home-made scones and the roses round the door of her quaint, thatched cottage. I used one word "granny" to trap you into misleading yourself. That's the art of the surprise ending.

The same principle is at the heart of a million jokes. The comedian lets you build the wrong mental picture before he destroys it with the (hopefully) hilarious punchline.

For example: *I went down to our local multiplex cinema the other day. I couldn't believe it. Sex, violence, ritual sacrifice and blood-guzzling zombies – and that was just the queue for the popcorn!*

Hold back a crucial fact

The idea isn't to conceal so much information that the reader becomes disorientated and distanced from the action – the secret is to keep one, and only one, important fact hidden.

In our go-go dancer's case the fact I kept hidden was her age. In other stories you could conceal the sex of the main character – Chris looked really great in the new pink dress. Unfortunately, his colleagues got a little worried.

Or maybe you can keep a relationship secret. The suave man spends most of the story chatting up the gorgeous woman he's spotted across the casino. They leave arm in arm for a night of passion. But at the end we learn they are husband and wife and that this is a little game they play on their wedding anniversary.

Or how about role reversal? The power-suited boss tells off the office cleaner for not vacuuming the boardroom properly. But the boss is a woman and the Mrs Mop is a man.

Don't lie

Twist endings depend on you conning the readers – wilfully helping them to jump to the wrong conclusion. And readers will see the joke in the skilful way you let them fool themselves. But you'll only antagonise them if you actively tell lies.

It's fine for me to say: *Chris looked really great in the new pink dress* and let you assume that Chris is short for Christine. I never said Chris was a woman.

But if I write: *Chris knew she looked great in the new pink dress*, I've told you she's a woman. If, later on, I try to claim that Chris is Christopher, you'll yell: *Hang on a minute, that's not right. You've cheated. You've changed it.* And you'd be right to feel aggrieved.

It's amazing how many stories fail because the writer's twist-ending contradicts the earlier information. You can't just move the goalposts to suit yourself.

Hidden clues

Surprise ending stories are a bit like whodunnits. With crime novels, readers want to see if they can uncover the killer before the detective does. In twist-in-the-tail stories, readers want to see if they can outwit the writer and spot the surprise halfway through.

For that reason, just like a whodunnit, you should have clues which give the reader a fighting chance. These shouldn't leap out from the text or be so obvious that everyone who reads the story guesses the ending in advance, but the clues should hint at the solution.

When the reader finds out that bus driving Malcolm is twelve he should say to himself: *Ah yes. So that's why he was sucking lollipops and had trouble reaching the pedals.*

You should give the reader the impression that he ought to have guessed the ending.

Devising effective clues is one of the most demanding parts of writing good twist-in-the-end tales. To give you an idea of the right way to seed these hints, it's worth looking at a story I had in *Chat* magazine entitled *Baby-Sitter Blues*.

Read it now and then we'll look at some of the sneaky ways I mislead the reader.

Roger blew into Jane's ear, making her jump. "You're miles away," he said to her accusingly.

Jane blinked, suddenly aware that she had been day-dreaming. "I was just thinking about Chloe." She made a face. "Well, *worrying* about Chloe."

She frowned at the thought of her baby-sitter and the mayhem she was probably wreaking. Jane pictured their front room littered with Coke cans and crisp packets, as music blared out from their CD player.

It had been Roger's idea to have Chloe babysit for them, after their usual sitter had let them down. Jane had reluctantly agreed because Roger was so looking forward to going out. But she wished they'd been able to find someone else – *anyone* else. Everywhere Chloe went, chaos followed.

There was no doubting that Chloe had a heart of gold, but she was so – well, irresponsible. And there was the awful music she listened to, and the ridiculous clothes. And then there were the gormless boyfriends. The last one had been caught in the high street, doing wheelies on his bike. Kate told herself that Chloe was at a difficult age, that it would soon all pass but it didn't help.

Roger sighed and touched her arm. "I'm sure you're worrying about nothing. Why not just ring home and check that it's okay?"

Jane shivered at the thought of it, and her hand trembled as she dialled the number. The phone rang for a long time, as Jane waited anxiously.

Eventually, the line clicked and Chloe answered the phone.

"Chloe! I've been ringing for ages," Jane complained, "Why did you take so long to answer?"

Chloe was evasive, "I ... I didn't hear it."

"You had your music on too loud, you mean!"

"Maybe," Chloe admitted, grudgingly.

"Is Scott all right?"

"Oh yes, he's fine. He wasn't sleepy, so I let him stay up a while longer. We were having a dance. He's in bed now, though."

Jane was about to ask if Scott had remembered to clean his teeth when she heard a laugh – a deep, male laugh. Her eyes narrowed suspiciously.

"Is that a man's voice I can hear?"

There was a long pause. "Er ... yes," Chloe replied. "It's just a friend. You know, Rick. He popped in on his way home from the youth club."

Jane fought to control her temper. How dare Chloe use her house as a rendezvous for dropouts!

"We're going to have a serious talk when I get home," she warned. "You'd better have some good excuses."

Jane slammed down the phone and stormed back to the table. She told Roger, but he seemed to find it all amusing. "Oh well, girls will be girls," he said.

"Not in my front room they won't," Jane replied. "Heaven knows what they're doing." She breathed in angrily. "That's it. We'll have to go back. Chloe can't be trusted. I knew something like this would happen."

Her husband groaned. "But it'll be midnight soon. We'll miss the last waltz."

Jane's expression was like bottled thunder. "I don't care. We're going home *now*."

Jane fumed on the drive back. "I knew it was a mistake," she snapped. "I knew it. I told you we should have had a responsible adult. Well, that's positively the last time she baby-sits."

Roger nodded, keeping silent. He concentrated on the road and winced at the thought of the confrontation to come. All too soon, they turned into their street and spotted Rick's bike parked outside their door. Jane spotted it too, and muttered furiously.

"He's still there," she said through gritted teeth.

The wall of sound hit them as they entered the house. Jane marvelled that Scott could sleep through the racket. She also marvelled that the neighbours hadn't called the police.

They found Chloe and Rick in the front room, both looking sheepish. Chloe immediately leapt up and switched off the music.

"Oh, I wasn't expecting you home so soon," she said.

"That's obvious," Jane said, her tone icy. She glared at Rick. "Isn't it time you were leaving?"

The bespectacled male nodded timidly and grabbed his CD collection of and his bicycle clips. Roger couldn't hide a smile as the youth-club leader hobbled away.

Jane turned her attention to Chloe. "Why don't you put your hearing aid in when you listen to music, instead of blasting it out?" she demanded.

Chloe's twinkling eyes misted under her grey hair. "I'm sorry, love," she said, shoulders slumping. "I forgot."

Jane wanted to scream. She looked across pleadingly at Roger. "Can't you talk to her? To explain things?"

Roger glanced at the merry widow and shook his head.

"I don't think so," he said. "I couldn't really tell her off. After all, Chloe *is* my mother!"

Well, were you taken in? Did I con you into thinking that Chloe was a wayward teenager instead of a problem pensioner?

Here are the pointers that help the reader to jump to the wrong conclusion. The deception starts when I said that Chloe would leave the front room littered with Coke cans and crisp packets. This is the type of snack food we'd normally associate with a teenager – but people of all ages eat crisps and enjoy soft drinks.

Then there was the mention of her playing her music loudly – but I didn't say what sort of music it was. It wasn't hard rock or chart toppers but was actually Vera Lynn.

The mention of her male friend doing wheelies on his bike was a bit naughty of me – but it wasn't a lie. You don't have to be young to be reckless on two wheels.

See how having used one small piece of misdirection, I then added on more and more until the reader was led up the garden path? The trap is completely sprung when Jane says: "*I knew we should have had a responsible adult.*"

The reader, mentally putting emphasis on the word *adult*, thinks this means that Chloe is a youngster. In fact, the reader should be putting the emphasis on the word *responsible*. Chloe is an adult all right, but wouldn't know responsibility if it foxtrotted with her.

The hardest part of making this deception work was to come up with a name that wouldn't give away the babysitter's age. I chose Chloe because it is a name that doesn't have any age connotations. As I said in chapter five, choosing just the right name for a character is vital in helping the reader to visualise what a character looks like.

I didn't want readers drawing any age inferences from the name Chloe, so that they would have to rely on the other information – the ambiguous information – to form a mental picture of what the babysitter looked like.

Put the sting at the end

Your sting is your punchline. Always have it as near the end as possible. It should be in the final two paragraphs. Some magazines insist on the sting being in the last six words.

Keep it tasteful

By the way, it's worth mentioning that sting-in-the-tail stories need to conform to the same taste and decency requirements as all other types of short fiction. Some people make the mistake of thinking that they need to have gory, nauseating or horrific elements in their sting ending. They feel that the ending won't be dramatic enough without some sort of shock factor.

The only shock you need is the reader's surprise when he realises that you mislead him. Remember: you're trying to entertain your audience, not terrify or sicken them.

Always have a plot

Never forget that a twist-in-the-tail story must have some reason for existing apart from just the tricksy ending. It must still work as a yarn even if the surprise climax is removed.

So don't let the tail wag the dog. The ending is merely a satisfying way of rounding off a story. It's still vital to have a realistic and intriguing conflict for your hero to deal with.

Endings in action

That's enough of the theory. Let's now look at the last few paragraphs of a selection of different types of short stories. Take special note of how the climaxes all bring the tales to a logical – and often ironic – conclusion. If they're doing their job properly, each should provoke a reaction – even if it's just a tortured groan.

In *Stage Fright* two young actresses are both after the same man. Their murderous rivalry comes to a head during a matinee pantomime performance of *Cinderella*. The principal boy, Lucy, has deliberately left the stage trap door open in the hope that her rival, Samantha, will accidentally fall down it ... but things don't go quite as she planned.

Lucy looked round startled, but there was no sign of Samantha.

"Where the hell is Cinders?" Lucy screamed at the audience, her fists balled.

Two dainty hands suddenly pushing into her back told Lucy all she needed to know. She tipped forward into the sinister gaping hole. Plunging through the darkness, she heard the children yelling: "BEHIND YOU!!!"

In *Everyone Needs A Hero* journalist Elaine faces the worst dilemma of her life. Her father is in hospital with terminal cancer. He desperately wants to see his eight-year-old grandson Peter one last time but she stops the child visiting. She's frightened Peter will be traumatised by the horror of seeing the old man so close to death.

Her stand, although taken for all the right motives, hurts everyone. As the story progresses she remembers the wonderful things her father did for her over the years, and how ungrateful she's always been. It seems she can't do anything but hurt him.

To take Peter's mind off her refusal to let him see his grandfather, Elaine arranges for the child to meet one of his footballing idols. She won't tell him who they are going to see, only that Peter's going to meet a "hero".

On the way to the football ground they have to pass the hospital. Suddenly, Elaine relents ...

Charlie took her hand and squeezed it. His red eyes began to moisten.

"You brought him after all." The voice was hoarse, but determined. "Thank you, Elaine. Thanks. You don't know what this means to me."

She shrugged, suddenly feeling flustered, embarrassed at this unaccustomed show of emotion.

"It's okay, dad. I owed it to you ... to both of you."

She turned to go. "I'll come back later. You two have a lot to catch up on."

Elaine was half-way through the door when Peter's voice stopped her. "Mum? I wanted to tell Grandad about the hero we're going to see. Who is it?"

His mother let her gaze fall slowly on the frail figure in the bed; the man who'd always been there for her, who'd held her when she was scared, who'd made sure she wanted for nothing and who was now fighting to hold on to the last shreds of his life.

Swallowing hard over the lump in her throat, she said softly: "You're talking to him ... "

Noah's Lark is a biblical shaggy dog story. Noah gets a surprise inspection visit by an angel of the Lord. The angel is naturally a bit puzzled by the putting green and ornamental rockery he encounters ...

"And what's this?" the angel demanded.

Proudly, Noah pointed across the flowerbeds to the bandstand. "That's the centrepiece. On Saturdays we have concerts."

"And this?"

"Mini zoo. Two of every animal – as requested," Noah replied, "the kiddies love it and their parents pack out the tearooms. Cream, scones and jam. We can't sell enough of 'em."

Bemused, the winged messenger consulted his clipboard. "There's obviously some mistake," he said. "I was expecting a boat of some sort. I thought God told you to make an ark."

Frowning, Noah adjusted his hearing aid. "Are you sure? I could have sworn he said park."

Poor old dad Dave finds himself *In The Doghouse* when he refuses to allow his six-year-old daughter Julie to keep a bedraggled stray she's found. Apart from the fact that Dave thinks dogs are smelly, make a mess and bark too much, he has a scar to prove they bite as well!

He's determined that *Bouncer* will be handed in but is given the cold, silent treatment by his wife and child. It all comes to a head on the way to the police station when he switches on the car radio and it starts playing *And They Called It Puppy Love.* Both the women in his life burst into tears, and the dog howls.

I knew I was beaten. The Donny Osmond song had broken my will. I'd been hounded into submission.

With a resigned tut, I announced "Okay, you win! The dog can stay. It's a big mistake but we'll keep the Hound from Hell."

In an instant the Ice Age disappeared. Grinning, Julie grabbed Bouncer and started squeezing the life out of him.

"Thanks, dad, thanks," she yelled excitedly. "You won't regret it. It'll be great. Honest, honest."

Kate threw her arms around me and gave me the kind of kiss that reminded me what I'd first seen in her.

"You're not such a bad old stick," she murmured. "I knew you'd come round ... eventually. You've made a little girl very happy." She kissed me again. "Not to mention a big girl ..."

I smiled – the kind of smile you have when you realise that losing can be more fun than winning.

On the way to the supermarket, I turned on the car radio again. It was Elvis Presley singing: You Ain't Nothing But A Hound-dog.

This time we all sang along ...

In *Fat Profit* overweight Sally is scorned by all the other women at an exclusive health farm when they learn that she's been secretly bingeing on food in her room. But she has the last laugh as there's more to this ample dieter than meets the eye.

Sally patted her partner on the back. "We've cleared nearly £2,000, Julia. As soon as those hungry hypocrites heard I had food in my room they were going bananas to buy it. People were knocking on my door every night – I've hardly slept a wink, I've been so busy."

The partners chuckled. It had been their most successful scam ever.

Julia sighed. "Those saps made it so easy. They couldn't admit to one another that they'd bought illicit grub, so no-one had an inkling what was going on."

"And we made an inflated profit on £60 worth of groceries." Sally grinned, thumbing the thick wad of banknotes. "We took the suckers for every penny they had and didn't even break the law. Now that's what I call living off the fat of the land!"

Sting in the Tale features elderly writer Miriam Hodges who is outraged that Jack, her young and very pushy publisher, doesn't like her work. He keeps sending it back asking her to change the endings. Finally she decides to take some very drastic action ...

She was consigning the letter to the bin when a thought struck her ... an unusually fiendish thought. Sting in the tail, eh? You want a surprise ending? Okay, sonny boy, I'll make sure you get one!

Smiling grimly she reached for her pile of envelopes ...

* * *

Not many came to the funeral. There was a big book fair on in Berlin at the time and the weather was atrocious, but Miriam preferred to see it as a sign of Jack's great unpopularity.

A few employees turned up, a couple of long-faced friends, but that was all. Only Diane, Jack's secretary, seemed upset.

"It's just not fair," she sobbed. "Jack was so young. He had his whole life ahead of him. No-one deserves to die like that!"

Miriam, watching the coffin being lowered into the ground, nodded absent mindedly. "No, I suppose not."

"I just couldn't believe it. Who could be so cruel, so cold blooded?" Diane blew her nose noisily. "I mean, who could have hated him enough to post him a live scorpion?"

Ouch – now that's what I call a real killer ending! Perhaps there's a moral there for fiction editors ...

Exercises

Take a short story from three different magazines and study each in detail. Note how the authors build up their stories to a climax. Pay particular attention to the point at which the denouement is introduced.

Now write an alternative ending in 150-300 words for each, making sure that you still tie up all the loose ends from the narrative.

Look at the story *Devoted Admirer* in chapter thirteen. Rewrite the story from the mid-way point, giving it a totally different ending so that Jo isn't a nun. What other reason could she have for not wanting to take the relationship further?

Write an 850-word sting-in-the-tale story keeping one, and only one, crucial fact hidden until the last sentence. See if you can fool the reader.

Summary

- ✓ How you end your story is important. It's the last thing people read and will be what sticks in their memory.
- ✓ So it's worth spending a great deal of time crafting and polishing the last few sentences to make sure they really work.
- ✓ The reader must feel the ending is a logical and satisfying culmination of the train of events.
- ✓ It must fit with the mood and pace of the story and must tie up any loose ends that would leave readers feeling puzzled.
- ✓ It should never be rushed or cramped, with the last events sketchily described or condensed.
- ✓ Nor should it be an abrupt cut-off as the writer realises he can't take the storyline any further.
- ✓ The ending of your story should be a climax – a punchline. It should elicit an emotional response.
- ✓ Ending your story swiftly is crucial. Know when to shut up. Make your tale conclude the moment the plot does.
- ✓ If a narrative starts the moment the main character faces a crisis, then it should stop the second that crisis is resolved.
- ✓ Don't give us epilogues, further adventures or a moment's thought to consider the moral of the tale.
- ✓ Always aim for an up-beat ending. Even a sad story can have a positive and optimistic outcome.
- ✓ Aim to make your hero change for the better. Let him learn and grow from the experiences he's been through.

- ✓ He doesn't have to beat his opponents or resolve the crisis to be a winner – finding inner strength or a lost innocence is a triumph in itself.

- ✓ Readers want your hero to overcome his difficulties by his own skill. They won't be pleased if a twist of fate gives him a helping hand.

- ✓ The worst of all endings is: *and then he woke up and realised it was all a dream*. Competition judges and editors hate this.

- ✓ Engaging sting-in-the-tail yarns are fun to write but you must follow the rules; otherwise readers will feel cheated or confused.

- ✓ The ending must develop naturally from the plot – it can't be bolted on as an obvious afterthought.

- ✓ And it can't ask the reader to accept something that is clearly ridiculous or which contradicts a fact given earlier in the story.

- ✓ Sting-in-the-tail stories work on the principle of misleading the reader – but not lying to him. You should use his own assumptions to trip him up.

- ✓ The secret is to keep one important fact hidden. It could be the appearance of the main character, his age or sex, his job, or his background.

- ✓ Readers like to have clues seeded through the text to give them a chance of guessing the ending. But don't make the clues too obvious.

- ✓ Your sting is your punchline. Always have it as near the end as possible. Some magazines insist on the sting being in the last six words.

✓ Don't make the mistake of thinking that there needs to be gory, nauseating or horrific elements in your sting ending. You are aiming to surprise – not shock or sicken.

✓ A sting-in-the-tail story must still work as a yarn even if the tricky ending is removed.

12

AVOIDING TABOOS

You can't blame anyone for being a little confused these days about what you can safely write about, and knowing what subjects are beyond the pale. Just one glance at the new wave of raunchy magazines on the market will convince you that the world's become a freak show.

Screaming headlines compete with each other to be more sensational, more shocking, more lurid:

I had a boob job at 50 and got myself a toyboy!
Ten ways to turn on your chick!
My mum, murdered with a bayonet.
"Get your car keys," hissed the maniac."We're going for a drive."
I'm marrying a girl I've never met.
Confessions of a lap dancing schoolgirl.

With all this seamy hard-sell going on, you can be forgiven for thinking that there are no boundaries – that anything goes as long as it titillates the reader, digs the dirt or offers a disgusting look at the darker side of human nature.

The truth is that although some of the racier men's and women's publications have gone out of their way to feature sultry semi-clad models, bawdy confession stories and sizzling "pep-up your sex life" articles, there are still a bewildering amount of taboo areas ... even in magazines which appear brazen and out to shock.

The same is true of small press magazines – traditionally seen as a freewheeling, liberal and experimental fringe world less hung-up on what is obscene or distasteful. Editors may look for gritty realism and stories with a dangerous feel, but they won't print anything too degenerate.

Horror and erotica magazines, for instance, always push the boundaries of what is acceptable, but they too have their limits. They feature a certain amount of sex and violence, but quickly draw the line at anything illegal or overly gratuitous or gory.

Even competitions have their decency guidelines. You may be more outspoken and daring in a competition piece than any other type of short story, but if the organisers are going to print the winning entries they won't be looking for material that is going to scandalise or sicken.

The message is clear. There are still some no-go areas for all writers, so before you rush to write anything – be it a grisly axe murder story or a sting-in-the-tail coffee break yarn – it's worth getting to know your market intimately. Study the guidelines for contributors and look at several issues of the magazine you want to write for. Get a feel for where the boundaries are drawn. Take time to discover what subjects are still likely to land you in trouble. It'll be worth the effort in the long run because no writer, in any field, can be a success if he offends his audience.

Don't believe the hype

Many mainstream publication covers have become so X-rated that it's surprising that newsagents don't hide our favourite magazines inside a plain brown wrapper. Even the fairly respectable magazines our parents used to read have learnt that sex sells.

But although it's undoubtedly true that there's much more steaminess in everything we read these days, there isn't half as much as the sales departments would have you believe. The hype machine is in full swing and it's easy to be taken in by it. Most magazines adopt a raunchy approach – like a fairground barker – but once you go beyond the overblown and often comical front page "teasers" you'll find that the contents of most magazines are reassuringly safe.

Well-known women's titles may have put on bright red lipstick and a figure-hugging satin dress, but underneath there's still a slightly bemused and cautious maiden aunt. At the first sign of trouble she'll run back to the cookery page and cardigan patterns.

The new crop of "in-your-face" lad-mags – aimed at blokes who know what they want and aren't afraid to ask for it – aren't much better. These hip-talking, fast-walking mags peddle an adult fantasy world of glamorous cars, dangerous sports, and easy sex but they're read mostly by teenagers.

No editor can afford to corrupt this young and impressionable audience (and antagonise their mums!) so even though the headline shouts: *How to bed big-boobed blonde babes* what it really says is: *You're sixteen, you haven't got a girlfriend and you're still a bit scared of girls.*

And what about the "no-holds-barred", feminist magazines aimed at the young, single woman out to prove she can be a career high-flyer and a sexual predator beating men at their own games? Usually the average reader is about 35 and although she may like the idea of being a wildly wanton winner in the dating game, she'd secretly like to be in a long-term relationship, preferably with someone who can cook.

I know what you're thinking. I'm supposed to be talking about taboos, not taking the mickey out of magazine readers or wrecking their illusions. But the point is that magazines aren't read by a new breed of liberated, licentious, pleasure-seekers out to explore the threshold of hedonistic ecstasy. They're read by people like you and me who rather like a little bit of raciness from time to time, but whose main pre-occupation in life is knowing when the supermarket shuts.

We're still British, we're still a bit reserved and we're still easily shocked. So there is a long list of taboos we don't want broken, thank you very much.

In this section we'll look at some of these problem areas and see just how far you can go in your fiction, depending on what market you're targeting.

A word about women's magazines

Before we dive into the nitty gritty, it's worth mentioning that writing for traditional women's magazines (you know the ones I mean) can be a frustrating business if you are keen to tackle tricky subjects or burning social issues. This section of the market is particularly taboo-bound and there are numerous restrictions on what authors can and can't write about.

Some titles set out to create a cosy, cloistered, unreal and untroubled world for their readers – many of whom are middle aged or elderly and brought up with values and attitudes very different from those of today. And if you try to inject a note of stark realism or social comment into your fiction it just won't be bought. This is definitely one market where you have to fit in with what is normally printed – no matter how bland and cotton wool it may seem.

D.C. Thomson titles, especially, have an old-fashioned and rather moralistic tone. The magazines verge on the prudish, and have a strong disapproval of such things as divorce and unmarried couples living together.

Even on more relaxed titles fiction editors go along with the myth of a family-based, secure, suburban world. They believe that readers look to their magazines for escapism – the chance to forget the worry and problems of modern life. The last thing most readers want is to be reminded of their anxieties and hardships. They want a gentler, more positive world and fiction exists to give it to them.

To the women's magazine novice, it must feel like there are nothing but wall to wall taboos, and it certainly does make writing acceptable short stories a challenging exercise. But it is still possible to write material with bite and impact.

I recommend looking at traditional women's magazines as they voraciously devour material and many publications do actively encourage submissions from newcomers. But if you think it's going to cramp your style or be too restrictive or stifling, then look for another market to write for. No-one will blame you. It's not everyone's cup of tea and hot buttered scone.

Watch out!

Okay, on to the danger topics. While it is impossible to give a full list of all the taboos in all magazines, here's a general idea of what *could* cause you problems.

Editors (even within the same market) all have different tolerance levels and what might be acceptable to one will be censored by another, so always do your own thorough research before sending anything off. This guide will help you – but it's no substitute for actually getting hold of the magazines and studying them.

Use this list as a working document. You may want to update or amend it as editorial policies become more liberal; or you may want to add headings of your own as you encounter new magazines with unusual or unexpected restrictions. Take note of any negative feedback from an editor because you've crossed the line somewhere and add this topic to your shopping list of taboos.

These are areas to take care with:

Rape: Most publications are unhappy to carry stories which feature a sexual assault, or which has rape as a central theme. Even erotic publications place great emphasis on all sex in stories being consensual.

You may be able to get away with a competition story on the topic but only if the assault is a crucial part of the plotline and isn't described in lurid detail. A sympathetic portrayal of the victim's ordeal and the emotional aftermath may be permissible, but anything written from the rapist's viewpoint is out – even if he expresses remorse. And under no circumstances include a rape merely to titillate the reader.

Prostitution: This is still a no-go area for most mainstream magazines, but you shouldn't have too many problems elsewhere.

Two points to consider – anything that seems to glamorise prostitution will be frowned on, and any story dealing with an underage prostitute may cause you headaches if you describe him/her in any sex act. It is illegal.

Under age sex: This follows the same basic decency rules as prostitution. Women's titles won't allow a story on underage sex, but you may be able to sell a tale elsewhere – providing it is an important and serious part of a plot and not just dropped in to excite the reader.

For instance, a girl on the eve of her sixteenth birthday feels she's not being treated as an adult by her parents and picks up an unsuspecting man in a pub to prove she's grown up. This then leads to big trouble for her and the man.

Even if you are using underage sex in this way, don't have long, lingering descriptions of love making.

You shouldn't have too many problems with a *Romeo and Juliet* style story where a 15-year-old couple have sex in a loving and innocent way. But it all gets much murkier if the underage boy or girl is having sex with an adult who is considerably older, or is using sex as a means of manipulating an adult.

I would make a big distinction between underage sex – a teenager who is very nearly at the age of consent – and paedophilia. Any story that deals with children being treated as objects of desire or being forced into sex is out. No editor or competition judge will tolerate it.

Incest: It's unlikely that anyone will buy a story that features incest – even erotic magazines stay well clear of this. The chances of a story with an incest theme winning a competition are extremely slight.

Phone sex lines: In all but the most conservative of magazines this topic should be okay, if it is dealt with in a humorous way. It's best to use it only as a plot device (husband has to hide the credit card statement from his wife because he's been ringing chat lines) and ensure that the story doesn't dwell on what the caller gets up to at his end of the line.

Promiscuity: This is easy – the more raunchy a magazine seems the more relaxed the editorial policy will be on fictional bedroom romps. But keep all sex clean, fun and free of any violence or coercion.

Some editors will be happy to have single people getting up to naughtiness but will frown on any storyline where a married person is cheating on his or her partner ... and is being seen to enjoy it.

The term promiscuity is open to interpretation. Some of the more old-fashioned magazines look upon any sex outside of marriage as a sin and won't allow it in their stories.

Fetishism: Since some male politicians have made dressing up in women's clothing almost respectable, you can get away with much more in print ... and in private!

Reference to toe-sucking and thigh-length footwear would have had most people reeling in shock twenty years ago but it's unlikely that the younger readership of a racy women's mag would be offended these days. Most small press readers and competition judges aren't likely to be shocked either.

However, it's still an area of disgust for most traditional publications, so do some checking before including anything kinky – even in jest. A couple of points to remember for all outlets: the fetish wear that you might encounter at a suburban Ann Summers party is okay, but don't go too far into the dark, specialist realms of whips, manacles and gags.

Don't describe fetish behaviour which "right-minded" people might find scandalous – eg piercing, savage bondage or sex acts which are banned by law.

Well, that's enough about sex. Let's move on to ...

AIDS: Sadly, many editors are still a bit uncomfortable with fiction that looks at this disease so it's difficult to say which markets are okay. Perhaps this is because even now the public doesn't fully understand the condition and is still scared by reading about it.

If your story deals with AIDS in a responsible and sympathetic way then take the risk and submit it. But be prepared for rejection. It won't mean your work is poor, just that the editor wants to steer away from a potential danger area.

If you are using AIDS for its shock value, or as an ill-considered plot twist, please think again. It's very easy to inadvertently offend. There is certainly no excuse for any thriller plotline where someone infects an enemy with AIDS just to get revenge.

Stalking: This is fine for most crime/thriller stories but avoid seeming to condone or advocate stalking. It's best not to have scenes where you describe a man lustfully watching his prey undressing, or where you tell the story in a prurient manner through the eyes of the stalker.

Drugs: This is one of the big taboos; so assume that a fiction editor won't handle material on this subject unless you find out otherwise.

Whatever your own personal views may be on the perils or pleasures of recreational substances, many readers are vehemently opposed to drug-taking in any form and you'll alienate them if you are seen to be advocating their use.

That doesn't mean that you are banned from showing characters, especially younger characters, taking drugs. But try not to suggest in the tone of the piece that this is commonplace, respectable or desirable.

In a science fiction story you may want to explore the premise that a world exists where all drugs are legalised and chart out the consequences. But what you can safely tackle in a futuristic or alternative setting becomes greatly restricted when you deal with a story set in the here and now.

Child abuse: No matter how sensitive the treatment, or how well meaning you may be, it's likely that a story dealing with child abuse is going to be hard to place. Most fiction editors think it's too dark and harrowing a subject for short stories.

That doesn't rule out writing about child abuse but you have to approach the project knowing your potential markets are very limited. Competitions offer the best chance of success.

Even if you want to illustrate the plight of abused children, resist the temptation to over-dramatise or have graphic scenes of assault. Hint at the abuse rather than draw a picture for the reader.

As with rape, it's unlikely that you'll sell a story that is told through the eyes of a perpetrator – even if he or she expresses regret.

Avoid having a story these days where an innocent friendship grows between a child and an older man or woman. It will be viewed with suspicion. Alas, the days of innocence are long gone.

Unmarried mothers: This is a forbidden subject only for the more staid of magazines, but one they feel very strongly about. The only way an unmarried mum would be acceptable would be if a final reconciliation – and marriage – with the child's father was the climax of the story.

Living in sin: This falls into the same category as unmarried mothers. It isn't as frowned upon as it once was, but some people will still be unhappy about the thought of a couple cohabiting who aren't legally wed.

Don't rock the editorial boat unless you have to. Unless there is a good plotting reason why your characters should both be single, marry them off. Be aware that even quite liberal-minded publications will balk at a story where an unmarried couple have children.

Divorce: This is another theme that's perfectly acceptable, except for the most stern and old-fashioned of titles. Although divorce is a fact of modern life, they try never to mention it. That's why so many of their romance stories feature middle-aged people who find themselves free to seek love because their partner has recently died. The mortality rate in romance stories is higher than an action film. Being a fictional spouse is a dangerous business!

Religion: Just like politics, this topic is one sure-fire way of starting a fight in a bar. It's also a good way to guarantee upsetting older readers and people from different cultural backgrounds.

It's fine to have religious figures in your stories, but not to portray them as being in any way underhand, two-faced, criminally minded or reprehensible. This will rule out selling your work to many publications.

Be careful not to be seen to be taking a pop at anyone's faith – even if it's by accident. And I strongly advise against you criticising the way a religion is run or attacking its core beliefs. You may not necessarily become the subject of worldwide death threats, but you will scare off most editors.

This whole area is a minefield. Think very carefully before trying to write a story dealing with religious intolerance, way-out sects, priests losing their faith or nuns feeling normal human emotions towards a man.

In chapter thirteen I've included the story *Devoted Admirer* which deals with an attraction between a nun and a man whom she meets at the school where she teaches. Despite it being innocuous and very "proper" in the treatment of the subject I couldn't get any magazine to touch it. It later went on to win first place in a national competition, which proves that it was the religious subject matter and not the manner of telling that was the problem!

The disabled: There is no reason why someone obnoxious shouldn't have a car crash and so end up as an objectionable person in a wheelchair. But if you try portraying that nasty character in a story you'll find many editors just won't want to know.

The general rule is that disabled people must always be selfless, courageous and inspirational. You'll stand little chance of selling a tale that has an unsympathetic disabled character. Some publications will accept a disabled person who is angry and treats those around him badly. But this can only be him hitting out in frustration at his plight. Later on in the tale he must make amends and put on a brave face.

Homosexuality: Forget what you have read in the papers, women's magazines know it doesn't exist. Even if it did, it wouldn't be a suitable topic of conversation at the dinner table. Publications aimed at an older readership are also unlikely to take any story with a homosexual element.

Apart from those two areas, there is a market for any narrative that has gay characters or homosexual relationships as its theme. In addition, you can target gay magazines which accept fiction.

Be a little coy in your treatment of the subject. Unless you are submitting work to a gay or erotic magazine, it's probably a good idea to keep descriptions of homosexual love making short and non-graphic.

One word of warning – no matter what outlets you have in mind, please don't, under any circumstances, have camp caricatures or limp-wristed characters in your stories. This causes grave offence.

Social irresponsibility: If pushed to define what type of characters fiction editors look for they'd all agree that they want people who are basically decent and caring.

That translates into main characters who are responsible. So no *Home Alone* parents out boozing while their kids are left unsupervised, no parents smoking over their babies, no people being cruel to animals and no people fiddling social security. This may sound a little quaint and naive, but most readers want people they can empathise with, not disapprove of, in their stories.

Some fiction editors take this idea to almost ludicrous extremes. I had a story for one women's magazine rewritten on social responsibility grounds. It concerned a man working as a department store Santa Claus because he loved children but he and his wife couldn't have any kids of their own. He gets his very own special Christmas present. His wife announces that she's finally pregnant. They're going to have a baby. It ends with the corny line: *So now you really are Father Christmas!*

What's wrong with that, you may ask? Simple – working as a department store Santa Claus is obviously a temporary job. How could a man even contemplate bringing a child into the world when he does not have a long-term, full-time job?

Now, I'm not joking here. This was put to me as a serious point. You and I may think it's crazy but someone was worried what readers would think about this irresponsible and scandalous behaviour.

Luckily, that is a very extreme example, but it goes to show that you need to be aware of what upsets the sensibilities of different editors.

Violence: This is another of the great taboos. Some fiction editors will accept violence as a regrettable but natural part of life, others won't. Even those that do, take great pains to stress that violence must be essential to the plot – and not just a gratuitous gimmick for injecting excitement or titillation.

Most editors only permit murder and mayhem in a jokey, cartoon way in twist-in-the-tail stories. Graphic depictions of realistic violence – especially against women – is a big no-no.

Domestic violence: Although it may appear that sting-in-the-tail yarns seem to feature nothing but outraged husbands and wives bumping each other off, anything that describes domestic violence in any emotionally moving or disturbing way is likely to run into problems with traditional mags. So no wife-beating, mysterious black eyes or girlfriends fleeing to refuges.

It's fine to tackle this subject for other markets. However, make sure that you don't go over the top and make the story sickening or overwhelmingly dark. Get the maximum reader shock from the minimum amount of violence. Again, this is an area where a story told from the abuser's point of view is going to be difficult to place.

Poverty: Graphic portrayals of living conditions tend not to find favour in more cosy publications. They are too depressing! Your characters can visit a run-down place or experience brief hardship but lingering, detailed descriptions of squalor aren't popular.

Don't worry about this restricting your atmospheric scene setting. Small press editors and competition judges will be delighted to accept "gritty" work.

Old people: Not surprisingly, those magazines with an older readership don't like elderly people being painted in a bad light. So stories with grasping grannies or cantankerous old men are going to miss the mark.

If you're writing for women's magazines, it's okay to have troublesome parents who are a worry to your main character.

However, you have to make it clear that no matter how trying mum and dad appear to be, their hearts are in the right place.

Minority groups: Magazines are so worried about appearing politically incorrect that they'll pounce on a story which seems to portray members of minority groups unfavourably. You may think that it's not worth the risk. I wouldn't blame you ...

Using black as a symbol of evil or depression: Personally I see nothing wrong with this literary device – the black in question refers to the night. But there are some who claim that this has all sorts of sinister, racist connotations. Don't get into a tizzy over it, but make sure you know the attitude of any editor you're sending work to.

Criminals not being allowed to succeed: You may laugh at this old-fashioned notion, but stop to think for a moment. No editor puts on his contributors' guidelines that criminals in stories must always fail, yet the vast majority of published twist-enders have the theme of wrong-doers getting their come-uppance.

So someone must be trying to tell us something. The subliminal message is that readers don't want criminals to benefit from their crimes.

Now I'm not suggesting for one moment that you have to slavishly obey this convention but it is useful to be aware that it still exists.

Well, that's a daunting list of subjects to be worried about! Trying to work your way round this lot might make you want to swear – but don't. Swearing is out. It's one of the biggest taboos of all!

Exercises

Look at several different types of magazines and see how explicit the subject matter is. Pay particular attention to how they deal with sex. Do they ignore it altogether? Is it included in "coded" terms? How far do couples go in the physical side of their relationship?

Now do the same exercise looking at violence. Make a note of which magazine has the most graphic or realistic portrayal of violence. Rewrite the story toning down the violence – but without losing the power and emotional depth of the narrative.

Send off for contributors' guidelines for six magazines and take note of their taboos. Are you surprised by the restrictions?

Look back at any old stories you've written and see whether you've inadvertently broken a taboo. If you have, rewrite the tale so that it won't cause offence.

Summary

- ✓ Even though magazines seem to be raunchy and daring, there are still restrictions on what subjects and themes you can tackle.
- ✓ No matter what the market, be aware of the taboos that will upset readers.
- ✓ Editors all have different tolerance levels so always do your own thorough market research. Study the guidelines for contributors.
- ✓ Look at several issues of the magazine you want to write for. Get a feel for where the boundaries are drawn.
- ✓ The biggest minefield is women's magazines. Many don't want to publish stories which feature stark realism or social comment.
- ✓ When submitting work anywhere, always consult your list of taboos to make sure you won't upset an editor.
- ✓ Always take note of any negative feedback from an editor because you've crossed the line somewhere.

13

PUTTING IT ALL TOGETHER

I'm not surprised if your head's starting to spin a bit by this point. I've asked you to pay attention to a lot of detailed information, advice and warnings. I bet you never knew there was so much theory to writing great short stories; so much to remember and think about.

Don't worry if it seems a bit daunting. Most of the writing techniques may sound complicated at first glance but they'll soon become second nature. You'll begin to do them without even realizing ... you'll even have fun.

I find it helps to think of it like learning to drive. In writing you have to worry about characterisation, dialogue, attention grabbing openings, viewpoint, plotting – all at the same time. In driving you have to keep your eyes on the road, be aware of other motorists, worry about which pedals to use, fumble about with the gear stick, know which lane to be in ...

Ask anyone who's put on 'L' plates. It's a nightmare. You don't know how all these different tasks can be done at once. Then suddenly, one day while you're picking your way through the traffic you realise that you have been driving without consciously thinking about it. Everything has gelled.

Well, it's the same for writing. The more you write, the more proficient you'll become at each different element and the more textured and professional your work will be. Suddenly you have compelling characters acting out a gripping drama, with the story starting at the most fascinating point and rushing on at a great pace towards a knock-em-dead finish.

So don't fret. Don't get wound up over any particular story-telling technique or way of approaching a plotting problem. Relax and let all the tips you've learnt file away in your brain. They'll be there when you need them. Sit back and enjoy the ride!

As we're at the half-way point in the book I thought I'd do the work for a change and give you a bit of a breather. Think of it as a metaphorical tea-break. (I take milk and no sugar in mine and I'll have a doughnut, if you've got one!)

Instead of launching into a new topic and hitting you with more information, we'll use this opportunity to consolidate what we've already learnt. We'll see how all this theory works when it comes to actually putting words on the page.

In this chapter we are going to take a closer look at two different stories and take them to pieces to see what makes them tick. After you've read each, I'll explain how the various elements work and mention any unusual or curious points worth special attention. The yarns are both mine – so please be kind.

Devoted Admirer – although a competition winner – was written originally as a women's magazine story. But the taboo-breaking surprise ending ruled it out for most editors.

Rat Pack is a small press science fiction tale which first appeared in an anthology.

DEVOTED ADMIRER

JO BLAKESLEY looked up nervously from her marking and watched the blue and white van pull up in the school playground. Through the smeary window, she recognised the words *Harris Photography*.

She'd been dreading its arrival all day, and now it was here she felt confused and edgy.

"Okay class," she said firmly to the huddle of nine-year-old faces staring up at her. "Start smartening yourselves up. The photographer's arrived to take your picture and I don't want you looking like you've been dragged through a hedge backwards."

Noisily, the kids produced combs and brushes and began tugging at their tangled locks. Jo allowed herself a furtive glance out of the window. She could see Bob Harris unloading cameras, lights and a tripod. His local shop had the contract to take all the class pictures and Jo knew it was the third and last day he'd be visiting the school.

That knowledge filled her with relief ... and sadness. It had only been 48 hours since the young schoolteacher had met the cheery-faced photographer, but it felt like she'd known him for years. In that short time she'd grown incredibly fond of his friendly smile, and the sight of him now filled her with excitement.

She bit her bottom lip as she remembered bumping into him on that first morning in the thronging hallway.

"You're new, aren't you?" he'd asked, studying her, "I'm sure I'd have remembered if I'd seen you before."

"I joined last term." She'd pretended not to notice his gaze. "I teach geography." She'd introduced herself and he'd told her that his first name was Robert. "But my friends call me Bob." Then, nodding at the children milling past, he'd remarked: "A right bunch of little devils, eh? You must have your hands full."

"Oh, they're good kids really," she'd replied, whipping the cap off a passing pupil. "Just a little high spirited."

"Well, I think you're a saint for putting up with them."

Jo had smiled wryly at that remark, and as they'd parted she'd realised that Bob Harris had made quite an impression on her.

Next day, Bob bumped into her again, and asked if they could have lunch together. Over a lukewarm shepherd's pie in the school's cavernous dining hall, they'd chatted about each other's jobs and interests. She'd been pleased to learn that they were both film buffs and they'd joked about some of the awful films they'd seen.

Bob did a passable Bogart impression and he made her giggle when he'd picked up a glass of water and said: "Here's looking at you, kid."

Jo had been a little shocked at first to find the good-looking photographer flirting with her. After her initial surprise, she'd found herself cheered and flattered by his attention. As an attractive, blonde 28-year-old she'd been used to appreciative glances, but that hadn't happened for quite a while.

"You should smile more often," he'd told her, "you've got a lovely face and it seems to light up when you smile. Even your eyes smile."

It was all nonsense, of course, but even though her brain told her so, her heart still responded.

She'd joked to cover her embarrassment. "You'll be telling me next that the camera loves me and I should be posing for you. I know all about photographers."

He'd laughed; a deep, warm, contented laugh. It was the kind of laugh Jo reckoned she could listen to forever.

That night, Jo couldn't sleep. Thinking about his sharp, blue-grey eyes, she felt herself being drawn in. He unnerved her in ways she didn't like to think about. She hadn't looked at a man since Roger had walked out years before. She'd promised herself that she'd never suffer that pain again. She'd vowed not to have anything more to do with men, and had felt more in control of her life because of it. More in control until now, that is. Until Bob – smiling and unaware – had walked into her life. The irony of it was, he probably had no idea of the effect he was having on her.

Suddenly aware that she was daydreaming, Jo shook herself and turned to the class. "Right, you lot. Leave your stuff here and get straight down to the gym. Be quiet, don't talk and don't dawdle. I don't want this picture to take all day."

Giggling and whispering, the kids filed out of the room. As the last child disappeared through the door, Jo stood and began to nervously pace the floor. She had time to get a coffee, or just enjoy the well-earned peace, but she couldn't shake the desire to go downstairs to see Bob.

It was ridiculous, she scolded herself. But she went down to the gym anyway.

Bob was busy organising her rowdy kids into two lines, and didn't spot her at first. When he did, his face brightened.

"Hi," he grinned, as he clipped one boy round the ear and shoved him back in line. "Keep an eye on this lot for a moment, will you? I've got to try to make them look respectable." He made a face. "Heaven knows how."

Jo nodded and clapped her hands. The kids obeyed her instantly. Bob's grin grew bigger, and he turned his attention to photographing the fidgeting children. He focused the Nikon and fired off several shots in quick succession, then changed position and shot off several more.

He seemed assured and professional: totally at ease.

Watching him work, Jo couldn't help wishing she could get to know him better. She imagined what it would be like to spend more time with him, to have dinner, to see a great movie together, but she knew it was impossible.

Soon the class picture was taken, the kids were dismissed and Bob was packing up. The last bell had gone; school was breaking up for the day. Against her better judgement, Jo hung around to see him off.

"You've been great. I'm really pleased we met," he told her, "maybe I'll see you again sometime."

"I'd like that," she replied, "but somehow I just don't see it happening."

"I suppose the job gets in the way."

"Something like that," she agreed.

He shrugged and frowned. "I understand ... I think."

Picking up his kit, he slung it carelessly over his shoulder. He held out his hand and she shook it. It felt warm and soft, and her fingers lingered for an instant longer than she'd intended.

As she watched him go, Jo had an urge to rush forward; to tell him how she felt. But something held her back.

The van door slammed and the engine coughed into life. Bob leant out and waved. Tears welled in her eyes, but she tried to blink them back. As he drove off, she ran from the room. She didn't want anyone to see her cry. That would invite questions and she feared to answer them.

Instead, she stopped in front of the mirror in the washroom and dabbed at her eyes with a paper tissue. Finally, satisfied that she was in control of herself, she adjusted her wimple and headed for the chapel.

It would soon be time for evening devotion, and Sister Josephine knew this night she desperately needed to pray.

Well, did the twist ending come as a surprise? I wanted this to read like a routine romance story for most of its length then to suddenly shock. I was very keen not to give the game away before the final two sentences – so it was a tricky business to dot clues in the text without them becoming too obvious or, conversely, too oblique.

I went as far as I could by having Bob Harris referring to the children as "little devils" and calling Jo "a saint" for putting up with them. They're innocent enough remarks when read at first, but they take on a different significance when we later learn that Jo is a nun.

It was important that the dialogue was also a little vague in a key section. I needed to put over that Jo's occupation was a barrier to their blossoming attraction – but not to say why.

"I suppose the job gets in the way."
"Something like that," she agreed.
He shrugged and frowned. "I understand ... I think."

This is a good example of keeping back information from the reader until it has the maximum effect. It's important, as the story-teller, that you know when to reveal crucial facts. Timing is everything.

This story follows the classic structure:

A. *Dilemma erupts for main character*
B. *Events leading up to the dilemma are recounted in flashback*
C. *Dilemma is resolved*

As my intention with the tale was to surprise readers but not to offend them there was only one "acceptable" way the dilemma could be resolved. Sister Josephine knows her duty to God and chooses the church.

If I'd been aiming the story at another market, her choice might have been different – we'll never know.

Two points to mention: even though this is a basically romantic tale, the plot starts right at the moment of conflict. As Bob's van pulls into the school playground Jo knows she has no time left – she has to make a decision right there and then.

I could have started the story at the point when they first meet and then follow it through chronologically but it would have killed the pace, suspense and drama.

A substantial part of the narrative is contained in the flashback. But despite events having taken place a few days before, I didn't just tell readers what happened, I showed them. I played the scenes out with all the description and dialogue. They got to experience the growing friendship – to see it blossom for themselves. If I'd just summarised it in a couple of lines, the story would have no depth, no power, no emotional pull.

Have another look at how I signalled that I was going into the flashback:

She bit her bottom lip as she remembered bumping into him on that first morning in the thronging hallway.

"You're new, aren't you?" he'd asked, studying her, "I'm sure I'd have remembered if I'd seen you before."

And see how I announced that I was coming back from the past to the present ...

Suddenly aware that she was daydreaming, Jo shook herself and turned to the class. "Right, you lot. Leave your stuff here and get straight down to the gym."

The signposts are there – unobtrusive but unmistakable – ensuring that readers never get left behind or confused about what time period they're in.

The reason why this story works (in my humble opinion) is because it has a great deal of sub-text. That means that there's more going on in the action than meets the eye – when the characters speak there are hidden meanings beyond what the words appear to say on the surface. We know right from the start that Jo and Bob are attracted to each other, even though neither directly admits it.

Sub-text is a fairly advanced technique so I wouldn't worry too much about it until you are very experienced and want to give much more depth to your work. It's not necessary to fill a yarn with sub-text for it to be an enjoyable read or for it to sell. In fact, most editors like their fiction simple, straightforward and uncomplicated ... a bit like they prefer their writers!

You'll be glad to hear that the next story contains no sub-text whatsoever. What you see is what you get.

RAT PACK

FRANK PETERS' voice had an edge of panic I'd never heard before.

"Jack, we've got trouble," he gulped, "the rats are out. Some lunatic's released them!"

Rubbing my eyes, I pulled the phone a bit closer. Frank, my deputy, wasn't the kind of man to get rattled. It must be serious for him to wake me at three in the morning.

"Say again," I instructed, switching on the small table lamp.

"The rats. They've been released. Gone. They're running loose somewhere ... "

I shuddered. I'd dreamt about getting a call like this one day. It was my most recurring nightmare.

"Have you got a location fix on them?" I asked, fighting to stay calm. "Are the homers working?"

"Negative, Jack. Whoever let them out removed the homers. The rats are off the base and we haven't a clue which direction they've taken. The security fence has been breached in three places and the control panel's flashing like a Christmas tree. It's a bloody shambles!"

Groaning, I told Frank to order a full alert – troops, police, the works. "Send the chopper for me, we can't afford to waste a second. If the rats reach a populated area before we can catch them it's going to be Hammer Horror Hour."

I dressed in a daze, a hundred images flashing across my mind – images of laboratory rats injected with God knows what, scampering across the darkened countryside. I prayed that they'd been infected with something relatively straightforward like Black Death or rabies. If the rodents had been injected with anything new – anything experimental – we'd be talking soldiers in silver sci-fi suits quarantining half the county.

For about the two-hundredth time, I began to regret accepting the security chief's job at the Institute. It had seemed like a cushy number at first: a doddle for someone like me who was cruising to retirement. But that was before the rash of break-ins, before the animal rights nuts got their claws into us.

Someone had told them about our experiments on rats, monkeys and beagles. Before long we had little commando parties of pissed students in camouflage jackets and balaclavas trying to cut through the fences. They'd set off the alarms and we'd call the local plod to come and arrest them.

I'd always thought of the protestors as a joke, but not now. Lives were in danger and, even if we could get the animals back, I knew my job would be on the line.

The dull thwacking noise of the helicopter's rotor blades snapped me out of my thoughts, and I rushed outside. The swirling downwash from the blades whipped me, making it difficult to breath. I cursed as I saw the damage the mechanical hurricane was doing to my rose patch.

We rose swiftly over the slumbering street, heading towards the distant lights of the complex. From the air, I could see the buildings stretching out across the 25 acres of the compound. By day it looked like a medium-sized industrial estate, a mish-mash of grey, concrete buildings and roads. Tonight, with the criss-cross mesh of security lights twinkling, it looked more like a town.

The chopper banked. Below, in an arc of sickly sodium light, I could see three figures. One was Frank, the middle figure was Dr Mitchells, one of the Institute's top scientists, but I didn't recognise the third person.

Frank came running as I touched down, head bowed beneath the spinning blades.

"God, I'm glad to see you, Jack," he yelled above the racket. "Unless we can get a lid on this, we're all going to be in the shit!" I nodded silently. Frank always was one for understatements. He dragged me by the arm to meet the others.

Dr Mitchells grunted a greeting. He looked shell-shocked, his grey hair dishevelled; eyes red and unfocused. I reckoned, like me, he'd been snatched out of bed. I flashed him a sympathetic look.

Frank nodded towards the dark-haired stranger. "This is Chief Inspector Turner, local CID. The Chief Inspector will be liaising with us on behalf of the civil authorities."

I shook the Chief Inspector's hand. The grip was firm, firmer than I expected.

"The name is Karen," she told me, making eye contact, "I'm the force's designated disaster management officer. I have a direct line to the Chief Constable. Anything you need, just ask."

I introduced myself, and tested the walkie-talkie that Frank thrust into my hand. "I'm in charge of this mess," I informed the woman. "That means it's my head on the chopping block."

She sniffed. "I'm rather more interested in recapturing these animals, than worrying about whose career is going up in smoke. Mr Peters tells me you've called in the army. On whose authority?"

I decided immediately that I didn't like Karen Turner. "It's standard operating procedure," I explained brusquely. "The MoD provides a major slice of the Institute's funding. Technically this is a military base."

I gave her a sour look. "But I'm more interested in recapturing these animals than worrying whose jurisdiction is being trampled on."

She blinked, startled, and I smiled to myself.

"Okay Doc," I said to Mitchells, "let's have a look at the labs. Every moment we stand around here gabbing these rats are getting further away."

THE RATS had been housed in an annexe to the main laboratory block. The pre-fab had only been on site a few weeks and as we ventured inside we were hit by the smell of new paint. There was another smell too – the sour, acid stink of animal house.

Frank and I screwed up our noses. Doctor Mitchells didn't seem to notice the strong gamey aroma, which I guessed wasn't surprising as he worked in it all day. Karen Turner wasn't bothered either – at least, if she was, she hid it well.

We hurried down the corridor, passing caged hamsters, gerbils and kittens; all squeaking agitatedly. Speaking loudly, Doctor Mitchells explained what animals were housed there, and what research they were used in. It was all fairly standard stuff – testing new drugs, cosmetics and foods.

"The more sensitive testing is carried out on the rats – in the secure section," he said, face clouding. "That's where we do the more hazardous ... biological tests."

I snorted at the mention of the secure section. What a joke. It hadn't been secure tonight.

Turning the corner, we reached the high-security rooms. To gain access you had to slide a coded plastic ID card through a sensor. I examined the lock, expecting to find it forced.

"That's odd," I exclaimed, "this hasn't been tampered with. Look, it's still working."

Frank gazed too. "But that's impossible. It must have been forced! There's no other way."

I swore as the full implication sank in. Unfortunately, Chief Inspector Turner beat me to it.

"They had a card," she ventured helpfully, "and were able to just walk in. Your security was breached. It was an inside job. Someone at the Institute helped the raiders."

There was no other answer. I began to feel very concerned. An infiltrator was all we needed!

The door hissed open and we hurried through. Doc Mitchells switched on the light and we stood, blinking, as the neon tubes flickered reluctantly into action.

"My God," he cried, pointing over to the cages. "Look!"

Our eyes followed his finger towards movement at the back of the banks of cages. Small, dark, beady eyes glared up at us. Whiskers twitched and a long tail swished across the sawdust.

"There are still some rats here," the doctor yelled.

"How many?" I demanded. "Quick, Doc. I need to know."

He counted excitedly. "Ten – no – twelve. Nearly half are still here."

"Well, at least that's something," Karen Turner muttered.

Frank ushered the doctor over to the animals. "Can you tell which animals are missing? We need to know what they might be carrying."

Doc Mitchells unlocked the filing cabinets and quickly pulled out folders, scanning them furiously. I watched, my nerves twisting. I was aware that fifteen minutes had passed since we'd entered the labs – we were taking too long.

I motioned for the Chief Inspector to join me and started to examine the cages. We checked each empty wire enclosure in turn. They were all the same – the same identical damage.

"This sounds crazy, but I don't think these rats were released," Karen Turner said, puzzled. "Look at the way the wires have severed."

I looked. She was right again. The wire hadn't been cut – it had been bitten: gnawed through.

"They escaped," I agreed, mouth falling open. "They bit their way out of the cages and high-tailed it out of the complex."

I got on to the guards at the perimeter fence, but I knew what they'd find. The wire hadn't been cut – it had been bitten clean through.

IT WAS difficult to make ourselves heard inside the helicopter's noisy interior so we all had to shout. Mitchells had finally located all the info we needed and had presented us with a classic good news/bad news scenario.

"The good news is that none of the escaped rats was injected with any diseases or bacteria. All the rats used for medical research are back in the Institute, tucked up in their cages," he said. "The bad news is that the escaped animals are in Project Alpha."

Project Alpha, he explained, was an MoD-funded experiment to artificially boost the intelligence of animals by using genetic engineering techniques. The idea was that they could be used in battlefield conditions where it was dangerous for humans.

"The missing rodents were all Alpha test subjects. Apparently the experiment has worked much better than we expected," he observed. "They somehow managed to open the security doors from the inside and evade the monitor cameras until they reached the fence. It shows amazing problem-solving capabilities."

That, I told myself, explained the mystery of the removed homers.

Karen Turner eyed the doctor disapprovingly. "So you're telling us that we're chasing a load of super-rats who are quite capable of out-thinking us and evading capture." She didn't try to hide her annoyance. "That's great, just great."

I was going to add my pennyworth, but the co-pilot's voice came over the intercom to tell us the rats had been spotted at a shopping centre five miles away.

"What are they doing?" I asked, "getting the week's groceries?"

BELOW, the flashing blue lights of the police cars gave the scene an unreal, fairy-castle appearance.

We hovered over the block of shops, watching as police and troops surrounded the area, then we landed at nearby playing fields.

Karen Turner talked steadily into her walkie-talkie, issuing orders to the assembled forces.

"The rats have broken into a pharmacy," she informed us. "My men have cornered them."

"Good," I answered. "The area's sealed tight. We can round them up without any of the public being involved. The Institute's sending men with tranquilliser rifles."

I felt relieved. Maybe I might just hang on to my job after all. At a signal from Turner, our party set off into the shopping mall.

It wasn't immediately apparent how the rats had forced their way into the chemists. The shutters on the windows were still intact. It was only when the waiting sergeant showed us the claw marks on the roof, and the missing slates, that it clicked.

"We found the rats in the storeroom at the back," he told us, "they'd been going through the boxes. If I didn't know better I'd have said they were looking for something."

None of us said anything. I gave Doc Mitchells a warning look. I didn't want him saying anything indiscreet.

The storeroom was a mess. The rats had done a thorough job. Boxes lay ripped open, contents scattered crazily across the floor. I'd seen tidier burglaries done by vandals on acid.

"That's the box they were attacking when we found them," the sergeant continued, "they scurried off when they heard us. We chased them into a cupboard. They're safely locked up, all except this one. We kept this one separate for you to examine. He seems to be the ringleader."

The policeman held up a plastic mesh carrying box. Inside I could see the black shape of a rat, sitting motionless, whiskers slowly twitching, eyes – deeply aware eyes – watching us; staring. The animal could have nibbled through the box in seconds, but he was choosing not to. He knew the game was up.

Tearing her eyes away, Turner examined the damaged carton. I knelt beside her. The box contained thousands of sticking plasters.

I frowned, puzzled, but she pointed to the logo printed on the side and suddenly it all began to make sense.

"Doc," I waved Mitchells over to us "are the rats engaged in other experiments – apart from Project Alpha?"

Baffled, Mitchells nodded. "Yes, some, but I can't see the relevance – "

"And are those experiments connected to cancer research?"

"Yes, but –"

Karen Turner knew what I was about to ask. "And does it involve cigarettes?"

The amused look on Mitchells' face showed that he finally understood. "Yes, but of course. We've been exposing them to sixty a day."

Frank still hadn't cottoned on. "I'm lost? What's this got to do with the break-out?"

I couldn't help smiling as I explained it. "It's all quite simple, Frank. The rats escaped for a reason. To get these." I motioned to the Nicotine patches lying strewn across the floor. "Project Alpha has been an amazing success, all right. It's bred animals that are smarter than humans. They want to give up smoking!"

This yarn is, of course, a shaggy dog story ... or if you prefer it, a shaggy rat story.

For the "sucker punch" denouement to work, the reader had to be taken unawares ... so the story up to that point was written straight with nothing comic or quirky to give the game away. In fact, it could well have been a classic horror tale with a gory ending as troops and super rats confront each other.

Because this yarn was aimed at the small press market, I included a fair amount of description but tried to ensure that it was short, fast paced and always working to build an eerie atmosphere.

The narrative could easily have been written in the third person, but I decided to tell it in the first person, to give more speed and immediacy. It saved me having to spend a lot of time describing Jack, the main character. The fact that he's cruising to retirement, cultivates a rose garden and dislikes successful women says it all!

Scenes in short stories where the characters introduce themselves to each other can be extremely slow and tedious, so I decided to get round this by having Jack and Chief Inspector Turner taking an instant and dramatic dislike to each other. This made their handshake a declaration of war instead of a mere pleasantry.

I couldn't resist pulling the "twist-ender" trick of making the reader mistakenly think for a moment or two that Turner was a man. The story would work without it, but it helps to make the start of the feud more memorable.

In a sci-fi story there's always a risk that the writer will bore the reader by having too much dialogue explaining the plot and background information. Jack's sarcastic exchanges with Karen Turner enabled me to put over the necessary exposition without (hopefully) lecturing the reader. The row is a wonderful camouflage.

A good example of this is the section:

"They had a card," she ventured helpfully, "and were able to just walk in. Your security was breached. It was an inside job. Someone at the Institute helped the raiders."

I'm telling readers information they need to know but with luck they don't consciously realise they're being briefed. What they will be concentrating on is the delight with which Karen Turner goads Jack, implying that he runs an incompetent security operation. Sneaky stuff, eh?

In several sections I ask the dialogue to work extremely hard. The intro is one example. In the opening I wanted to put over a lot of scene setting exposition, get the story off to a flying start and also to introduce a feeling of excitement. Dialogue seemed the most effective way to achieve all three aims.

"Have you got a location fix on them?" I asked, fighting to stay calm. "Are the homers working?"

"Negative, Jack. Whoever let them out removed the homers. The rats are off the base and we haven't a clue which direction they've taken. The security fence has been breached in three places and the control panel's flashing like a Christmas tree. It's a bloody shambles!"

I could have put over this information in narration – in a straight description of the scene – but it has more power and impact coming from a character's mouth.

Later on I use a quick snatch of dialogue to increase the feeling of urgency ...

"There are still some rats here," the doctor yelled.

"How many?" I demanded. "Quick, Doc. I need to know."

He counted excitedly. "Ten – no – twelve. Nearly half are still here."

"Well, at least that's something," Karen Turner muttered.

Every time a character speaks it's moving the story along. Even the punch-line is in dialogue ...

"Project Alpha has been an amazing success, all right. It's bred animals that are smarter than humans. They want to give up smoking!"

Now, I've spent a great deal of space and time outlining the "rules" of short story writing – giving guidelines which I hope will help you construct entertaining and commercial fiction. And I'd like to think you'd follow them as much as possible. But I don't want you to follow every rule slavishly.

There will be times when it's right to break a rule, when ignoring conventional wisdom gives you a better narrative. If that happens – great. You should always do what creates the most dramatic effect, what's best for the story – not necessarily what will keep your writing tutor sweet.

One piece of conventional wisdom is that it's boring to start off a story with the main character asleep in bed. Another is that you should never have a character explain the plot set-up to another person over the telephone.

I've broken both these rules – and got away with it. By having Jack being rudely awoken by a panicky phone call, the story kicks off with a sudden, jagged, *emergency* feel. We get swept along with the action as he stumbles out of bed, dazed and confused. It creates the effect I was after – it sets the mood and pace of the story.

Now, don't think because I've ignored it that conventional wisdom is wrong or stupid. It's just that it doesn't apply in this particular set of circumstances.

If Frank Peters had been calm, the opening wouldn't have worked. The phone call would have been dull and leadened. Likewise, if Jack had woken up normally at seven, yawned and stretched, had breakfast and then got a phone call the story would be ponderous.

I got away with breaking the rules only because the two elements worked together. When you *occasionally* do your own thing by ignoring the guidelines, please do so because you have a particular dramatic effect in mind, not just because you don't like being told what to do, or think all creative writing advice is baloney.

Well, that's all I've got to say about *Devoted Admirer* and *Rat Pack*. I hope you liked them. They're not perfect, but I have a soft spot for both of them. I hope by taking them to bits I've given you an insight into some of my thought processes when I was writing them.

Always try to put yourself in the writer's place when you read a short story. Ask yourself – why did he write it that way? (Or if you hated it – why did he write it at all?) See if you can work out where he got his original inspiration from and note how he used dialogue and description to help move the conflict along. Study how he created his characters and what small details he's used to show their personalities, backgrounds and mannerisms. See what tricks he's used to make the story different.

You can learn a lot by studying the stories you read for fun. But don't go overboard with this *deconstructing* lark. Don't take it too far – especially when you're gazing critically at your own creations.

After all, you can pull a butterfly apart to see what makes it beautiful and end up with just a load of insect parts! If a story *flies* don't agonise over why, just enjoy its graceful flight.

14

PERFECT PRESENTATION

It's very important to realise that you are up against full-time writers who are ruthless professionals and so you must do everything in your power to compete on even terms. That means getting your manuscript right before sending it off. It must look like it's come from a "pro". So no crumpled pages, handwritten text or faintly printed copies; no fiddley binders and no coloured paper.

Pastels are great in bathrooms but the kiss of death in an editorial department. Stick to good, honest, simple white paper and have your pages loose, only held together by a paper clip.

Don't under any circumstances send work containing fussy layout gimmicks or clip art graphics. You may be especially proud of your super duper state-of-the-bank-balance computer, but it won't dazzle a fiction editor. In fact, stories illustrated with gruesome daggers and headstones or cutesy bunnies and smiley faces are more likely to go straight into the reject pile than any others. They announce to the world that the writer is an amateur.

Make sure your work reads well, so no first drafts. Polish, polish, polish – and then polish some more. Make sure every word earns its keep. Cut out the flab. Never submit stories that appear hastily written or thrown together.

Check that the piece is structured properly – that it has a coherent start, middle and end. Check that the *denouement* or climax is both credible and flows logically from the facts given and events described. If any vital information is missing, insert it – but not in a clumsy way which reveals that it is an afterthought.

Reread the text, putting every scene and every encounter between characters under the microscope. Ask yourself: is it all crucial to the plot? If not, take it out. Don't allow flabby dialogue or baroque descriptions to get in the way or slow the pace.

Be critical. Demand that each scene works on several levels – advancing the plot, aiding the characterisation and providing vital background.

When you've finally done all that and you can't improve the yarn, no matter how hard you tweak it, then (and only then) it is ready to send off. You only get one crack at an editor; so don't blow it. And *please* no apologetic little notes asking for special treatment. If your story isn't good enough to be accepted on its own merits, no editor will buy it just because you've spun a hard luck story. Trust me on this, editors don't have a better nature, so don't try to appeal to it.

Be smart

Your work must be perfect. Nothing less will do. Pretend you are sending your story to a job interview. Don't send it looking scruffy. Make sure it wears its best suit.

If you're thinking of sending a photocopy of a story – don't. You're wasting your postage money. It just won't be read. The editor will know the story has been rejected elsewhere. Why should he take something another editor wouldn't touch?

The same goes for dog-eared, coffee-stained carbons and sheets of paper yellowed with age. By sending shabby, second-hand work you're being discourteous. It takes little time to retype or reprint a story so that an editor receives a fresh and inviting copy.

If you are submitting work electronically (after checking with the editor that this is okay) make sure that it is in exactly the format requested. Most editors prefer ASCII plain text or Microsoft Word. Most prefer the words to appear in the body of the e-mail and not be submitted as a separate attachment, but find out.

Title sheet

Always have a clear title sheet (see the example overleaf) showing your name, address and telephone number, the name of the story, the word count and the words *First British Serial Rights*. (I'll talk about Rights in the next chapter.) Don't put anything else on the title sheet. It should look like this:

16 Camelot Close
Housing Estate
New Town
Ayrshire
AY1 22T

Tel: 0632-365551

A KNIGHT TO REMEMBER
by Arthur Pendragon

(1200 words)
FIRST BRITISH
SERIAL RIGHTS

Avoid pen-names

It amuses me that new authors feel compelled to adopt some sort of silly alias. I've known individuals agonise for days over what their *nom-de-plume* should be.

Perhaps I'm missing something here but I can't see why anyone would want to conceal their identity – unless they are hiding from the Mafia in a witness protection programme, owe their ex-spouse an astronomical amount of alimony or are so ashamed of what they write that they don't want to be publicly associated with it. Well, fine if you are a vicar who peddles pornographic tales while on the run from your Italian ex-wife's hit-men, but for the majority of us *normal* people a pen-name is just an affectation.

You don't need a pen-name. Even male writers submitting stories to women's magazines can use their own names. So stick to your ordinary moniker. It's what people know you by. Why complicate matters pretending to be someone else?

If you must (really must) use a pen-name then make it clear to the editor what your real name is. In brackets under the author's name on the title sheet put the words: *Such and such is the pen-name of ...* Otherwise, the magazine will issue a cheque made out to your alter ego and you'll have the devil of a time convincing the bank manager that Tristram de Pseud really is you, good old Tommy Smith.

Appearance

Always use A4 paper of no less than 80gms weight. Plain white copier paper is ideal. It is available from high street stockists and the larger discount stationery stores.

Type on one side only and double space your work, leaving a wide margin (about an inch) all round. The text should look as though it is surrounded by a white frame. Try to use short paragraphs (long paragraphs can look dark and ugly when set across a magazine's narrow column measure) and indent your second and subsequent paragraphs.

Some people will tell you that it's fine not to indent, as long as you leave a clear white space between each paragraph. This is okay for articles and readers' letters, but isn't really suitable for short stories where a clear white space between sections of the text is used to denote a change of scene or passage of time. If you indent, there is no danger of ambiguity or confusion arising over just what the white space signals to the reader.

Catchline

Make sure your work has a catchline in the top right hand corner of the page which clearly identifies it and differentiates it from anyone else's. One word from the title will do.

If your story is called *Gnome is Where the Heart is*, use the word *Gnome* as the catchline and then make sure each page is numbered so that the catchline reads *Gnome 1* on page one, *Gnome 2* on page 2 and so on.

Also, have the words *More Follows* or *Continues* in the bottom right hand corner of the page. On the last sheet use the word *Ends*. This labelling device tells the editor immediately that if the last sheet he is holding says *More Follows* then there are missing pages. Your layout should look like this:

Gnome 3

"Can you give me a description of the missing ... article?" The constable tried hard not to smirk.

George shrugged. "You know, sort of garden gnomish. Two feet high, with a pointed hat, red waistcoat, beard, fishing rod and green wellingtons."

"Any distinguishing features?"

"A small chip on his shoulder."

George could have sworn he heard the policeman mutter: "Haven't we all."

The PC closed his notebook with a flick. "We'll keep a lookout, but I don't hold out much hope. I reckon you're right about it being kids. Sounds exactly the sort of prank they'd pull."

/More Follows

Gnome 4

As he left, the policeman asked them if the gnome was insured. George shook his head and Margaret rushed from the room sobbing.

Next day, George decided to take Margaret to the garden centre to buy a replacement gnome, but his wife refused to go.

"It just won't be the same," she protested. "No-one can ever take his place. There'll never be another Gnomie."

Just then the morning post arrived. It was the usual pile of bills, offers and assorted junk. Absent-mindedly, George was about to throw it away when he noticed a postcard, hidden away at the bottom.

/More Follows

Catchlining your work may seem a terrible fuss, but it is necessary. With a fiction editor handling several stories at once, accidents can happen. If pages from three stories become muddled up, it will be impossible to sort them back into their respective piles if the pages have not been adequately tagged and numbered. If an editor can't sort them out, they'll all end up in a filing cabinet – or the bin! And it will be the fault of the three writers, not the editor.

Clean text

If you make a mistake, retype the page. Don't allow anything to leave your desk covered in correction fluid, scorings or ink amendments. Any blemish will detract from the story's impact.

Check your work

Make sure your punctuation and spelling are correct. Nothing destroys credibility quicker than a story which is littered with silly spelling errors or apostrophes in the wrong place. If you know your spelling is suspect and you're a bit unsure about using commas, full stops, dashes, etc then consult one of the reference books listed at the back of this book.

Even if you think you can spell well, the chances are that you can't; so please use a dictionary to double-check everything you write. About 95 per cent of people regularly misspell even simple words.

If you have a computer, use the spell checker regularly. It's a useful tool, but still look in the dictionary as a back-up. A spell checker has its limitations. It will tell you if a word is spelt incorrectly but it won't tell you if you've misunderstood what that word means and are using it in the wrong context.

For example, it won't know that *Little Boy Blew* should be *Little Boy Blue* or that *their was a huge explosion* should really be *there was a huge explosion.*

Also be aware that most computers feature an American dictionary – so many spell checkers think *socks* should be spelt *sox* and *neighbourhood* should be *neighborhood.* But you can usually alter your computer to a British setting – if in doubt read the manual.

Good layout, spelling, punctuation and grammar aren't just desirable – they are crucial. Work containing mistakes will be rejected. In the old days a good story that contained several grammatical errors might still have been bought and worked on by a magazine's sub-editors. But in these leaner times, magazines are cutting back their editorial departments and haven't got the staff, time or inclination to mess about with sub-standard scripts.

Covering Letters

Opinions differ about whether a covering letter will help. Some fiction editors like to know exactly who they're dealing with, while others reckon that if they receive a short story through the post the writer is obviously submitting it for consideration. It's self evident.

Personally, I always send a covering letter. I think it's only polite. The object of the exercise isn't just to sell a single story but to get yourself known, and develop a good working relationship with a particular magazine's fiction department. It's difficult for a fiction editor or a small press publisher to build up a good rapport with you if all you are is a name on a page; especially if it's a pen-name.

For that reason I always recommend enclosing a covering note – with one stipulation. If the letter is going to destroy your credibility or make you sound like an out and out wally, don't bother. Editors are always receiving gauche, gushing, embarrassing covering letters from inexperienced writers that seriously damage their case.

Remember that this is a business letter, so be brief, confident and factual. Don't apologise for the story – it's not the time for false modesty – and don't make exaggerated claims for it either.

Always find out the fiction editor's name. If it isn't printed in the magazine, ring up and ask the switchboard. Even if his name is listed in one of the reference books, call to check that the fiction editor hasn't changed recently.

Address your letter to him by name. Nothing beats the personal touch. Introduce yourself and ask if the fiction editor would be kind enough to consider your story for publication. Be polite and mention the publication's story slot by its name – it shows you've read the magazine.

If you are dealing with a small press editor you might mention a couple of stories in a recent issue that appealed to you. That will flatter his ego. After all, he chose them. But don't insult the fiction editor or publisher by explaining what your story is "really" about. He's not stupid, he'll work it out for himself.

Don't say that your wife/husband/mother/auntie/cat/dog or budgie liked the story. Unless they are trained commissioning editors their opinions count for nothing. If an agent or another magazine liked your story, then maybe that point is worth mentioning. Also say if it has done well in a major competition.

Include any fact that gives you credibility – other work published/writing prizes/creative writing degree/any relevant training etc. If you haven't got a strong track record keep the letter short. Also, be respectful and don't be flippant or over-familiar.

Have a look at the following two examples of covering letters. The first one is a classic example of how to wreck your chances and make yourself look rather silly. I promise you that although this particular letter is made up, it closely mirrors dozens of cringe-making letters I've seen.

The second example is short, direct and to the point. It "sells" the writer and inspires confidence in her.

Example A

Dear Sir or Madam

I enclose a copy of my spooky mystery story "Cat With Nine Lives" which I'm sure you'll want to consider for your magazine. I haven't done an exact word count but I think it's about 2,000 words. I expect that's the length of story you normally print – if not, feel free to slash it back.

The story tells what happens to a vet when he kills a cat and then finds himself being menaced by a mysterious presence which pads around behind him in the dark. (Actually it's the ghost of the cat.)

I wouldn't normally send a story to a publication I don't read but a friend told me she'd seen an item in a writing magazine which said you were looking for well written tales. Well this should fit the bill nicely. I'm too modest to say it's a masterpiece but my friends all like it and I got a very favourable response when I read it out at my writer's circle.

I'm sorry the printing is a little faint, but the ink cartridge on my computer is nearly empty and I haven't had a chance to go out and buy a new one. (I've been too busy writing this story in fact.) I'm sure you can always get someone to retype it at your end if it's a problem.

A few points I'd like to mention. Firstly, can you send me a copy of your guidelines for contributors. I'd like to study them before knocking off my follow-up story for you. Secondly, I need to know about payment. Can you let me know how much I can expect for "Cat With Nine Lives"? And lastly, can you drop me a note to assure me that you will keep my story away from prying eyes. I'd hate to think of someone pinching it!

Well, I must dash. I look forward to hearing from you and getting your reaction. I'm sure it will positive!

Bye now

Rebecca Jane Claremont

PS My real name is Beckie Brown. Can you make sure the cheque is made out to me and not my pen-name?

Ouch! This is what I'd call a suicide note ... every sentence makes things worse. The writer obviously doesn't know the editor's name or sex, admits she hasn't read the magazine or seen the fiction guidelines, tells the poor editor that the story is great and explains what it's about in case he is too thick to spot it for himself.

All that is bad enough, but do you notice the tone of the letter? By using expressions like *slash it back* and *knocking off* a follow-up, the writer is signalling that she doesn't take any of it seriously – it's just a jolly game, a mildly amusing diversion.

But perhaps this writer's worst crime is implying that the editor has no choice but to buy the story. She's sure that he'll want to consider it and that his reaction will be positive. Oh no, it won't! The one guaranteed way to get your story rejected is to imply that the editor is barmy if he fails to appreciate the treasure you've so generously sent him.

Example B

Dear Barry Edwards

This is a short note to introduce myself and ask if you'd be kind enough to consider my 1,500-word story "Cat With Nine Lives" for the *Spooky Mysteries* slot in *Eerie Tales* magazine.

I'm a regular reader of *Eerie Tales* and have been a writer for three years. My stories have appeared in *Midnight Creeper* magazine, *Twilight Zone Monthly* and *Graveyard Shift* fanzine. I was a runner up in this year's national horror writer's competition run by *Graveyard Shift*.

Fellow writer Gregory Spencer – a regular contributor to your magazine – was kind enough to look over "Cat With Nine Lives" for me and said I should send it to you. I've tried to stick to the style and feel of the *Spooky Mysteries* slot and have followed all the advice in your fiction guidelines.

I hope you like the tale. If not, I enclose a sae for its return. Many thanks for your attention. I look forward to hearing from you.

Yours sincerely

Beckie Brown

It's short, sweet and up-beat without being brash or over-confident. This letter shows Beckie in a good light. She knows the magazine, has studied the guidelines and written the piece to fit what is required. In addition, she has a proven record of success and knows exactly who she is writing for.

Just like the first example, she is saying that someone thinks the story is good but this time it's a regular contributor to the magazine – someone whose judgement is worth listening to; someone whose opinion the editor is likely to value.

Notice the deferential tone of the letter? She asks the editor if he'd be *kind enough* to look at the story, and thanks him for his attention. At no point does she even hint that this sale is a foregone conclusion.

Even if she had never had anything published before, the editor would still think this was a writer with the correct attitude, someone to take seriously. Try to make your covering letter create the same good impression.

Send a stamped, addressed envelope

In this second example, Beckie mentions that she's enclosed a sae (stamped, addressed envelope) for the return of her work. This is vital. No magazine is going to subsidise you.

Don't think that a huge publication can afford the postage anymore than you can. If a fiction editor paid for the return postage on 200 rejected stories every week he'd have no cash left to buy any. It's worse for small press magazines which can often struggle to find the funds just to pay the printing bill.

Story length

Always round-off story lengths to the nearest 25 words – a story is 1,000 words, not 996 words. You may think that it is commendable to be as precise as possible when counting words but ironically such accuracy isn't necessary. No-one cares if a yarn is a few words over or under as long as it is roughly the right length. Only beginners give exact lengths – it's a real give-away.

An editor handles dozens of stories each day and will know at a glance when a script is much longer or shorter than the title sheet states. So don't be tempted to try slipping through a 1,500-word story claiming it is only 1,300-words. You will get caught.

Trim the piece to fit what is required. Don't hope that no-one will notice or that someone will take pity on you and cut it down later. They won't.

End note

I know all the advice in this chapter sounds a bit fussy, but good presentation is more important than most people realise. Shoddy work won't impress an editor and there are plenty of other writers who take special care to ensure their manuscripts are crisply and cleanly presented and easy to read. Don't let them get an edge over you.

Exercises

Go back to a story you submitted for publication more than three months ago, but has been rejected. Reread it. Were there any mistakes? Was every sentence well written? Did the story have a clear and logical structure? If your tale was less than perfect, why not rewrite it and then resubmit it to another publication and see if you have more success.

Create a title sheet for the story as shown in the chapter. If you are working on a word processor, take a separate copy of this and keep it as a template for all future stories.

Write a short, businesslike letter to accompany your tale. Include any relevant details about you and your writing career Compare your letter with the example given in the chapter. Have you managed to sell yourself without making exaggerated claims?

Make a copy of the letter on disk and use it as a template for all your covering letters.

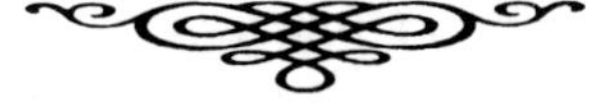

Summary

✓ You will be up against full-time writers who are ruthless professionals so your work has to be well presented. No dog eared, coffee-stained carbons and sheets of paper that are yellowed with age.

✓ Avoid crumpled pages, handwritten text or faintly printed copies – no fiddley binders and no coloured paper.

✓ Always use white paper – and have your pages loose, held together only by a paper clip.

✓ Don't send work containing fussy layout gimmicks or clip art graphics.

✓ Polish, polish, polish. Make sure every word earns its keep. Never submit hastily written stories.

✓ Check that the piece is structured properly – that it has a coherent start, middle and end.

✓ Check that the *denouement* or climax is both credible and flows logically from the facts given and events described.

✓ Don't enclose an apologetic little note asking for special treatment. No editor will buy it just because you've spun a hard luck story.

✓ Always have a title sheet containing your name, address, telephone number, the name of the story, the word count and the words *First British Serial Rights.*

✓ Only use a pen-name if it is essential. If you must adopt a pseudonym make your real name clear to the editor.

✓ Always use A4 paper of 80gms weight. Type on one side only and double space your work, leaving a wide margin all round.

- ✓ Use short paragraphs and always indent your second and subsequent paragraphs.
- ✓ Make sure your work has a catchline in the top right hand corner of the page which clearly identifies it.
- ✓ Have the words *More Follows* or *Continues* in the bottom right hand corner of the page. On the last sheet use the word *Ends*.
- ✓ If you make a mistake, retype the whole page. Don't allow anything to go out covered in correction fluid, scoring or ink amendments.
- ✓ Make sure your punctuation and spelling are correct – and don't just rely on your computer spell-checker.
- ✓ It's a good idea to send a covering letter but keep it short, businesslike and to the point. Address it to the editor by name.
- ✓ Mention the magazine's story slot by name – it proves you have done your homework.
- ✓ Don't say that your friends or family liked the story – their opinions count for nothing.
- ✓ Include any fact that gives you credibility – other work published, writing prizes, a creative writing degree, any relevant training etc.
- ✓ Be deferential but avoid being over-familiar.
- ✓ Always enclose a sae for a story's return.
- ✓ Round off lengths to the nearest 25 words. Never lie about a story's length.

15

THE ART OF SELLING

Competition to get into magazines is fierce. Everyone wants to see their prose in a well-known and prestigious publication. Because so many writers try to sell their work to the mainstream commercial magazines, the slush piles on most fiction editors' desks are enormous.

Some slush piles are so huge that freelance copy readers are brought in to help sift the rubbish from potential sellers. The copy readers present the fiction editor with a shortlist of possibles.

To give you an idea of the scale of the task, just consider that many magazines receive between 150 and 200 unsolicited scripts a week. If you multiply that figure across all the big name magazines that regularly publish short stories, there must be about 2,000 unsolicited stories arriving each week.

Yet it is the same small band of writers, perhaps as few as a 100, whose names appear regularly. Some even have several stories appear simultaneously in rival publications. So why do they seem to beat the competition while others fail?

The answer is that, like professional gamblers, they've done everything possible to reduce the odds against them. They've made sure that their work is polished, accurately targeted, well timed, excellently presented and stands out from the herd. And that's what you have to do if you hope to take them on.

Bookmakers don't quote odds on a new writer getting his work into print. But I'd suggest that a competent newcomer, with a good plot, who has done the necessary market research and tailored his work to fit what a particular fiction editor wants, will have about a 1 in 7 chance of making it through the slush pile. When he becomes known to various fiction editors and they come to trust his work and look out for it, that figure may come down to 1 in 3. Having an agent helps beyond measure, of course, and the odds come down to about 50/50. I'll talk about agents, what they do and how to get one in the next chapter. But in the meantime, let's see how you – as a relative beginner – can ensure that you aren't a 200 to 1 shot outsider.

Beating the odds

I'm assuming that you have already done extensive market research before writing your story, as I advised in chapter two. I'm also assuming that you've got hold of fiction guidelines and followed them to the letter. If not, you don't really deserve to sell your work.

The next step in improving your chances is to look for magazines which publish several stories in each issue. They are worth special attention because, as they print more stories than anyone else, they buy more stories than anyone else. It's not just a question of numbers. They'll also be looking for variety – a mixture of story styles – and you might succeed because your yarn neatly contrasts with others already bought.

D.C. Thomson titles are good markets to try as they often print several stories in a single issue. Also think about offering stories for the spring, summer and winter specials of women's magazines. These bumper issues frequently contain eight or more stories and are an excellent way in for new writers. Sometimes a tale that is good but thought not quite in house style or too quirky for a magazine's normal weekly issues will be bought for its seasonal supplement.

Don't just focus on magazines you find in the newsagents. Small press magazines – most available by subscription – usually print more than half a dozen stories an issue. These magazines are worth your special attention because (a) there are so many of them and (b) some are relatively obscure and aren't targeted by masses of would-be contributors. You'll be competing against maybe only a handful of other writers.

Target poor payers

Go for magazines that pay the least – professionals won't touch them. Don't go for top payers like the household name magazines and big name tabloids. The competition is cut-throat. As you are a beginner up against the cream of the writing game, your chances of getting something accepted are negligible. Aim at more modest targets – targets which are so small or pay so badly that most people shy away from them.

As I've already said D.C. Thomson titles, seasonal specials and small press/independent mags are all worth considering because they take so many stories. But they're also worth your attention because they pay so little. In fact, many small press magazines only offer a complimentary copy of the issue your story appears in – but these outlets are an invaluable first step in your writing career.

Take it a step at a time. Getting into print is the main thing, not getting rich. (That can come later!) Be happy if you are offered £50 for a story. Take it – never argue over payment or demand more. You'll be told to go take a running jump.

Another important point to make while we're looking at payment: be prepared to wait quite a while for your cheque. Many magazines pay on or immediately after publication, not on acceptance. I'll talk some more about payment and rights later on in the chapter.

Make sure your timing is right

Timing is crucial for any short story writer. You have to understand the buying cycle of magazines. You have to know what time of the year fiction editors will be looking for a particular type of story. There's no point sending a tale about spring-time lovers when a magazine is looking for an autumn story – possibly about a bonfire-party romance.

In practice, fiction editors tend to work anything up to six months in advance. So while you are pulling crackers and kissing under the mistletoe, a magazine's fiction department is already thinking about what stories to buy for its summer special.

This means that you can't leave it to the last minute to submit tales with a seasonal setting or which tie in to important dates like Valentine's Day, Mother's Day, New Year's Eve, Christmas, Bonfire night, Halloween or April Fools Day. No matter how good they are, if they miss the six-month-in-advance deadline they will be rejected. Also, there's little point leaving it until the last possible moment to submit your Christmas or Valentine's Day story because hundreds of other writers will have beaten you to it.

Don't think that the fiction editor will hang on to your late arriving story until the next year. He won't. There isn't room in his office to have a story library and he'll send it back rather than risk it getting lost. Besides, he'll want to choose from the best possible selection next year; so even if he held on to your story it wouldn't get preferential treatment. It would go back into the slush pile to slug it out with 200 others.

So why is there such a long lead-in time for stories? Why do they take so long to make it through the system?

There are three main reasons:

1. It takes a fiction department a while to read through a huge mountain of scripts – even if there are several people scrutinising them and when they probably know from the opening paragraphs that most stories are stinkers. Your story is only one of several hundreds being read that month.

Some magazines can't afford a large fiction department and the fiction editor may be working single handed. He may not have a deputy to run things while he is off sick or on holiday, so stories start to stockpile. Even if he likes your work, it's likely that it will go to a second reading where other members of staff will look at it and comment. Two or three months can be eaten up just getting through the selection processes.

2. Having bought your story the fiction editor has to find an available slot for it in his publication schedule. Magazine contents are chosen well in advance and he'll want flexibility to select the most suitable time to use it. The more time he has, the greater the choices open to him.

3. The story has to be sent to a freelance illustrator for him to draw the cartoon or picture that will accompany the story. This will take several weeks.

It's a similar situation in the small press world. Many subscription-only magazines are run by one-man-bands or small groups of friends who produce the titles as a labour of love in their spare time. The magazine will have to fit in with work and family commitments and may be issued on a fairly fluid basis.

Stories can tend to hang around for a while before getting a thumbs up or a refusal – there's only one person to read through them. Then the same delay happens while the story has an illustration drawn – sometimes by an artist who is working for the magazine in his spare time.

Patience is the key word. No-one will ever deliberately spin out the process, and you have to remember that a few weeks may not seem a long time to an editor even though you're going up the wall with suspense.

How long to wait?

It's impossible to judge with any great accuracy how long it takes a story to be bought or rejected, but the rule of thumb is that the longer it's out there the better. Stinkers are rejected quickly, but possibles are kept so that the fiction editor can re-read them and show them to other members of staff.

If you haven't heard anything from a mainstream magazine after eight to ten weeks, it's usually a sign that the story is doing well and might just make it. Whatever you do, don't ring up and ask about its progress. Be cool, be professional and be patient.

If, after twelve weeks, you still haven't had a reply, drop the fiction editor a polite note enquiring about the story and saying that if you haven't heard anything within a fortnight you'll assume you are free to offer it elsewhere.

With small press magazines I'd double the time scale. Give the editor 24 weeks to make up his mind. Even working just in the evenings and at weekends, he should have had a chance to look through his slushpile.

Don't try to speed-up the process by sending the same story to several magazines simultaneously. Editors expect you to offer your work to them exclusively and would be extremely angry to think you'd offered it to several magazines at the same time. You could find yourself having some awkward explaining to do if two rival editors wanted to buy the same story. You could end up blacklisted. Wait until a story is rejected before offering it elsewhere. And don't send several stories at once to a fiction editor. If he hated the first, it's likely to colour his thinking about the others.

Important: Don't ring up a few weeks after you've sold a story asking why it hasn't been printed or pestering to know when it will be used. That gives you away as an amateur.

Know which doors are open

Some magazines are happy to look at unsolicited scripts, while others only buy stories submitted through literary agents. As a newcomer, there's no point sending your story to one of the "closed door" magazines – they'll send it back unread.

Consult either the *Writers' and Artists' Yearbook* or *The Writer's Handbook*. They identify which magazines are "open" and which are "shut". You can find these guidebooks in most reference libraries, but I'd suggest you splash out on your own copy as they aren't very expensive and it's worth having them to hand as you never know just when you need to check the details of a magazine. Most high street bookshops will have copies of both reference books or can order them for you.

Consult the books on every possible occasion. Don't just guess or hope that a fiction editor will take pity on you and make an exception in your case. He won't. So a few minutes market research like this can save you the cost of wasted postage and a red face.

Remember: while your Valentine's Day story is sitting for a couple of weeks on the desk of a fiction editor who won't read unsolicited material, it's missing its sales slot somewhere else.

If you are still in doubt after consulting the reference books, phone the editorial department (but **not** the editor) and ask if the magazine will accept unsolicited stories. It only takes a couple of minutes and will remove any uncertainty you might have.

Double check your story

Make sure it's the best you can do. It has to stand out from the crowd. Read it again before submitting it – this time with more critical eyes. Is it well structured with a finely honed plot? Are your characters and settings lively and bright? Have you avoided cliches and tired images? Is it tightly written and fast paced?

Make it the best story you have ever written. Check that every scene, every character and every line of dialogue really works. Then give it to someone to read who isn't blinded by your dazzling personality and charms. Preferably someone who views writers, and everything to do with them, with suspicion.

Let that person scour the script for any weaknesses. If your severest critic says it's fine then you'll know it's ready to send off.

Learn from your mistakes

Don't just throw away your rejection slips. Study them. They offer invaluable feedback. They often contain hidden messages – fiction editors haven't got the time or inclination to nanny along inexperienced writers. So if they go to the trouble of sending you a personal rejection letter, or scribble a quick note on the rejection slip, they're signalling to you that you're near to the target.

Always take their advice and act upon it. Never take the huff – you will only hurt yourself. If you're told to change the ending – change the ending. If you're told there are too many characters – do a cull.

Reread your story until you see the flaws that the fiction editor has identified. Learn from the experience. Make sure you don't make the same mistakes twice. Practise any technique that you aren't fully comfortable with.

Follow up immediately on successes and near misses – get yourself known (for all the right reasons). If a magazine has been impressed by your work, send them some more, but don't inundate them. Show that you think and act like a pro.

Sympathetic response

One of the great attractions of writing for small press magazines is that you'll usually get a sympathetic and encouraging response from the editors – many of whom are also authors in their own right. They know what it's like to be on the receiving end of rebuffs and rejection slips, so they try to be as friendly and helpful as possible.

Whereas an editor of a large magazine may be so busy that he can only send you a short and impersonal "stock" rejection letter, a small press publisher may take the time to point out why he didn't like your story and may offer suggestions on improving it or your writing style. Some magazines even send a critique back with every story. So it's worth targeting this end of the market if you're still a little unsure of yourself and are looking for expert advice and a more chummy response.

Don't get me wrong – not everyone in the mainstream world is hard faced and cold hearted. D.C. Thomson magazines pay modestly but the company's fiction departments are well known for their kindness, patience and encouragement. The staff are wonderfully supportive to new writers and will often write a lengthy critique of a story that has narrowly missed the target.

The magazines are rare in that they will happily take a second look at a story provided that the author has made the amendments suggested. I, and many other successful writers, owe a debt of gratitude to D.C. Thomson staff for help and advice when we started out. Thanks guys – I won't forget you!

"Rights" and wrongs

Many newcomers get into a terrible tizzy over money, invoices, what serial rights to offer and whether copyright will protect them from having their work stolen. These worries are usually groundless, but they cause genuine concern so let's look at them and see if we can put everyone's mind at rest.

Let's start with rights. These seem to cause more confusion than just about anything else. Actually, once you look at them, it's quite simple.

When you submit a story to a fiction editor you are offering him "the right" to print it. Think of it as another term for "permission".

Usually writers offer *First British Serial Rights.* This means that a magazine has the right to print the story once (and only once) in the UK. By offering *First Rights* you are telling the editor that this is a fresh, original story that hasn't been published or broadcast in Britain before.

What you are doing, in effect, is renting out your story for the editor to use on one occasion. You keep the copyright and after that, it's yours to sell again – if you can.

This arrangement sounds great but it's worth mentioning that although you retain the overall ownership of the story, you don't have control over how it is used. You rent out your story for an editor to do as he likes with it. He may change character names, cut the length, re-title it or even completely revamp the ending.

I know lots of authors are mortified at the thought of this tinkering, but there's nothing you can do. My advice is: take the money, smile sweetly through gritted teeth and quietly re-instate the altered passages next time you offer the tale. You are in a buyer's market and there's no room to be precious or act the tortured artist. And to be fair, most times the amendments will have improved the story ... or at least won't have fatally wounded it.

If you are lucky enough to be able to re-sell the story to a another UK magazine you then offer the next editor *Second British Serial Rights*. He rents the story in the same way for a single printing.

Re-sales don't happen often as most editors aren't keen to take a story that has appeared before in a UK magazine unless there are unusual circumstances or the story is going into a collection or an anthology. However, some editors will look at a story which first appeared on radio or in a magazine abroad.

It's important that you don't try to trick an editor into thinking he's getting first crack at a story if it has already appeared elsewhere. Be honest in your covering letter. If he finds out he's been conned, he'll be furious.

There's an increasing tendency for mainstream magazines to demand that writers sign over *All Rights* when they offer a story. This means that you are handing over your story forever, selling it instead of renting it out. It loses you the chance of being paid for repeat printings.

I really can't give you any definitive advice on this except to say that you should think very carefully before signing over *All Rights*. Once they're gone you can't get them back. Only agree if you think you won't be able to re-sell a story a second or third time; if you are desperate for the cash offered or if you are at the stage where you need published work more than you need to worry about maximising your income from it.

One important bonus you'll give away if you agree to sell *All Rights* is the chance of overseas sales. Just because your story has appeared in the UK doesn't prevent you from later offering it abroad and you'll kick yourself if you give up this potentially lucrative extra income. There are eager markets for

English language short stories in South Africa, Australia and North America and their magazines pay extremely well.

This is definitely worth considering if your short story has universal appeal, isn't tied too much to one culture, religion or racial group and has a setting and characters that aren't too blatantly British. (Look in writing magazines which publish an *Overseas Markets* page, and consult *The Writer's Handbook* and other reference guides for more details.)

If you are selling work abroad, don't worry too much about what rights to offer. The principle is exactly the same as submitting a story to the UK market. If, for example, you are sending your story to an Australian magazine, for its first publication in Oz, simply offer *First Australian Serial Rights*. If it's going to America or Canada for the first time offer *First North American Serial Rights*. If you are selling a story for its second publication in Australia offer *Second Australian Serial Rights* and so on.

One final point about print rights. Apart from putting the expression *First British Serial Rights* on your title sheet (as shown in the last chapter) don't mention them in your covering letter or any other correspondence you may have with the editor. It's a dead giveaway that you are inexperienced.

Your rights on the Internet

So what if you intend to submit work to an Internet magazine? What rights do you offer to a publication that exists only in cyberspace? How often can an E-zine reproduce your work and what restrictions are there on selling your story elsewhere?

The simple answer to these questions is that there's no simple answer. As with many things to do with the Internet, the facts about *Electronic Rights* are still a little hazy at the moment. This is because editors have all taken different approaches, and it's a heated and constantly evolving issue.

Some editors don't seem to care about rights, others don't understand them and a few think that once they've paid you for a story then it belongs to them forever.

Eventually things will settle down, but in the meantime my advice is not to worry about it. Think of an Internet outlet as basically just the same as any other magazine, but instead of offering *First British Serial Rights* offer *First World Electronic Rights* or *First Exclusive Electronic Rights.*

This means that the editor gets first crack at reproducing the story on the Web and after it appears you'll feel free to offer it to anyone else who'll buy it. But be aware that reselling a story might not be so easy after it's appeared on the Web. Some editors of conventional print magazines may consider that publication on the Internet means that the story isn't fresh any more and that they are getting second-hand goods. (This is especially true if an E-zine keeps your story on its web page for months on end.) So it's probably a good idea to target the more traditional markets before turning to the inducements of E-zines – especially as many Web publications don't pay for material.

Copyright

So much for rights, but what about copyright? How can you protect your work from being stolen?

Well, to be frank, you can't – not really. There is no copyright on ideas, only on the exact way the words actually appear on the page. So unless someone lifts whole sections out of your story, word for word, there's no real way to prove you've been robbed. You can sprinkle copyright notices all over your work, but it offers about as much protection as crossing your fingers and reciting a magic spell.

This sounds awful but in reality it's no big deal. The truth is that although new writers are often paranoid about having their ideas nicked, this happens so rarely that you have more chance of being savaged by a runaway yak than of having a plotline pilfered. It's not worth losing any sleep over.

You'll hear people mutter darkly at writer's circles that they know someone who knows someone whose sister's next door neighbour had the idea for a best-seller nicked, but it's just another urban myth. Honestly. Don't get me wrong, there are plenty of people out there who genuinely believe they've been the victim of manuscript muggers but more often than not they're deluding themselves.

Look at the evidence. Most stories deal with the same twelve basic dramatic themes, have similar characters and conflicts, and feature fairly hackneyed settings and predictable outcomes. Nearly every tale is a reworking of the same age-old material – only the details alter, and even then writers all tend to plump for fashionable social problems, "in vogue" dilemmas and issues they've read about in the newspapers.

This often happens when the writers are all targeting the same big-paying mainstream magazines. Everyone follows the same recipe – writing for a particular age group, background and gender – working within narrow story-telling parameters set out in the guidelines.

Is it any wonder that your story sounds a bit like someone else's? If you ask me, it's not at all surprising that there are suspicious coincidences between different tales. The surprising thing is that it doesn't happen more often. You try writing a truly original Christmas story!

I see it all the time. In any given competition, I'll find five stories basically identical in plotline and general setting. Of course, there's no way that these five writers have pinched ideas from each other, but if one of these yarns won and was printed, don't you think the other four people would be yelling: *Hey, hang on a minute, mate – you nicked my storyline*!

So please don't get neurotic about it. Covering your work with copyright symbols is pointless. If you feel you must put a copyright notice on a script, only put one line, in small type, at the end of the story. Don't put one on every page – again, it screams that the story's been submitted by an amateur.

What about protecting your work if it appears on the Internet? The same principle applies as with print magazines. Your work is protected in theory but actually doing anything about theft is virtually impossible.

Be philosophical. Ask yourself: is it worth trying to sue someone for breaching your copyright if they live on the other side of the world and getting them into court would bankrupt you?

Chasing up payment

What about not getting paid for a story? That's another worry that people frequently voice. Once again, it's not something that's worth getting your blood pressure soaring.

If you submit work to household name magazines or long-established small press publications you shouldn't have any problems. These well known magazines are all scrupulously honest and will send you a cheque either on acceptance of your story or within a few weeks of it being printed.

If there is a lengthy delay – it's four months after the story appeared and you still haven't seen a penny – it's more likely to be a genuine mistake rather than anyone trying to pull a fast one. After all, we aren't talking about a fortune and such magazines have their reputations to think about. A polite reminder note will usually do the trick.

If you're concerned, consider submitting an invoice. (Some magazines now ask writers to send one as a matter of course.) This will help the fiction editor to chivvy the accounts department on your behalf if your cheque has gone missing or hasn't been dispatched.

Keep it simple, on a single sheet of paper. Something like the one on the next page will do:

INVOICE

16 Camelot Close
Housing Estate
New Town
Ayrshire
AY1 22T

Tel: 0632-365551

December 15th this year.

For short story "A Knight To Remember" by Arthur Pendragon, printed in August edition of Wow-Wee! Magazine – £300, as agreed by fiction editor Abi Rhode.

Please make cheque payable to G. Smith
(Arthur Pendragon is a pen-name of Giles Smith)

Many thanks

That's all you need to put – who you are, why you have submitted the invoice, the amount agreed, who authorised it and to whom the cheque should be made payable. It's all very straightforward.

Folding titles

The non-payment problem only tends to arise when you are submitting work to newer, less well-established magazines. These are high risk publications – the ones that spring up overnight, last a few issues and then fold ... often without warning. Usually they close because they're under-funded, the editor doesn't have the expertise or he suddenly realises how much hard work it is.

What can you do if your story has appeared in one of these and the magazine has closed before you've been paid? The answer, I'm afraid, is not very much. You can, in theory, take the editor through the small claims court but even if you win a judgement there's no guarantee that you'll get your cash. If the magazine folded because the owner/editor was broke, he won't have the money to pay you.

Just be philosophical. Small press mags rarely pay huge amounts for stories so you won't be that much out of pocket and you'll still have the cutting to cuddle up to on a cold winter's night.

The whole question becomes that much trickier if you encounter a rogue editor – one whose magazine is still happily publishing but he won't part with the fee he promised you. Thankfully such people are quite rare. The small claims court approach isn't foolproof, as I've said, and it's unlikely that he'll be worried about your angry phone calls and letters so, galling as it sounds, there's little you can do.

The one note of consolation is that you'll have learnt a valuable lesson and won't get conned in that way again.

Now, I don't want all this to scare you. Non-payment is fortunately the exception to the rule. Even so, you can stop yourself being caught out by using a little common sense. Only deal with large or long-established magazines, and ask around at writer's circles about publications and editors to avoid. Also keep an eye on the letter's pages of writing magazines. You'll read about others' bad experiences and know which titles to keep away from.

Exercises

Go into a newsagents and see if you can spot magazines which publish several short stories in one issue. Have a good look through them. If you can afford it, buy a couple of copies to take home to study.

Have a look in either *The Writer's Handbook* or the *Writers' and Artists' Yearbook* to see if the magazines you chose are listed there. Do they accept unsolicited manuscripts? If so, send off for guidelines and then write a suitable story of the requested length and submit it.

Is there a small press magazine listed in the reference books that captures your attention? If there is, send off for its guidelines – plus a couple of back copies – and write a story suitable for it.

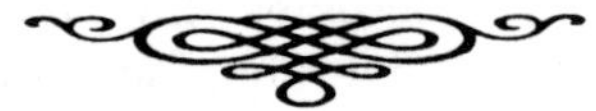

Summary

- ✓ Competition to get into magazines is fierce.
- ✓ Make sure your work is polished, accurately targeted, well-timed, excellently presented and stands out.
- ✓ Look for magazines which publish several stories in each issue. They buy more than anyone else and look for a variety of styles.
- ✓ Also look out for the seasonal specials produced by some women's magazines.
- ✓ Aim at more modest targets. There are lots of small press magazines, some relatively obscure, which are overlooked by the mass of contributors.
- ✓ Learn the buying cycle of magazines. You have to know what time of the year fiction editors will be looking for a particular type of story.
- ✓ They tend to work up to six months in advance. So don't leave it too late with seasonal or anniversary tales.
- ✓ If you haven't heard from a mainstream magazine after eight to ten weeks it's usually a sign that the story is doing well.
- ✓ If you haven't had a reply after three months, write to the fiction editor. Tell him that if you haven't heard anything within a fortnight you will assume you are free to offer it elsewhere.
- ✓ With small press magazines give the editor 24 weeks to decide.
- ✓ Don't send the same story to several magazines at the same time.

- ✓ And don't send several stories at once. If an editor hated the first, it's likely to colour his thinking about the others.
- ✓ Always make sure you send work to magazines which are happy to look at unsolicited scripts. Consult *The Writer's Handbook* for details.
- ✓ Reread your story before submitting it. Let someone who is critical scour the script for weaknesses.
- ✓ Don't throw away rejection slips. Study them. They offer useful feedback. A personal note shows you are close to the target.
- ✓ Always take an editor's advice and act upon it. Never take the huff.
- ✓ Make sure you follow up on successes and near misses. Get yourself known.
- ✓ Target small press magazines where you are more likely to get a friendly reception. Or go for mainstream magazines which have a reputation for being kind to new writers.
- ✓ Always offer *First British Serial Rights*. By doing this, you keep the copyright.
- ✓ An editor has the right to tamper with any story he buys; even having sections of it rewritten or altered.
- ✓ Don't try to trick an editor into thinking he's getting first crack at a story if it has already appeared elsewhere.
- ✓ Only agree to sell *All Rights* if you don't think you'll be able to re-sell the story at a later date.
- ✓ There are eager markets for English language short stories abroad and they pay extremely well.

- ✓ Don't go on about rights in your covering letter or any other correspondence. It shows you are inexperienced.
- ✓ There is no copyright on ideas, only on the exact way the words appear on the page.
- ✓ Copyright notices don't offer that much protection, but the chances of having an idea stolen are slim.
- ✓ If you must put a copyright notice on a script, only put one line, in small type, at the end of the story.
- ✓ If you submit work to household name magazines or long-established small press titles you shouldn't have problems with being paid.
- ✓ If you haven't been paid three months after publication send a polite reminder note. If you're concerned, submit an invoice.
- ✓ If a magazine goes bust or the editor refuses to pay you, be philosophical. Chasing up bad debt is expensive.
- ✓ You can protect yourself by only dealing with established and reputable publications.
- ✓ Listen to any gossip/warnings from other writers who have grievances against particular editors.

16

DO YOU NEED AN AGENT?

I'm a great fan of literary agents. Writing can often be a lonely, confidence-sapping business, fraught with rejection and disappointment and nothing beats the reassurance of knowing that there is someone out there who believes in you and is fighting on your behalf.

I look on the day that my agent took me on as being one of the big milestones in my career. I had been enjoying regular success under my own steam but things really took off once I was "represented". The number of magazines I could sell to doubled, the payments which I received for stories soared and unheard of riches like foreign sales and Radio 4 offers came my way. It was as though I was working in a completely different world. Instead of fearing the morning post in case it contained a dreaded rejection slip, I eagerly waited for another letter from my agent outlining sales successes or leads to follow.

Her advice has always been useful and, more importantly, accurate. And the encouragement I've received over the years has been invaluable.

It's been more than just having an "insider" working to further my interests, it's been like having a friend to rely on – someone who really understands what it's like.

Do you need an agent? Do you think your writing career is at the stage where it could benefit from a similar boost? This chapter looks at the role of agents and how to get one.

Are agents necessary?

You don't need an agent to be a successful short story writer (especially in the chummy and less rigidly structured small press world) but having one certainly helps swing the odds in your favour with mainstream magazines. Not only do agents have access to "closed door" titles who don't accept unsolicited scripts but they usually have excellent links with the fiction editors on most of the other major publications.

Fiction editors are only human and must become dispirited at the thought of sifting through 150 or more unsuitable – and sometimes incomprehensible – scripts to find the handful of short stories worth considering. Agents help them enormously in their struggle to find acceptable stories by offering an easier alternative.

When an agent sends a folder of stories, the fiction editor knows that each story has been thoroughly read and selected by an expert. Not every story in the file will appeal but he knows that each yarn will be a cracking tale, well written by an experienced author. Put yourself in the fiction editor's place. Which appeals more to you – the horrors of the slush pile or the hand-picked winners?

After hearing this, I'm not surprised that you're thinking: where can I get an agent? The answer is that, sadly, it's not that easy.

There are hundreds of thousands of people wanting to be writers and only a limited number of agents. Only a handful of these agents are prepared to work in the short story market because it involves a great deal of hassle and paperwork for sometimes quite modest returns. For this reason, agents can afford to be extremely choosy about whom they take on, and won't handle beginners or one-hit-wonders.

Unless you can demonstrate that you are capable of writing consistently good material, in sufficient quantities to make it worth an agent's while, you won't be an attractive proposition. This may sound harsh, but writing is a business and agents can't afford to lavish time and effort on writers who won't earn a sensible return.

Betting on a winner

I have heard some writers say disparagingly that agents are punters who bet on the winning horse after the race is run. They don't really want to know you until you have become a successful writer; then they are only too happy to cash in.

Personally, I think that claim is both cynical and unfair. You are asking a stranger to gamble a lot on you and if you are an unknown writer there's no way an agent can tell whether you have the right attitude and discipline to make it as a professional. You may have written one great short story, but can you keep producing the goods – time after time? You need to supply some sort of evidence and if you already have several short stories published then you've proved you have what it takes.

What does an agent do?

Basically an agent has four roles:

1. To sell your stories, getting the best price possible for your work.
2. To offer you help and encouragement.
3. To help fiction editors by acting as a filter, ensuring that only good stories are offered for sale.
4. To act as a barrier, cushioning the writer from the pain of rejection and negative feedback.

The knowledge

Because agents deal regularly with fiction editors they know when a magazine is particularly short of stories and exactly what type of tale is most likely to succeed.

Using good market research and magazine guidelines, you should be able to deduce a great deal about what is commercial but you won't have "the knowledge" – the trained nose of an agent. Nor will you have the contacts. Agents have the benefit of actually talking to fiction editors.

Expert advice

As the first trained eyes reading your story, an agent will spot flaws or see elements in the story that may harm its chances. He will make suggestions for alterations and rewrites.

When you consider that script doctors and other critiquing services charge a minimum of £20 a time, this free feedback from an agent is invaluable. So always take an agent's advice and make any changes requested.

Commission

Short stories are fiddley to handle for an agent. They may have to be offered round several outlets before a magazine bites and may generate a great deal of administration for a relatively small return. For this reason, a great number of agents won't handle short stories.

Those that do tend to charge 15 per cent commission. This may sound a high percentage but, believe me, an agent earns it. He may get you as much as double what you'd be offered as an unrepresented writer.

An end to rejection slips

One of the great benefits of having an agent is that you avoid the agony of opening returned manuscripts. Your agent will automatically send on the story to the next magazine he thinks will be suitable.

Some of your stories may still be unsuccessful but you won't end up with piles of rejection slips. In your regular up-date, you'll be told where the scripts have been offered and failed but it doesn't have the same psychological effect as handling the rejection slips yourself.

Good agents are always up-beat and encouraging and try to tell you about failures in the same letter as they inform you of a sale. The sale cushions the blow – so much so that you probably won't even realise that the letter contains bad news.

How to interest an agent

There are three main ways to attract an agent (four ways if you count offering yourself as a sex slave): recommendation, cold calling and being head hunted.

1. **Recommendation**: If you know a successful writer who likes your work, see if he will recommend you to his agent. Agents are always on the look-out for new talent to sign up and a word in the right ear can do wonders. If he values your friend's opinion, the agent will take a serious look at your work.

There is the advantage that you aren't working blind – your writer friend can tell you a great deal about the agent and how he operates. You can decide whether he sounds like the kind of person you'd be happy to have representing you.

2. **Cold Calling**: This method can be soul-destroying! Go through the appropriate section of the *Writers' and Artists'*

Yearbook and put together a list of agents who sound promising and write to them. Don't ring!

Most will only be interested if you have several – probably six – published short stories. Unless you have the potential to earn good money from your stories (£250 and above) you won't be worth an agent's time

3. **Being Head-Hunted:** If you have several stories in a high profile magazine or on Radio 4, it's possible that an agent will contact you. Pat yourself on the back for being talented enough to have come to his attention, but do some research into the agent before signing up.

Several of the large, national short story competitions offer the bonus prize of the winning entries being read by a top literary agent. This is an excellent way to come to an agent's attention. Your story may only be *Highly Commended* but if he likes it and sees potential, you may be taken on.

Be on your guard

It may seem flattering to be head-hunted but please exercise caution when dealing with anyone who gets in touch and offers to represent you. Many are genuine but some, unfortunately, are not.

Beware agents or "literary" companies who contact you making wildly exaggerated claims: *Hey, nobody's heard of you but that doesn't matter. We can sell your work by the lorryload*!

Be suspicious of agents who advertise for clients – with hundreds of thousands of writing hopefuls all chasing agents, why would a good agent need to advertise?

Beware people who contact you after you've had a modest competition win. The chances are that they are ambulance chasers. They hope to make a few quick pounds out of you, but are unlikely to develop your career or point you in the right direction. They'll sell the best pickings of what you've got, then dump you.

Don't ever part with cash for a "registration fee" or a "development fee" or pay money to put your name in some mysterious writer's directory. Legitimate agents make their money through selling your stories and then taking a set-rate commission from the money the magazines pay. They deduct their commission before passing on the balance to you. They get money **for** you not **from** you. If anyone purporting to be an agent gets in touch with you and asks you to part with your money – run a mile.

Reading fees

I have to be honest and say I'm not keen on reading fees, but I understand why some agents feel they need to charge them. Being inundated with floods of badly written and shoddily presented scripts, they must have some way of scaring off time-wasters.

The idea is that amateur writers who are just messing about will be reluctant to pay £20 or thereabouts to have the agency check over their work. Thus only the truly committed writer will submit material.

It sounds reasonable as many agencies employ professional readers to work through the scripts and they need to be paid. Many agencies offer to refund the reading fee if they later take on the writer as a client. But I'm still uneasy with the idea of people being asked to part with money. Surely if it was so necessary all agents would charge? Speaking purely for myself I'd never pay a reading fee – refundable or not.

One fact I don't like is that it scares off perfectly competent writers who just don't have the cash to squander. Why should they be penalised? Agents have so many risk factors removed for them already that I feel that going through a few scripts for free isn't too much to ask.

So, to pay or not to pay? If you know your work isn't up to par but are just looking to get some feedback, I reckon you'd be better off going to a professional critiquing service who will give you a detailed report for your money and not just a "yes" or "no". But if you think your work is good enough, then the decision has to be one of personal choice.

No-one can advise you. Writing is a bit of a lottery. The question is do you feel like paying for a ticket?

Selecting an agent

How can you be sure that you're going to get a good agent – one who is trustworthy, genuinely cares about your writing and will work hard for you?

I've already mentioned asking more experienced authors for their recommendations about who to approach, but there are other ways of investigating. *The Society of Authors* (84 Drayton Gardens, London, SW10 9SB) carries out an annual survey of members asking them for feedback on how good their agents are. This "consumer testing" gives a valuable insight, pointing out agents who have many satisfied customers and those who don't. Ask the Society for information from their most recent survey. It isn't foolproof – you may still find that you don't get along with a popular agent – but it does offer some help in avoiding anyone with a bad reputation.

Another thing worth checking is whether an individual or agency belongs to the *Association of Authors' Agents.* This professional body has a code of conduct and this should provide peace of mind for writers. You'll find member agencies marked with an asterisk in the *Writers' and Artists' Yearbook* and *The Writer's Handbook.*

But a point worth mentioning. Going for an Association member offers many safeguards but it still isn't a hundred percent guarantee that something won't go wrong. It shows that members have promised to abide by the rules – not that they've been endorsed for their hard work, skill and cleverness.

Also, membership is a matter of choice. Some excellent and highly ethical agents (mine included) aren't members of the Association. So don't make the mistake of thinking that all good agents belong to the group and bad agents don't – it isn't that simple.

Perhaps the best word of reassurance I can offer is that picking a bad agent isn't the end of the world for a short story writer. If you have someone bungle a million pound best-seller novel sale, then it's something to feel upset about. If the sale of your short stories is mishandled you will lose a few hundred pounds at most. I'm still of the opinion that even a lacklustre agent is better than none. The great thing is that once you are represented you have made it safely through the credibility barrier, and can always change agents later on. After all, if one agent knows another agency took you on, then you're obviously worth bothering with. You are no longer an unknown and untried outsider.

End note

Agents are great and it's definitely worth having one if you intend to make a career of writing or tackle it as a serious part-time activity. They take away tears and heartache, give you encouragement and put extra money in your bank account. Now, that's what I call a friend!

Exercises

Get hold of a copy of *The Writer's Handbook* or the *Writer's and Artists' Yearbook* and draw up a list of agents who handle short stories. Make a note of those agents on your list who charge a reading fee and those who don't. File the list for future use.

Make a list of your background and achievements that you think would interest an agent. Concentrate on your major selling points. Write a letter to an agent introducing yourself and asking if he/she would be interested in representing you. Include the selling points you identified earlier. This will be good practice for when you are more experienced and actually want to contact an agent.

If you have already had several published short stories – post the letter and don't forget to include copies of the stories!

Summary

- ✓ Writing is lonely and confidence-sapping. It's reassuring to know you have an agent who believes in you and is fighting on your behalf.

- ✓ An agent can multiply the number of stories you sell, get you more money for them and give you an "in" to radio and foreign sales.

- ✓ Having an agent isn't compulsory, but it helps swing the odds in your favour with mainstream magazines.

- ✓ Agents have access to "closed door" titles and usually have excellent links with the fiction editors on many of the major publications.

- ✓ Getting an agent isn't easy. They can afford to be choosy and won't handle beginners or one-hit-wonders.

- ✓ Only a handful of agents handle short stories.

- ✓ You need to have proved yourself before an agent will consider you. It's not worth contacting anyone until you've had six published stories.

- ✓ An agent has four roles: (1) To sell your stories for the best price. (2) To offer help and encouragement. (3) To ensure that only good stories are offered for sale. (4) To cushion the writer from negative feedback.

- ✓ Because agents have the right contacts they know when a magazine is particularly short of stories and what type of tale is likely to be sought.

- ✓ As the first trained eyes reading your story, an agent will spot flaws and make suggestions for alterations. Always take his advice.

- ✓ Short stories generate a great deal of admin for a relatively small return. For this reason, agents tend to charge 15 per cent commission.
- ✓ There are three main ways to attract an agent. These are: recommendation, cold calling and being head hunted.
- ✓ If you know a successful writer who rates your work, see if he will recommend you to his agent.
- ✓ Alternatively, look through the writers' reference books and draw up a list of agents who sound promising. Write to them, don't ring.
- ✓ If you have stories in a high profile magazine, it's possible that an agent will contact you. Great – but check him out before signing up.
- ✓ Be suspicious of any agent who advertises for clients. Also beware of "ambulance chasers".
- ✓ Never part with cash for a "registration" or "development" fee.
- ✓ *The Society of Authors* lists agents with a good reputation. Also check if an individual belongs to the *Association of Authors' Agents.*
- ✓ Going for an Association member isn't a hundred per cent guarantee, and some excellent agents aren't members.
- ✓ Some agencies charge a refundable reading fee for unsolicited manuscripts. It's up to you whether you deal with them.

17

WRITING FOR RADIO

Most short story writers would love to hear their work being broadcast on the radio. It's what we dream of – the pinnacle of many authors' careers, a sign that they've made the big time.

There's nothing that compares to the exquisite thrill of hearing an actor reading your story, bringing your fantasy world to life – giving voice and intonation to the people you've created from your imagination. The first time is so exciting you want to explode. You have to fight the insane urge to run out into the streets yelling at people to turn on their radios and listen.

When you listen to your work it seems different; somehow more professional than you'd ever imagined. It's as though it was created by someone else. A totally new tale emerges as the trained theatrical narrator finds new meanings and subtleties in the text that you weren't even aware were there.

It's a buzz that every new writer should experience at least once in his life. So if you have only ever thought of producing fiction for magazines, think again. Radio is the great untold secret of the short story world. Some people ignore it, others never even consider it – yet it's a wonderfully expressive and fulfilling medium which can offer huge prestige.

Tuning in

I know it's fashionable for young writers to think radio is a bit fuddy-duddy and lame, but they couldn't be more wrong. It's enormous fun, offering the new writer a phenomenal attraction – instant credibility. Nothing looks better on your CV than a story on Radio 4, and a broadcast yarn is an immense help in convincing an agent that you've got what it takes.

It even pays well! The BBC only offers a modest amount – even for a story broadcast on the national network, but the Beeb has a lovely habit of repeating stories again and again. Every time it is put out, you get a repeat fee. Some stories are broadcast for the first time on a weekday afternoon and then immediately repeated that weekend. How many magazines will pay you twice in a week?

Then there are syndication rights over the BBC's World Service and the possibility that the corporation will sell your story to another country's radio stations. I've had one tale used by the Beeb so many times that I've made close to £1000 from it. Not bad for a day's writing!

And the good news doesn't stop there. Having a story go out on the radio doesn't stop you selling it to a magazine later on. Many editors are happy to print a story that's been on the air. I've even heard of writers being approached by magazines who've said: *We heard your piece on Radio 4 and loved it. Can we use it too?*

A tough market

Now I'm doing a hard sell here – I'm obviously a "wireless" convert. But I must strike a small note of caution. It's only fair to point out that radio is a small and highly competitive market which takes only the best. This is what makes it so hard to break into and what consequently makes it so prestigious.

It isn't a closed door – far from it. Anyone can submit a story, regardless of their experience or whether they have an agent, but standards are extremely demanding so you really have to make sure you're sending in your best work. Be honest with yourself. Be your own strongest critic. It may be that you're completely new to the writing game and you'd benefit from cutting your teeth on a few competition and magazine stories before attempting anything more ambitious. But if you do think you're ready, then give it a whirl.

In this field, more than any other, it's crucial that you carry out detailed market research right from the outset. That means finding out who broadcasts short stories, what they're looking for and what you need to do to make your fiction stand out from everyone else's.

We'll talk about a recipe for a great broadcast story in a few moments, but I think it would be useful to look first at the main outlets for radio fiction.

The best place to start looking is in *The Writer's Handbook* or any other reference guide. (The small number of entries for radio work may scare you a little but don't give up.)

Of about a hundred independent local radio stations only four broadcast short stories and then only infrequently. One has an annual competition. BBC local radio stations – which are less music based than their independent rivals – tend to offer more opportunities. Of approximately fifty stations across the country, ten regularly broadcast short stories. But even then the stories must have a relevance to the locality. Some stations prefer the tales to be by local authors.

So there are only fourteen local radio stations who will look at your work. You can begin to see now what a niche market this is. But don't despair – we haven't looked yet at Radio 4.

Four play

It's difficult to talk at the moment with any great certainty about Radio 4. Although traditionally it had always been the best market for broadcast short stories, the station was drastically revamped to attract a wider audience and the traditional 4.45pm afternoon story slot was axed.

Since then short stories have been broadcast on a regular – if erratic – basis in a new 3.30pm miscellany slot, which also features poetry, biography readings and novel serialisations. But it's not clear how many stories the Beeb intends to broadcast in future and how many of those will be from new writers as opposed to those penned by famous authors.

This is a little frustrating but the station is still a partly open door and is worth targeting as the kudos of having your work on Radio 4 is immense. Not only that, but it broadcasts stories in a wide variety of styles. It's quite possible to hear a rip-roaring comedy one day and an emotionally charged tear-jerker the next.

The station also runs an annual short story competition which gives five lucky winners the chance to have their tales read out by household name actors. For details of the "Dot-dot-dot" competition it's worth keeping an eye on the Radio 4 section of the BBC web site at *www.bbc.co.uk* from late spring onwards.

For details on submitting stories to the 3.30pm slot, write to The Commissioning Editor, Afternoon Reading Slot, Radio 4, Broadcasting House, London W1A 1AA. Local radio stations tend not to have a formal submissions procedure so just send your story to the Station Manager or Head of Content with a brief covering letter.

Story length

Most local radio stations like their stories to fill about ten minutes of air-time. (Check what your local station prefers.) Radio 4 takes stories that are 13 minutes 45 seconds – that comprises a fifteen minute slot, minus the opening and closing announcements.

So how do you know your story is the right length? The easiest way is actually to read it out loud and time how long it takes. This isn't an exact science but it will give you an idea of whether your piece is near enough.

Broadcasters work on an equation that the average person speaks at the rate of three words per second. So if you know how much time is allocated for the reading, multiply the number of seconds by three. This means a ten minute slot has 600 seconds. Multiply 600 seconds by three and you get a total of 1800 words. Take off a ten per cent margin for error and you end up with a piece that should be roughly 1600 words long.

Remember that people speak at different speeds, but this formula will bring you close to an accurate figure. A good actor can always talk faster if your story is a tad over or talk slower if it is a little short. Some actors prefer a story to be a bit "under" so that they can have dramatic pauses!

What makes a winner

Okay so that's the main market, and the length of yarn you need to submit. But what makes a good radio story? How does it differ from a magazine yarn?

There are quite a few differences, but the biggest is that your text must appeal to the ear instead of the eye. It must be melodic – it must have cadence. The words must flow smoothly from one image to the next.

Chatty

Worrying about how a piece sounds rather than how it reads is a new experience for most of us so don't be surprised if you find it a bit odd at first. A good aid is to think of the short story as a speech. It must mirror the rhythms, beats and patterns of normal conversation.

Read your work out loud. Listen to how it sounds. It should appear perfectly natural – if there's anything that comes across as stilted or awkward change it. Your language should be as active and as punchy as possible, even if it means including slang and split infinitives. There's no room for jargon, passive phrases or stuffy formality.

Never say: *A good time was had by all* when what you really mean is: *We all had a great time* or *We all thought it was brilliant.* Likewise, never say: *It was decided we should leave* when what you really mean is: *We decided to leave.*

Remember, an actor has to actually read out loud what you've written. He has to speak the words *naturally* as though he is taking part in a normal conversation with his friends, recounting events that really happened. No-one in the real world talks in precise, clipped, grammatically perfect tones, so let your work reflect this informality. Don't be slovenly, but aim to be relaxed and chatty.

Colour

A radio story has to hold a reader's attention for ten minutes or more, which is a long time to concentrate on someone speaking, so the words have to be colourful and intriguing. Characters and settings have to be just that little bit larger than life. There has to be a trace of the exotic or mysterious.

You are aiming to create a strong sense of location and era just as you would in a more literary magazine piece. You're trying to transport the listener to another world. You need to describe that world in sufficient detail for the audience to picture it perfectly – from the cobbled streets to the droplets of spring rain dripping from the guttering on the church tower.

Characters must be strong, charismatic and described in ways that enable your listener to visualise them instantly. They must burst with life and vitality. Radio is one of the most colourful of all mediums when it works at its best, and it's up to you to paint vivid and vibrant images.

Not only must you create a dazzling backdrop for the story to play against, you also have to imbue the narrative with a powerful emotional drive. If the story is one of impending menace and doom, you have to make the listener wriggle on his seat with anticipation and dread. If you are telling a comic story, the sense of fun and excitement must shine through.

It must all be there in the writing. Unlike a radio play which can use sound effects to create atmosphere and put over vital background, your text must do all the work necessary to sustain the drama. It's asking a lot, I know, but that's why radio stories have such power, and can leave such a strong impression on the listener. It's story-telling at its most potent.

Plot

It's more difficult to concentrate on material that is spoken rather than written down, so a radio story isn't really the place for a dense plot crammed with red-herrings and nuance. A basic story, powerfully told, has more impact than any amount of twists and turns.

You are already devoting a great deal of time and energy to building up mood, characterisation and setting, so it leaves little space for plots that are too intricate and challenging. Keep it simple but never simplistic or trite.

A straightforward *will he or won't he*? dilemma will grip the listener. So will a mysterious stranger whose identity is kept to the very last moment or a clever sting-in-the-tail where the victim turns out to be more than people bargained for. Ironic endings are particularly effective and shaggy dog stories can work stunningly when an actor's silky tones help build a tenser and tenser atmosphere, luring the audience on towards the ambush of an unexpected and humorous denouement.

Dialogue

There's no ducking it – a radio story needs dialogue and lots of it, otherwise it will sound slow and ponderous.

Your dialogue needs to be sharp. It has to be as clever and exciting and emotionally powerful as you can make it. In a magazine piece you might just be able to get away with dull, predictable exchanges if the plot is strong and other elements of the story compensate. But on radio – with the lines being spoken out loud – every flaw is magnified. Every dreary expression seems to draw attention to itself.

Enjoy putting in as much sizzling dialogue as you can. The actor reading your story wants to be more than just a routine narrator – he wants a chance to act, to have fun bringing the characters to life. He'll relish a story where he gets to say interesting lines in a dramatic way and show off his talent for characterisation. He's hoping that a producer will hear him read your story and will rush to cast him in the next big radio play!

Pace

One of the delights of having nearly 14 minutes of air-time is being able to let a story run at its own pace, to let the mood and subject matter dictate the speed at which the narrative unfolds.

If your story is a gentle domestic tale, it doesn't have to zoom along at breakneck speed. And you don't need to dive straight into the conflict. There's room at the beginning for a little bit of scene-setting – provided you don't overdo it and end up writing travelogue, poetry or overblown character studies. A more relaxed pace is a luxury, so don't squander it. Don't be so languorous that you kill the drama or send your listener to sleep.

I pointed out in an earlier chapter that you can inject breathlessness and excitement into your story by making the sentences and paragraphs become progressively shorter and more staccato. This gives the feeling of the story hurtling faster and faster towards its climax. As this technique apes the gabbled way that people talk when they become agitated or afraid, it's particularly effective on radio.

Viewpoint

One of the big decisions to make is whether to go for *First Person* or *Third Person* perspective. Will your actor be telling the story as the hero, or will he be a distanced narrator, looking down on events from a god-like position above?

Either approach is acceptable, but *First Person* viewpoint stories work extremely well on the radio. It seems natural for someone speaking out loud to be actually talking about himself. Remember what I said about a broadcast tale being a bit like a speech?

A powerful and compelling format is the dramatic monologue. This is where the actor makes no pretence of being a narrator recounting a story. Instead, he gives a dramatic performance. He becomes a character who rabbits on in a seemingly directionless and gossipy way. At first, it sounds as though you're eavesdropping, accidentally listening to someone chatting in a bus queue. Nothing of any great consequence is being said – or so you think. But the more you listen, the more you find out about the character.

In a good monologue the person talking has a dark or sad secret that is slowly revealed. The woman is on her own because she hasn't been invited to her son's wedding; the bonus the sales rep boasts of winning turns out to be his redundancy pay-off; the business tycoon being given a humanitarian award is secretly hated by his colleagues; the man who has got a dating agency to fix him up with a girl isn't single but is really cheating on his wife ...

The more the character talks the more we realise that he is deluding himself. He is unaware of his own failings and shortcomings and we see him as he really is, not as he sees himself. As all this goes on a story slowly emerges.

Monologues are enjoying a big comeback and even if you aren't a regular radio listener, you'll probably have seen this story-telling technique used to great effect in Alan Bennett's evocative Talking Heads series on TV.

Monologues are great fun to write but you have to bear in mind a few points:

- Characterisation is everything – the story stands or falls on how strongly the hero's personality and mannerisms come across. You don't have another character for your hero to react to or to give clues to your hero's background. Everything must come from him, from the words he says. He must be an interesting character – he can't afford to be bland or ordinary.
- There must be a coherent story, not just a series of random mutterings. Even if it takes a while to become clear, the plot must involve the character in some form of predicament and this dilemma or problem must be important to him.
- A monologue must have a definite structure. A good, simple way is to begin with the predicament, tell how it came about, then move on to the resolution or the unexpected ending. Of course, as the plotline is being gradually revealed the pace of the piece must be slower and more relaxed than a typical magazine story.
- Your dialogue must be convincing. You have to know exactly how people speak. Your hero's vocabulary and voice

patterns must be right for the age, gender, nationality and background of the character you've selected. Every word he says must sound like normal conversation.

- The ending must be a climax. You can't afford to have the story drift to an end. The closing sentences must be a logical and dramatic resolution of the events. The listener must know that he's hearing a denouement.

Examples

Okay, that's enough theory for a moment. Let's look at two different types of radio story. (It would be nice to actually hear them – but this is a book!) Both are comic pieces but are different in style, pace and mood.

The first one, *Driven To Distraction*, is a monologue about a maniac woman driver. The second, *What The Dickens*, is a quirky update of Charles Dickens' *A Christmas Carol.*

I hope you like them ... I'll talk a little about each afterwards.

DRIVEN TO DISTRACTION

Now I don't like to boast. It's not in my nature. But I've always been a good driver. Not flashy or fast, but safe. You know, reliable.

I'm what you might call a motoring natural. The minute I sat behind the wheel and reversed into those dustbins, I knew I'd finally found my niche in life. It was "Hazel – go forth and motorway." I was meant to be out on the open road.

I came to driving a little late in life but my instructor said I had bags of energy and enthusiasm so it didn't matter. I also had bags of money which seemed to help.

I reckoned I was his best student. Well, you don't do 85 lessons without picking up a thing or two. He was a lovely man. Never shouted or raised his voice. Not once – not even with that business with the milk float. Just sat there rigid, staring.

I told him: "There's no use crying over spilt milkmen" but he didn't smile. Very serious man, he was. It was a shame when he had to retire like that. Nerves, they said. Well, it's a stressful job with long hours and I'm sure he must have had some hair-raising experiences. After all, not all his students could have been as safe as me.

I can remember the last thing he said to me. "You've got a talent, Hazel. A God-given gift. You can do things with a car that even the manufacturers hadn't thought of. One day you'll be famous." He never did explain exactly what he meant by that.

Well, I passed my test – after a couple of false starts. The first time I failed wasn't really my fault – the cyclist swerved in front of me. He even had the gall to say I shouldn't have been on the pavement in the first place!

The second time there was a mix-up about my emergency stop. The examiner was very good about it. Said broken noses were all part of the rough and tumble of driving tests.

The third time, it went like a dream. It was wonderful. I even got a mention on the radio! A traffic flash. I didn't know the police did that sort of thing. Gave out my registration number and everything. I thought that was nice of them.

All the other drivers seemed to know it was a special day for me. You know, it was great – they all got out of my way and tooted their horns. Some of them even waved. I wish I could have heard what the taxi driver was mouthing at me. He looked very excited ...

Notice in this monologue how Hazel is totally unaware that she is a menace to all the other road users. It's her lack of self-consciousness that makes her so dangerous.

The humour works here because the words are coming from her own mouth. If someone else – a narrator – was telling you about Hazel's disastrous driving, it would seem snide. We'd be sneering at her lack of motoring skill. Instead, we're smiling (kindly) at her "unworldliness" and naivety. We feel protective towards her. We want her taken off the road – but not to get into any trouble. Monologues are a great way of getting you to sympathise with, and even like, a troublesome character – even if it's someone who probably doesn't deserve it.

Did you notice how much you learnt about Hazel as a person – just through the way she spoke and the attitudes she demonstrated. Even as we took on board the gory details of her near-misses and prangs, her character became clear.

WHAT THE DICKENS!

BOB CRATCHIT groaned loudly, loudly enough to be heard over the buzz of the counting house computers. "But Mr Scrooge, it's just not fair! You do this to us every Christmas. We just want to go home and be with our families!"

Ebenezer Scrooge swayed on the ladder in surprise and let the highly-coloured tinfoil streamers drift downwards like snow-flakes. His light-up Santa Claus hat slid perilously over one eye.

"But we always have a Christmas party," he told his senior clerk. "It's a company tradition. You know – egg-nog, mince pies and a good old sing-song? The big binge. Furtive flings behind the filing cabinet. Secretaries faxing photocopies of their back-sides to our Birmingham office. Punch-ups in the car park. It's a great night."

Bob Crachit sighed. "For you maybe, but not for the rest of us. We appreciate the thought, and don't think we're not grateful. But none of us likes Christmas any more. We think it's a terrific waste of time." Ebenezer's mouth fell open. "But everyone loves the Chrissy party blow-out. It's the highlight of the year!"

Bob silently waved a hand around the high-tech trading floor of Scrooge and Marley International Investments PLC. There wasn't a Christmas card, a clump of mistletoe or an Advent calendar in sight. Even the usual dog-eared artificial tree had gone – manhandled earlier through the office shredder.

"Sorry, Mr Scrooge," he said, "but we're sick of it. You're the only person left in Canary Wharf who looks upon Christmas as anything more than a pain in the wallet. This year we're all giving it a miss."

Blinking in surprise, Scrooge held up his sprig of holly. "But what do I do with this?"

Bob Crachit bit his lip and shrugged, resisting the over-whelming temptation to reply with the obvious, painful answer.

* * *

THAT NIGHT, as he enjoyed a televised carol service, Ebenezer couldn't help feeling sorry for his trusty staff. Getting them into the festive spirit was going to be a problem and no mistake, he told himself, but he was determined not to be beaten. He was about to ring Bob and invite him over for a Yuletide drink, when the TV picture unexpectedly vanished – replaced by a snowstorm of interference.

Tutting, Ebenezer fiddled with the controls, but couldn't get the picture back. Instead, as he watched, a face formed in the swirling dots ... a face he knew well – it was his old partner Jacob Marley.

Ebenezer thought he was going to faint. "I-I-I don't believe it," he gasped, "you're dead. Buried. Gone. It can't be!"

Jacob grinned. "No-one dies on television, you know that. There are always reruns." The phantom winked. "Think of it this way. I've been sent to give you a message."

"A message? What message?"

"A message from our sponsor. Mend your ways, Ebenezer Scrooge. You must abandon all this Christmas nonsense before it's too late!"

Ebenezer was baffled. Christmas nonsense? When Jacob was alive, he'd enjoyed the annual knees-up more than anyone.

"Ah, but I was a fool, an empty-headed fool," the spirit told him, reading his thoughts. "Like you, I savoured the delights of plum pudding and crackers. I, too, watched the Queen's Speech and bought over-priced wrapping paper. But I was wrong – oh so wrong. Christmas was my undoing and it shall be the end of you, Ebenezer!"

Shaking his head, Ebenezer told himself that he was having an hallucination. Snatching the TV remote, he flicked to another station, but Jacob's features continued to stare at him. Anxiously, he flicked through the channels but the ghost image remained chillingly the same.

"Learn by my mistake," his dead partner pleaded, "remember my festive fate. I died at the office Christmas party, choking on a mince pie while groping Mavis from the typing pool. That nibble did for me. Don't let it happen to you ..."

Ebenezer was terrified, but he stood his ground. "You've got metaphysical sour grapes," he said. "Just because your Christmas didn't work out, there's no reason why I shouldn't enjoy mine."

At that Jacob wailed, almost knocking Ebenezer off his feet. "You're a fool, Ebenezer, completely Christmas crackers. I see there is no alternative but to show you the error of your ways." His voice dipped low and menacing. "Tonight you shall be visited by three spirits ... "

"Spirits? Oh goody, I love a nice spirit – especially that one with whisky and cream. What's it called?"

"DO NOT MOCK!!" the screen boomed. "These spirits will show you things that will chill your blood. Things that will touch your very soul. Fear their coming, Ebenezer Scrooge, fear them."

With that, the television switched back to the carol service.

* * *

AFTER several drinks, including the one with whisky and cream, Ebenezer convinced himself that he'd been the victim of one of Bob Crachit's famous practical jokes – like the exploding toilet seat in the executive loo during the wages dispute.

"I'll have to think up some prank of my own to play on him," he thought happily, as he fell asleep clutching his copy of Delia Smith's Yuletide Yummies.

He was dreaming about revenge when a hand fell on his shoulder and a rasping voice whispered: "Wake up Ebenezer. It's a spook at bedtime!"

Blinking, he sat up groggily and gazed in shock. In an instant he was wide awake, shaking. There, floating above him, towering above him, swirling above him, were three incredible visions from Hell.

The first nightmarish figure was decked out in flashing Christmas tree lights while the second wore a garish orange sweater, several sizes too big, and sported a necklace made up of bottles of cheap aftershave. The third wore only a black hooded shroud. Together they looked like a Stephen King version of The Three Stooges.

"W-w-who are you?" Ebenezer demanded.

"I'm the ghost of Christmas Past," the twinkling apparition said, "and this ..." he pointed to his nearest companion, "is the ghost of Christmas Present."

The second phantom gave a little wave.

"And the character on the end is the ghost of Christmas to Come. He doesn't speak much."

The shrouded figure on the end nodded slowly – like a coffin lid being lowered.

Ebenezer grasped the duvet tightly. "Wha-what do you want with me?" he stammered. "I've done nothing wrong. You've got the wrong bloke. I love Christmas. I can't get enough of it."

"That," said the first ghost, "is the problem. You've got it bad. You're suffering from acute tinselitis."

* * *

"LET ME get this straight," Ebenezer said after the apparitions had spent half-an-hour explaining things to him, "you're here to make me despise Christmas?"

"That's the idea," the spirit of Christmas Past agreed, "we've only got one night to save you from yourself so we're keen to get cracking. Haunting's not cheap and we charge double time after midnight."

Ebenezer shrugged. "Sounds a bit bizarre if you ask me, but go ahead. But you won't find anything in the past to upset me. I remember the Christmases of my childhood, and they were all wonderful. Lovely times, warm, friendly times ... joyous times."

The phantom made a face. "Joyous times? I've never heard such sentimental clap-trap in all my life."

It soared over to Scrooge's side. "Memory plays tricks, my schmaltzy old friend, and it's done a whole Paul Daniels routine on you."

With that, it snapped its fingers and Ebenezer felt himself lifting, being sucked towards the grandfather clock. Swirling round and round, he gazed as the clock's hands whizzed backwards and he was transported back through time – back to December 25th 1946.

The swirling stopped abruptly. He gasped, watching himself at the age of six, sitting by the Christmas tree, sobbing.

"You don't remember this, do you?" The spirit whispered in his ear. "You don't remember getting a smack because you wouldn't kiss your Great Auntie Enid. Remember her horrible moustache and how sick it made you feel?"

Ebenezer swallowed hard. He had forgotten that. The ghost pressed on. "And what about the nauseatingly cutesy pixie suit your mother made you wear. Remember what a fool you felt in it, and how the other boys used to jeer?"

Scrooge shivered at the recollection. "And what about the Christmas party piece you had to sing for all the adults. Little Boy Blue. Yuck!" Suddenly, Ebenezer felt hot. The ghost's prompting brought back a tidal wave of bad memories. How could he have forgotten all those awful family parties with his hateful cousins and grandmother complaining all the way through lunch that the sprouts were too hard for her false teeth? "Okay," he conceded, "perhaps it wasn't all that great back then, but I've had some fantastic Christmases as an adult."

Sighing, Christmas Past brought them back from Scrooge's childhood. The apparition patted his colleague on the back. "Over to you, Present old lad. Tell it like it is."

"I am the ghost of Christmas Present," the second spirit announced, "or rather, I am the ghost of Christmas Presents. The spirit of all those naff, totally tasteless, useless gifts people give you at Christmas." He clapped his hands, and the flat began to fill with a treasure-trove of tat.

"Behold," he said, "the flotsam and jetsam of Christmas consumerism. The over-priced, tweely packaged, cringe-making stuff no-one would ever buy at any other time of the year."

Gazing at the huge mountain of packages, Ebenezer gasped. There were space-age silver Christmas trees, tablemats with Dickensian street scenes, a plastic nativity scene with light-up baby Jesus, a Mr and Mrs Snowman cruet set, a Santa Claus jewellery box that played Rudolf the Red-Nosed Reindeer, ceramic cherubs, artificial candlesticks, a family-sized tin of Monarch of the Glen shortbread – enough Yuletide yuckiness to fill a dozen mail-order catalogues.

"And that still doesn't include socks, hankies, individually packaged Olde Worlde English Marmalades or ... " The phantom pointed sadly to his jumper and aftershave bottles, "the old favourites."

Stunned, Ebenezer realised that the ghost was right. Most Christmas gifts were over-priced rubbish – useless items even a junk shop wouldn't handle. He had cupboards full of stuff he'd never even opened.

Confused and suddenly depressed, he looked across at the third ghost. "Of all the spirits, you are the one I truly fear the most," he said, with a gulp. "Show me what horrors are to come."

Silently, the shrouded figure pointed a bony finger towards the television set and it flared into life. On the screen Ebenezer could see the Crachit family.

The scene in their front room was bedlam. Bob and his wife knelt on the floor, hands over their ears. All around them chaos reigned as the kids re-enacted the Battle of the Somme.

A karaoke machine boomed out *Here It Is – Merry Christmas,* electronic toys beeped and whirled, computer games screamed, and the kids yelled at the tops of their lungs, trying to be heard over the ear-splitting din.

The children berated their parents for not buying enough batteries, while Bob tried to explain that the shops were shut. The kids were in no mood to listen! Even saintly Tiny Tim jumped up and down in a tantrum, snapping his walking stick.

"Is this the future then?" Ebenezer asked, shuddering. The ghost didn't answer, but Ebenezer needed no reply. He gazed hollow-eyed at the three spirits.

So this was the true face of Christmas. The face he'd never seen. Childhood misery, cheap shoddy gifts and an electronic nightmare to look forward to. Now he knew why most people groaned at the mention of the word Christmas.

"Okay," he told the rapidly fading phantoms, "you win. I'm convinced."

* * *

EARLY next morning, Ebenezer leapt out of bed and phoned his secretary in a panic.

Glenda sounded surprised: "A flight? Today? But where?"

"Anywhere," Ebenezer replied," Timbuctoo, Outer Mongolia, the South Pole. I just want to escape this Yuletide lunacy. Away from crowded shops, turkey leftovers, family quarrels, department store Santas, piped carols and the 100th rerun of *The Sound of Music.*"

Glenda was convinced that her boss had flipped, but she promised to do her best. She rang back after an hour.

"I've managed to get you booked one-way on an Air China flight to Shanghai," she announced. "It wasn't easy at this time of year, but I pulled a few strings."

He hung up before she had a chance to wish him Merry Christmas, and began packing. Somehow he managed to block the idiotic festivities from his brain, even getting the taxi driver to stop humming *I Wish It Could Be Christmas Every Day* with the promise of a large tip.

At last, Ebenezer was safely on the plane. He settled back in his seat, relaxing, letting every thought of Christmas drain away. As the engines roared into life, he allowed himself a satisfied smile. He'd done it! He'd escaped the Boxing Day blues. He was leaving the mistletoe madness behind.

"Boiled sweet?" the stewardess asked, thrusting a small basket at him.

Gratefully, he popped one into his mouth. The sweet's musty flavour took a moment to burst on his tastebuds, but when it did he started to gag. "Bah," he spluttered in disgust, "humbug!"

This 2,300-word story – at nearly 14 minutes long – has been broadcast several times on Radio 4's afternoon story slot. (A good tip here – if you want to have something repeated often, give it a Christmas theme!)

Although zany, the piece has a much more orthodox format than the monologue, because the actor narrates a recognisable plotline, explaining events chronologically as he goes along.

The piece is packed with comic descriptions and exchanges of dialogue. It features an army of odd-ball characters, offering the narrator plenty of meat to get his acting teeth into. Much of the humour of the story comes from the role reversal trick of making Scrooge the Christmas fan and everyone else bad-tempered party-poopers. The yarn has a fast pace – with gags following on in quick succession. This speed is necessary because the author would be sunk if the listener stopped to think how awful the jokes are.

Because most listeners will already be familiar with the characters and basic storyline of *A Christmas Carol*, the descriptions are able to be short and snappy. It works well when the descriptions are jokes in themselves – the three phantoms looking like "*a Stephen King version of The Three Stooges*".

Content

I've used comic examples here, but your radio yarn doesn't have to be humorous or flippant. Broadcast stories can deal with serious and sometimes harrowing issues. You'll find the BBC more willing than most mainstream magazines to handle gritty material. Producers won't shy away from stories that deal with social problems or which pose difficult moral questions.

Explicit sex and graphic violence are out – as are sexual swear words – but you'll find most subjects will be acceptable as long as they are tackled in a responsible manner and don't feature anything depraved or illegal. The point to remember is that Radio 4 stories are broadcast at a time when children could be listening so use your taste and common-sense about what is permissible.

Get on the right wavelength

I hope this chapter has fired your enthusiasm for radio. It's a great medium to write for – and offers a whole new set of challenges. For one thing, you need to think more deeply about your characters and how to portray them. For another, you'll find a radio audience more discerning, more critical and often better educated than an average magazine's readership.

To be a success you'll need to produce material that every listener feels "speaks" to him individually and which talks with a clear and distinctive voice. Your own personality must shine through.

There are lots of books on writing for radio, BBC-sponsored workshops you can attend and helpful sections like this in creative writing manuals to absorb. But there's no substitute for sampling the real thing. Nothing will give you a better feel for what appeals to producers than switching on your radio and listening.

If you can, tape-record a few stories and play them over and over. Concentrate on how the writers have achieved their effects. Do they have techniques in common? Do they use any tricks of description or characterisation? Do they have a feel for language and rhythms?

Each time you listen to a story, you'll spot something new. The more stories you hear, the more your "radio ear" will develop.

It's worth the effort – a keen listener picks up all sorts of writing tips and secrets. So make yourself a cuppa, put up your feet, and reach for that dial.

Exercises

Contact your local radio stations and ask if they accept short stories. If so, find out what length they look for and what type of material is suitable. Tune in and do your market research. Then write a story to fit and submit it.

Tape three different radio stories. Play them over a few times, compare them and make notes of any stylistic points or techniques that you feel work well.

Write a 2,000-word story suitable for broadcast in this slot, using as many of these techniques as you can. Send it off.

Pick a story from a women's magazine and rewrite it as a 1,500-word monologue, as though you are the main character describing what happened to you.

Summary

✓ Writing for radio is great fun but it's a small and highly competitive market which takes only the best. That's why it's so prestigious.

✓ Only four independent radio stations and ten BBC radio stations regularly broadcast short stories. Radio 4 is the most prestigious outlet.

✓ Having a story broadcast on Radio 4 is a sign that you've "made it" and is an immense help in attracting an agent.

✓ The BBC only pays a modest amount but will often repeat stories again and again. Each time you get a repeat fee.

✓ Radio 4 broadcasts stories in a variety of styles. It runs an annual short story competition to attract new writers.

✓ Read your story out loud and time it to see if it is the right length. It is better to be slightly under than over.

✓ To work out how many words you need, assume that people speak three words per second, then take off a 10 per cent margin for error.

✓ A radio story must appeal to the ear instead of the eye. It must be melodic – it must have cadence. The words must flow smoothly.

✓ Think of the short story as a speech. It must mirror the rhythms, beats and patterns of normal conversation.

✓ Characters and settings have to be a little larger than life. They must be colourful – described in ways which make them instantly visualised.

✓ Aim to create a strong sense of location and era, and imbue the narrative with a powerful emotional drive.

- ✓ A basic story, powerfully told, has more impact than any amount of twists and turns – so keep it simple.

- ✓ Dialogue should be sharp, clever and emotionally powerful. Give the narrator a chance to act, to bring the characters alive.

- ✓ Ensure the pace is right for the subject matter. The more action you have, the faster the story. Use short, breathless sentences to create excitement.

- ✓ If you are opting for a *first person* viewpoint, the dramatic monologue is a powerful format. The narrator becomes the main character. The more he "gossips" the more a story emerges.

- ✓ Broadcast stories can deal with serious and sometimes harrowing issues – grittier material than you'd find in magazine fiction.

- ✓ But remember that many Radio 4 stories are broadcast at a time when children could be listening.

- ✓ Do your homework. Listen to radio. Tape-record stories and play them over and over to study the writing style and techniques used.

18

COMPETITIONS

There's something about short story competitions that's almost impossible to resist. Perhaps it's the tantalising suspense of sending off several stories and then waiting for sleepless weeks to find out if you're a winner.

Maybe it's the idea of finding fame and glory – of showing all those doubters that you are not only an accomplished writer but that your stories are better than anyone else's.

For some of us more mercenary characters, it's the lure of major prize money.

Whatever motivates you to enter, there's no getting away from the fact that short story competitions are compulsive. And with hundreds to enter and tempting cash prizes it's likely that if you aren't already hooked, you soon will be.

Since the 1980s, the number of comps has exploded. Once there was only a handful of writing contests. Now it seems, almost every writers group in the country is running one. And even the most unassuming local competition with modest prizes can attract hundreds of stories.

In this chapter we'll have a look at why competitions are so popular and offer some do's and don'ts. Most importantly, we'll tell you how you can improve your chances of being a winner.

What's the big attraction?

It's difficult to explain to someone who isn't addicted just what a buzz you get from pitting your literary skills against your rivals. The uninitiated are baffled why anyone would think it's okay to spend days – and a small fortune in entry fees – just to win third prize in a writer's circle competition.

It's difficult to explain – but ego, vanity, excitement, hope, tension and desperation all play their part. If pressed to justify my addiction I always answer that competitions aren't a waste of time and money. In fact they help keep the world of short story writing alive. Writer's circles, charities and small press magazines use competitions as a way to boost their coffers, gain publicity and attract new members/readers.

The advantages to competitors are just as tangible. Large national contests offer prizes which are easily two to three times more profitable than selling your story to a mainstream magazine. Entry fees are cheap and many organisers offer bulk discounts for multiple entries.

But it's not just the cash that's the draw. Competitions are an easy alternative to long, grinding and sometimes expensive market research. There is no need to buy costly magazines or spend hours reading through them trying to glean snippets of useful information about editorial policy and the likes and dislikes of readers.

You have no need to research your target market because quite simply *there is no target market.* Every competition is different, every judge is different, there are no fashions or trends to tap into and even the same competition may have different themes, styles and aims each year.

Another big plus is their "openness". It's not just that anyone with a typewriter and a few pounds can enter, but judges tend to be more flexible in their thinking. Fiction editors have to be rigid in what they accept. They look for stories which are identical in tone and style to the ones their magazines always print.

But a judge has no audience to pander to, no preconceived notions of what readers are looking for. He only has himself and the organisers to please, so he's more likely to be on your wavelength if your style isn't routine, mainstream magazine fodder.

For instance, you can use sex in a competition story – as long as it's important to the plot and isn't just a gratuitous pornographic romp. In fact there are even erotic short story competitions for writers who have an earthy and more robust approach to story telling.

Competitions give writers a chance to use more realistic characters and gritty settings, examining heart-rending themes and social issues in a non-compromising way. For example, you'd struggle to sell a story on child abuse to a magazine but you could win a competition with one. (As long as it didn't condone or glamorise abuse.) In general, competition stories can be a little more unsettling than magazine stories – exploring the dark, harsh and sometimes unacceptable side of human nature.

If you detest the formulaic "writing-by-numbers" nature of magazine stories, competitions offer scope for work that's more literary and experimental. Basically, as long as your yarn contains clearly recognisable characters and a cohesive plot, you are free to explore any subject area in any style that appeals. And you aren't bound by the length restrictions of the 1,000 word magazine story. Some comps allow entries up to 3,000 or 4,000 words long. This gives you more room in which to let your story breathe and more time to develop the main character and his or her conflict.

Feedback

As well as all these big attractions, many competitions offer critiques on entries. The judge – or some other professional writer – will analyse various key aspects of your work, pointing out any technical shortcomings in the story. This can provide invaluable feedback on your writing skills and storytelling techniques – the kind of vital feedback that fiction editors haven't the time (or often the inclination) to give.

Sometimes a critique will be given free. At other times the organisers will make an additional charge of a few pounds. This is an optional extra. If you don't want a critique then that's fine and you should send only the basic entry fee.

Such critiques are usually value for money. Professional critiquing services tend to be more expensive. If you study a competition critique and act on the advice given they can be hugely helpful in honing your writing.

But beware of critiques that consist merely of forms with category boxes (dialogue, characterisation, plot etc). These are ticked – good, average or poor. It may be of some help to know that your dialogue, for instance, is rated as poor. But it's not as useful as receiving a properly written individual critique where the judge highlights exactly what's wrong with it and makes suggestions for improving the way your characters speak.

If you can, ask the organisers what type of critique is being offered before parting with any cash.

Boosting your career

If all that isn't enough, a competition win can be just the type of recognition and acknowledgement you need to interest an agent in your work, especially if you've done well in a lucrative, big-prize contest where you've been up against the cream of the writing world.

Even if your achievement is more modest, a competition "mention" can be a thrilling experience. Nothing beats seeing your name in the list of winners or having your story appear in an anthology. That "highly commended" can be a real boost to your ego and spur you on through difficult times. It's a pointer that you're heading in the right direction.

Some large national competitions are so prestigious that merely being short-listed is enough to establish your writing credentials. You only have to mention your success to have most other short story writers looking at you in awe. You'll find general details of these major competitions in *The Writer's Handbook*.

One long-established competition boasts the attraction that all winning entries are read by a top London literary agent.

Finding competition details

Okay, so I've sold you on the idea of becoming a competition junkie. Where do you look for details of forthcoming contests? The good news is that it's easy to find out what comps are being run and what type of entries organisers are looking for.

Writing magazines and arts board publications are packed with news on competitions. In any given issue you'll probably find more mentioned than you'd have time to enter. Many magazines aimed at writers such as *Freelance Market News* run their own in-house competitions as well.

Reference libraries and arts centres often have details of competitions – especially comps with a local relevance. And if you aren't already a member of a local writer's circle it's worth thinking about joining one. Most competition organisers send out details to club secretaries.

One important point on which competitions to target: the smaller the prize money, the fewer people will enter. So it's worth concentrating your efforts on contests with modest prizes at first. The odds will be much better – but the glory of winning is just the same.

Impressing the judge

So what exactly is it that will have a short story judge rushing to award you that coveted first prize? What is the secret ingredient that will make your yarn stand out from the other 700 entries? There are as many different answers to that as there are competition judges.

I can only speak for myself and my own prejudices, quirks and whims. When judging, I like a short story I can lose myself in – one that has a gripping plot, charismatic or unusual characters, and a satisfying (and hopefully surprising) ending. I suppose I would describe it as a cracking yarn rather than a literary masterpiece.

My detailed checklist of winning elements would look like this:

- ***Originality*** Like any other reader I want novelty. I want to be surprised. It's amazing how many similar stories will pop up in one competition. I'll deal with hackneyed plotlines in more detail a little later in this chapter.

- ***Story telling skill*** I want to believe that the writer is in complete control of the story, spinning a narrative web that will catch me and hold me firmly in its grasp.

  Some short stories seem to sag in the middle. This is because they have no internal framework – no real sense of direction and design. The writer has worked out his starting point and his conclusion but is a little hazy about how he's going to get from one point to the other.

- ***A sense of daring*** I want to read a yarn that is different, that challenges me, that dares to be exciting and take risks. Competitions allow you to deal with normally sensitive or taboo subjects. It gives you a wonderful opportunity to write in a more realistic way about life, and the human experience.

- ***Emotional depth*** The story must be packed with emotion. I want to feel the characters were truly experiencing the upsets and anguish the plot puts them through. Because the writer really lived the story he could make the reader live it too.

- ***A sense of humour and fun*** Hey, if I'm going to have to read 700 short stories I want them to be entertaining. Sometimes the subject won't lend itself to slapstick but a tiny ray of ironic humour can lift even the most depressing tale.

- ***A sign that the writer is professional in his attitudes*** I want to see a manuscript which is well-presented and neat, that isn't covered in spelling mistakes, scribbles and correction fluid. I don't want to feel I'm reading a rough first draft or something dashed off in a hurry.

- ***Flair, style and verve*** A competition is a chance to show just how well you can write, unshackled by the restraints of fiction editors' demands. So make the text zing. Rise above the ordinary. That means especially no clichés, no stereotypical characters, no mundane scenes or conversations. Be dramatic.

  Too many people repeat old formulae, recycling second-hand and shop-soiled ideas. Don't let the judge think you are writing by rote.

- ***Plenty of dialogue*** It's amazing how many people enter stories which contain little or no dialogue. Dialogue is vital. It gives a story pace, tension and dramatic force. Characters don't really come alive until they speak.

  Make sure your dialogue is crackling with excitement. People in your stories must say something worth listening to – something that moves on the plot, tells us something new and fascinating about the characters, or which builds the suspense.

- ***Attention-grabbing*** You're fighting an uphill struggle with a judge who is wading his way through a mountain of mush. Your entry has to stand out from the rest. You can't allow yourself to be boring. A lively intro and clever, attention-grabbing title are every bit as important for a competition story as anything written for a magazine.

It's worth dispelling a myth here and now. Some people will have you believe that it's vital to do background research on the competition judge in order to give your entries an edge. They tell you to read the stories he's written and find out what he likes so that you can get inside his mind and tailor your material to fit what he's looking for.

Well, if you want to do that then great, I won't stop you. But it really isn't necessary or foolproof. I often award prizes to stories which tackle topics I wouldn't touch, written in a style totally divorced from mine. Judges always pick the best stories from the bundle – not the ones that most resemble what they themselves would have written.

Anyway, there's a strong likelihood that the organisers will have given the judge some hints on the type or style of story they would like to see win. This is particularly true of comps run by magazines where they'll be publishing the winning story and the editor doesn't want to shock or offend readers with something too radical or unsuitable.

Unless you were privy to the notes the judge was given, you won't have a clue what he is looking for. It's far better to spend your time polishing your stories to make them as sharp and entertaining as you can.

A few don'ts

Just because competitions are more open doesn't mean that absolutely anything goes. There are still some general guidelines to follow.

For a start, a short story competition isn't really a market for stories which have failed to reach publishable standard. If your tale is too unpolished, unfocused or amateurish to interest a fiction editor it certainly won't impress the judges. They'll be looking for a clever story with more depth to it. They'll expect a plot that has unexpected elements – something that makes the reader stop and think. If anything, the story that wins a competition will be better written and more imaginative than many which make it onto the pages of mainstream magazines.

And it's just as important that you don't send any old story to a themed competition. If the comp calls for contemporary stories set on a tropical island – that's what the organisers want. It's no good changing your Victorian gothic romance set in 1880s Birmingham to include a few palm trees, a sandy beach and mobile phone references.

You can't just add a few lines to try to make an unsuitable tale relevant. The judge will spot it a mile off. I can always tell when a story was written for another market and the writer has tweaked it in a couple of places to try to adapt it. Trust me on this – a judge knows when you have used the "search and replace" keys on the computer to skip through the narrative changing the *he's* to *she's* and the *horse-drawn carriage* to *rocket ship.*

Equally as obvious is when a story meant for another niche has been cut to make it fit the length requirement of a comp. It's difficult to cut a yarn without butchering it or drastically altering its tone, pace or atmosphere. You'll end up with a stilted story – hardly likely to be a winner.

Something else to avoid is using a competition story as a platform for preaching or moralising. Give your tale a moral by all means, but don't let it get in the way of the narrative. Don't bore the poor judge or make him think he's being lectured.

If there is one golden rule, it is: *write a new, fresh and relevant story especially for the competition.* Don't try to make do with an old has-been yarn dragged out from your bottom drawer. But if you're going to ignore this important advice, at least be smart enough to reprint the story before entering it. Don't signal to the judge that it is a battle scarred and often-rejected yarn going out for one more futile bout. It saddens me every time I see a dog-eared entry, on yellowing paper complete with coffee stains and dirty thumb prints.

The message this gives is: *I don't think your competition is important enough for me to make the effort.* Nothing is more likely to guarantee your failure.

Not that old chestnut again!

Perhaps the one thing that kills a short story quicker than anything else is a hackneyed plot. Judges can forgive writers a lot of things, but not a lack of originality.

Unfortunately, in my experience the same old chestnut stories keep popping up time after time. I've lost count of the number of entries I've read (and rejected) where the sting-in-the-tail denouement is the narrator turning out to be a cat or a dog. Close behind come the haunted mirror, the haunted house, the haunted computer, the haunted anything really ...

The worst of the ghost story clichés is the motorist who breaks down in a remote village late at night, and is taken in by the kindly old woman who later turns out to be a ghost. In any given competition there are likely to be three stories on this theme. Other old favourites include:

- The man who mistakenly thinks he's won the lottery and tells his boss to go take a running jump.
- The man who mistakenly thinks he has won the lottery and tells his wife he is leaving her. "*By the way,*" he adds, "*I've been having an affair with your best friend.*"
- The man who mistakenly thinks he's won the lottery and gives away all his possessions.
- The man who mistakenly thinks he's won the lottery and well, you get my point. As a rule, lottery stories have had their day and should be avoided.

Other tired oldies are:

- The wife who thinks her husband is having an affair because he is acting strangely and is making mysterious phone calls. Guess what? He isn't seeing another woman, he's actually planning a surprise wedding anniversary treat.
- A passionate romance where the sting turns out to be that the love-lorn relationship is between two five-year-olds.
- The story of Helen's big wedding day, complete with descriptions of her lovely dress and flowers, and how beautiful her proud father thinks she looks. Of course, Helen isn't the bride, she's the eight-year-old bridesmaid.
- Any "turning-the-tables" stories where conmen become the victim of a fraud, or people plotting a murder are themselves slaughtered.
- Any sci-fi or horror tale where the narrator turns out at the end to be a vampire, wolfman, Frankenstein monster, alien or bogeyman.

A particular dislike of mine is any bizarre or outlandish plot that suddenly ends: *Sorry I can't write any more. The men in white coats are coming round now with my medication.* This approach is a favourite with writers who find their narratives have lost all plausibility and they need an escape route. They are, in effect, saying: *Hey folks, the story was unbelievable but don't worry – it was all the fevered imaginings of a lunatic.* Yeah right!

There's only one thing worse and that's the: *And then I woke up and it was all a dream.* Do me a favour! This juvenile cop-out isn't even acceptable in a 12-year-old's school essay, and it's guaranteed to get up the nose of any competition judge.

Carelessness rules okay!

New writers often ask me: *How can I improve my chances of winning a short story competition?* and I always reply quite simply: *Read the rules.*

They immediately look at me as though I'm mad or have said something outrageous.

But it's a fact that between a quarter and a third of all competition entries are disqualified before they're even read because people have failed to study and follow the rules. So if you make sure that your story is presented and submitted in the way asked for, you'll already have beaten up to 33 per cent of your rivals.

So what are these all-important rules that can make or break a competition entry? They do vary from competition to competition but usually cover the following areas:

Presentation: The stories must be set out in double line spacing, on one side only of white A4 paper and must be clearly numbered and catchlined on every page. Often a competition will insist that entries be typed.
Length: Entries mustn't be longer than a stipulated length. The word limit is often 2,000 words.
Originality: The story must be the author's own work, and not have won a prize in another contest or been previously published.

Anonymity: The work should be anonymous. There should be no identifying marks on the text and the author's name and address must not appear anywhere. (This is a safeguard so that the judge will view all stories on their merit and won't be influenced by knowing who wrote the piece.)
Relevance: The story must be on the theme stated in the competition details and the work must be a short story – not a poem, play or article.

These rules don't sound too onerous or difficult to follow but people ignore them in droves. Why? I honestly don't know. Maybe writers get too excited and forget to read the rules, or leave it to the last minute to enter and haven't time to study the paperwork.

Sadly, I suspect the largest number are those who simply think rules are silly and don't apply to them. Well, I have news for them – the rules apply to *everyone*. Every time writers ignore competition rules they are automatically disqualified and lose their entry fees. Maybe I'm being a little harsh, but it does seem a rather elaborate and pointless way to throw away money.

Case study

I know that even now there'll be some people reading this who think I'm exaggerating about the vast numbers of competition entries which are immediately disqualified. So I thought it would be illuminating to look at one competition I judged for a well-known magazine a little while ago. What I'm about to tell you is typical – please believe me.

Of the 472 entries, 114 were weeded out on the first sift. These included:

- 59 people who had single-spaced their work. One entry was a solid block of black type with no margins or white space top or bottom. It looked like one of those 3-D puzzles where, if you stare at it long enough, a picture emerges.
- 18 people submitted stories with identifying marks. These included complete names and addresses, people who put copyright marks at the end of their stories, one woman who put her

name *and phone number* on each page (no, I didn't follow up on that one!) and one person who not only put his name on each page but made himself the main character in the story.

- 11 stories which had the name and address of the author tippexed out. There's little point hiding the identity of the writer if the judge can see it every time he holds up the page to the light.
- 2 hand-written entries. Not owning a typewriter is a huge handicap in this day and age. Even so, couldn't these entrants have got a friend to type out their stories for them? Writing magazines are full of adverts for inexpensive typing services.
- 9 stories which greatly exceeded the 1,500-word limit. That included one story that was 1,000 words longer. A judge will know just by looking when a story is overlong. He'll certainly know when it's nearly twice as long as it should be.
- 10 entries which were totally unintelligible. Alcohol may be a great stimulant to the muse, but please don't try writing a competition entry when you're drunk ... or worse!

In addition there were the entries that had been tattily photocopied; entries produced on a typewriter with missing or clogged-up keys; stories printed on a ribbon so faint they were unreadable; people who sent in poems, plays and snatches of autobiography; and the entrant who not only identified herself but submitted an article together with photographs.

Six competitors managed to get themselves disqualified for breaking two separate rules and one enterprising individual managed to have his story eliminated on three different counts.

It wasn't just the rule breakers who needed to have a serious think about their professionalism. I won't dwell on it, but a third of all entries were marred by serious spelling, punctuation and grammar mistakes and half of all the stories entered didn't have any dialogue whatsoever. What depressed me especially was the high number of stories where the author hadn't even bothered to give his characters names.

Competition etiquette

Just as it's vital to read and obey the rules, it's also a good idea to stick to the accepted etiquette of short story competitions. That means not doing anything that's likely to upset a judge or land you in hot water.

The most important piece of etiquette is not sending the same story to several competitions at once. You could end up with the embarrassing problem of two rival competitions both selecting your story and the different organisers publicising it unaware that you hadn't offered it to them exclusively. As well as having some difficult explaining to do, you could find yourself disqualified from both contests and your name blacklisted.

Don't think that you wouldn't get caught. Often you'll find that the same person judges several competitions in a year, sometimes more than one at a time. I've recognised the same story entered in two simultaneous competitions. As it happens I didn't blow the whistle, but I did automatically disqualify the story from both contests.

On a similar note, don't send the same story to the same competition two years running. Groups who run competitions tend to use the same judge year in and year out. He will remember your story from the year before – even if he has to read a page or two of it before it jogs his memory.

Once again I've seen the same story from the same writer two years running. What made this particularly irritating was that I'd given the individual a detailed critique of why the piece didn't work and he hadn't bothered to alter a word. The yarn was completely unchanged.

Multiple submissions (sending several entries to the same competition) are a great way of keeping your costs down as the organiser will often reduce the entry fee for second, third and fourth stories. But they can also have a negative effect. If your entries are kept together it means the judge will read your tales one after another. If he hates the first, it will colour his thinking towards the others. So even if a later story in your bundle is a knockout, the judge won't be reading it impartially.

It doesn't matter whether all entries are anonymous – he'll still spot the same typeface and layout and the fact that the paper it is printed on is identical. He will know it is from the same competitor. Usually I can tell because the stories all have the same spelling mistakes.

My advice – unless you're very strapped for cash – is to send in entries in ones and twos on different days. I know this is an extra hassle but it should mean that they all appear in different parts of the judge's reading bundle.

The worst breach of etiquette of all is to submit a story which you have already had published elsewhere or which has already won a prize in an earlier competition. People insist on doing this, but invariably get caught as soon as the list of winning entries is published.

If you're tempted to try this ploy, be sure that someone, somewhere will recognise your story and get straight on the phone to the organisers. Believe me – you'll be stripped of your prize and your "cheating" will be publicised. It's not something you can easily live down – so don't do it.

Anthologies: a word of warning

You've won a prize in a competition and the organisers offer you the opportunity to see your story in print – as part of an anthology of winners. Obviously you want several copies of the book to give to friends and relations. Who wouldn't?

But before you rush off to buy half a dozen copies, please take a few moments to think about whether you're going to be ripped off. Most groups who publish anthologies are genuine and merely want you to have a keepsake of the contest. But there are sharks around who are only after your money and it's vital that you be on your guard against them.

How do you spot these sharks? Easy – genuine groups make little or no profit on anthologies and sell the volumes for just a few pounds each. The sharks, on the other hand, charge huge amounts for anthologies. They'll organise a competition merely to give them a pool of willing victims to whom they can sell anthologies.

I've heard of volumes made up of photocopied sheets being sold for more than £20 a copy. It isn't illegal but it is morally reprehensible and isn't something that any writer should co-operate with or encourage.

I know it's difficult to turn down what may be your first chance of seeing your name in print, but if you have to pay an exorbitant amount for the privilege then is it really worth it? How would you feel if you bought half a dozen copies of that photocopied booklet – at a total price of £120 – knowing that it cost less than a pound a copy to produce?

And how would you feel if you learnt that all 700 people who entered the competition had received a letter telling them they were a lucky "runner-up" and that all 700 stories (no matter how awful they were) appeared in the anthology? Is a booklet like that worth having? It merely marks the fact that you entered the competition. It doesn't say anything about your skill, story-telling talents or success.

I had a student at one of my workshops who wrote fairly average poetry which she submitted to various competitions. She was thrilled when she received a letter telling her she was a lucky winner and could buy a deluxe anthology containing her poem – at a ridiculously expensive price.

I advised her against wasting her money – especially as the letter contained a sentence saying: *Can you let us know what lines 3, 7 and 8 said as we couldn't read your handwriting*!

So what do you do if you are told your short story is going into an anthology? My advice is to buy a copy only if you are familiar with the group who ran the competition.

If you aren't sure, ask to view a copy on approval. See how many stories it contains. If it contains more than about 50, alarm bells should ring.

Only buy the anthology if it is inexpensive, well produced and you know that it represents the cream of the work entered in that contest.

Be cautious. Even if you ultimately want six copies, only buy one as a tester. Have a good look at it. If you like what you see, and think it represents good value for money, buy the other five.

Vanity publishers prey on the egos and weaknesses of the gullible. Don't make them any richer than they already are. Never part with cash to anyone who asks you to make a contribution towards the production costs of an anthology. It's not your responsibility to see that an anthology is published or that it makes a profit.

Exercises

Have a look in a writing magazine at the competition details printed. See if you can spot a contest with small prizes. If any of the competitions have a theme which appeals to you, send off for an entry form and rules – and have a go.

If you don't have enough time to write a fresh, new story, try to find a competition with no definite theme, then look through the stories you've written (but which haven't been published or won any prizes) and see if any are suitable.

Eliminate those which aren't sufficiently quirky or different to interest a judge. Only send in work which is of the right length and style. If you're resubmitting a competition entry which has failed to win elsewhere, put yourself in the judge's shoes. Write down why you think it didn't succeed. Be brutally frank with yourself.

If you like the idea of entering competitions, start to build up a list of the ones that appeal to you. Many are run annually so you can keep a diary of when to prepare your entries and the closing date for each. Some competitions you enter will mail you the following year with up-to-date details.

Summary

- ✓ Short story competitions are compulsive and there are hundreds to enter, some of them offer extremely tempting cash prizes.
- ✓ Large national contests offer prizes which are easily two or three times more profitable than selling your story to a mainstream magazine.
- ✓ Judges tend to be more flexible in what they'll accept so they're more likely to be on your wavelength if your style is unconventional.
- ✓ Competitions give you a chance to use realistic characters and gritty settings, dealing with heart-rending themes and social issues.
- ✓ Stories can be a little more unsettling – exploring the dark, harsh and sometimes unacceptable side of human nature.
- ✓ They offer more opportunity for experimentation, self-expression, and "literary" language and descriptions.
- ✓ You aren't bound by the shorter length restrictions of the magazine story. Some competitions allow entries up to 4,000 words.
- ✓ Many competitions offer critiques. The judge will analyse various key aspects of your work.
- ✓ A major competition win can be just the type of recognition and acknowledgement you need to interest an agent.
- ✓ Writing magazines and arts board publications carry details of most competitions. Reference libraries and arts centres often have information on local contests. Writer's circles are worth trying too.

- ✓ The smaller the prize money, the fewer people will enter, so concentrate your efforts on contests with modest prizes.
- ✓ Aim to impress the judge with originality, polished work, a sense of daring, emotional depth, a sense of humour, flair and plenty of dialogue.
- ✓ Don't bother researching the judge. He'll probably pick a story which is nothing like the material he writes.
- ✓ Competitions aren't a market for rejected magazine stories or for stories which failed to reach publishable standards.
- ✓ Always write a new story for a competition if you have the time. Don't butcher an unsuitable existing story to fit the theme or length required.
- ✓ Avoid using a competition story as a platform for preaching or moralising.
- ✓ Learn what the hackneyed plots are and avoid them.
- ✓ Always read and obey competition rules. A quarter of all entries are disqualified because people break the rules.
- ✓ Don't send the same story to several competitions at once, and don't enter the same story in the same competition two years running.
- ✓ Never enter a story that has already been published or won a prize elsewhere.
- ✓ Only buy a copy of a winners' anthology if it is inexpensive and you are happy that it represents good value for money.
- ✓ Never part with cash to anyone who asks you to make a contribution towards the production cost of an anthology.

19

EROTICA

It's easy to believe that erotic writers have really got it made. Imagine having a perfectly acceptable alibi for sitting around all day having rude thoughts. Imagine being able to indulge your greatest carnal fantasies – on paper at least – and being paid for it! It's no wonder that many people secretly consider having a go at erotica – even if they daren't admit it to their friends and family. But they soon find it's not for the faint-hearted!

Get the mix wrong and sexual fantasy can come across as Carry On farce. Misjudge the market, make your sexy story go too far, and you can repel the very readers you're trying to appeal to. So spinning that sensuously enticing tale is an art. That's why skilful erotic writers are in demand. If you can turn out a raunchy tale that captures the lascivious mood of the moment and has the reader panting for more you'll never be out of work or out of print.

And the good news is this is a market where women writers equal and often outshine the men – in numbers, profile and success. Think it's worth a whirl? Want to take a walk on fiction's wild side? In this chapter we'll tell you everything you ever wanted to know about erotic writing – but were afraid to ask.

So what is erotica?

To many people the terms erotica and pornography may appear totally interchangeable. There's a mistaken notion that erotica is merely the polite, socially acceptable term for pornography. But there's actually a great deal that separates them – even though both obviously deal with sex.

Pornography is the nuts and bolts end of the market – the graphic depiction of sex that leaves nothing to the imagination. Erotica, although it will often have descriptions of love making, is much more cerebral. It's a celebration of sexual thoughts and feelings – lust, attraction and desire. Stories deal with the magic of sexual passion, the allure of the forbidden – not just the mechanics.

Good erotic writing is filled with suspense and emotionally-charged. Stories take the reader into an unpredictable and uncharted world where sex offers a tantalisingly tempting range of dangers and desires. Fantasy is the key. Erotica isn't about sex as it is – it's about sex as we secretly dream it could be.

Great market

Erotica is seen as a small "niche" genre with few outlets – *The Writer's Handbook* and *the Writers' and Artists' Yearbook* give information on only a handful of "adult" publications. However, look elsewhere and you'll find a number of magazines here and abroad which regularly print steamy stories, specialist erotica short story competitions and publishers who bring out anthologies of sexual fantasies.

It's not the sort of thing you'd probably want to ask about at your local reference library or writers' circle, but don' t worry – you can research this fascinating market without blushes. A quick skim through the Internet reveals a number of magazine outlets both here and in America.

A particularly useful web site is run by the *Erotica Readers Association (ERA)* – which offers a wealth of market information and writing hints. As well as guideline details for erotic magazines and publishers, it tells writers when particular publications are actively seeking submissions. There's a gallery of steamy stories and poems, so you can get an idea of what is suitable. The web address is: *http://www.erotica-readers.com/*

Embarrassed?

So could you write erotica? If you're someone who blushes when you read something risqué and X-rated films have you rushing to switch channels, then the answer, quite simply, is no. But what if you like to think of yourself as modern, liberated and easy going? Surely, penning a few sizzling sex scenes won't present many problems?

The answer is probably yes, but it's a good idea to make sure that embarrassment doesn't creep up behind you. Be honest with yourself. Are you *really* as liberated as you'd like to believe? It's difficult to write stories of wild, abandoned sex and hedonistic indulgence if secretly you disapprove of the characters or what they are getting up to. You have to be totally relaxed about the idea of describing lustful couplings, or some hint of your squeamishness and discomfort will show through, no matter how well you try to hide it.

The best way to find out is to have a go, and see how it feels. Just write for yourself. Don't worry about showing it to anyone else or what they might say. See if you find erotic writing fun or if it makes you squirm. You may find that you're not cut out for steamy storylines and describing naked antics, but then again ... you might just discover that there's a racy writer lurking inside you.

What will the neighbours say?

A lot of people say they'd like to have a go at writing adult material but are scared of what people might think of them.

Well, that's perfectly understandable. It's a very British attitude to imagine that there's something strange or perverted about talking about sex – never mind actually writing about it. But you'd be surprised at the ordinary, respectable individuals working in this genre.

You don't have to be a sex maniac to write erotic stories. Just because you have your leading characters indulging in raunchy romps in exotic locations it doesn't mean that you do the same in reality. Just like any other kind of writing, you can use your imagination. After all, if you were getting up to all that sort of naughtiness you wouldn't have time to turn out short stories! I know this will come as a disappointment to some people who'd rather hoped that erotic writing would offer them the excuse to indulge in a little "research"!

But if you're seriously worried about what people will say – don't tell them. It's none of their business. And don't worry about someone spotting your name in a magazine and blowing the whistle on you. This is one of the few occasions when using a pen-name is both sensible and permissible. It can be a secret between you and the editor ... the vicar need never know.

Challenging genre

There's a misconception that erotica is somehow easier to write than other forms of fiction. Some people imagine they can get away with shoddy, badly constructed work, as long as it has lots of sex in it. Nothing could be further from the truth. In fact, it's one of the most demanding types of story-telling.

Erotic writing is about creating atmosphere, tension and sexual frisson. This requires a subtle, skilful touch. It's the anticipation and titillation that makes a story work – not a graphic description of the acrobatic antics. In fact, it's quite possible to write an erotic story where sex never takes place – it's the promise of intimacy that drives along the story. The art is in creating a powerful effect with a gentle touch. The more subtle the sex – the more it's a turn-on. The scene where a woman slowly teases a stranger by seductively licking her lips can be far more powerful than a straight description of their lovemaking afterwards.

As well as a gentle touch, you must be able to maintain the balance between fantasy and credibility and give the reader intriguing characters that he can care about, a gripping and unusual setting, and blistering dialogue that builds up the sensuous mood.

There are only a few basic plot set-ups so the writer has to be extremely imaginative to keep devising fresh, new, lively settings and conflicts. The idea of an erotic story may be to show two (or more!) people having sex but you need to make the reader feel that he's never read anything like your tale before. The mixture must be new and ingenious. There's no room for formula writing. Each element must be original and sensual.

Think sexy!

Perhaps the most difficult part of erotic writing is getting yourself into the right frame of mind. It may be a doddle to think sexy thoughts after a romantic candlelit dinner and a couple of bottles of wine, but putting yourself into an amorous frame of mind to order is quite another thing – especially on a wet Monday morning. Try crafting a sheet-melting fantasy when you've run out of milk, got a dentist's appointment in the afternoon and you've just washed the kids' PE kit. Life is full of petty distractions and hassles – all designed to remind you that reality is many things but rarely sexy.

To be able to write erotica that escapes the mundane world, you have to escape that world as well. So, plan to write at a time when things are quiet in the house – early in the morning, late at night or when everyone else is out. Find somewhere that, even if it isn't sexy, has a romantic or *hidden away* feel. It's better to write erotica in a bedroom than at the kitchen table. Clear your mind of everyday troubles and annoyances. Allow yourself a little time for nothing but fantasy and day-dreaming.

Be prepared for the occasional frustration (in the writing sense). Things don't always run smoothly. Thinking up sexy scenarios and images is one thing. But bringing them to life is another. They don't always survive the journey to the page. What seems a sensuous idea in your head can seem odd or cold when translated into words. Fantasy can easily become French farce. Erotica is about magic, and spells can be broken.

Setting

The magic starts with the right setting. It's important that you come up with a location for your story that lends itself to sexual opportunities.

That doesn't just mean a place that's quiet and discreet where characters can jump on each other in a mad passion. It means coming up with a location that is sexually charged – where there's a feeling of lust, desire and danger in the air; a place where readers can believe wanton abandon is just one chance encounter away.

Make your location as exotic, intriguing or glamorous as possible. Penthouse bedrooms, luxury hotels, yachts, casinos, tropical islands, a Bedouin's oasis encampment all have a sultry, sensuous feel. Place your tale in any of these locations and half the spell-weaving work is already done. Set your erotic story in a fish market and you have an uphill struggle.

Perhaps the most sexually charged settings are "power" situations – stories set in places where important decisions are made, where power, fame and glory are there for the taking. Strong, influential people are sexy – especially when they have a cold, ruthless side to their nature. Fame is an aphrodisiac. Rich, reckless characters who don't care about convention ooze sensual danger.

So set your erotic encounters in the boardroom of a multinational, the changing rooms of a Premier League football club, the private offices of a Government minister, or the polo stables of a large country mansion and you're guaranteed a story that will crackle.

Then there is the darker side of power ... that hint of corruption, evil and vice. The dominance of a policeman over a suspect, the menace of a gangster, the jailer with desires who turns a lustful eye on his prisoners. Any situation where one person has command over another has sexual sub-text. Any story set in a place of confinement has carnal overtones. Use this latent sexual energy to make your tale a stunner.

One point to remember about settings. You want your story to be as refined as possible so avoid the squalid and the seedy. In real life people may have sex in toilets, but it's not the stuff of elegant erotic dreams ... even if the toilet is on Concorde.

Era

The second stage in creating the magic is deciding *when* you should set your story – what period or era you should choose. It's perfectly acceptable to have contemporary tales, but you might – like many writers – feel that the past is always more romantic, more mysterious than the present. It offers morals and settings less familiar to a modern audience.

Certainly there are eras when sex was very much "on the agenda" – from the libidinous intrigues of the eighteenth century French Royal Court to the free love days of the hippy sixties. Even a period like the stern and proper Victorian Age offers huge sexual potential. Society was supposed to have been very respectable then, but underneath bubbled a forbidden frenzy of lust.

Without doubt, the biggest attraction of a historical setting is the scope to have your female characters dressed in any manner of enticing garments. From bosom-heaving gowns to figure-hugging basques and corsets, historical women have a dazzling array of erotic clothing to model. They even get to indulge in sexual escapades at large country house balls where their identity is kept secret behind discreet masks.

On a more comic note, you may think that the past is better for your story if you intend to write about the corruption of innocence and the seduction of an unwary virgin. Readers may be a bit cynical about your evil seducer finding any girl who is sexually naive in this day and age!

Mood

The third element is mood. When you write an erotic story you should create a mood of danger and excitement, whisking the reader away to a sexual fantasy world. You cast a spell and then have to do everything in your power to make sure that spell remains unbroken.

The biggest stumbling block can be a writer using language which is inappropriate, or which grates or seems incongruous. There's no point spending a lot of time and energy creating a poetic wonderland where angelic figures flit majestically from scene to scene if you suddenly have one character refer to the other as *a plonker*. It destroys the atmosphere in an instant. So does language that is obviously modern in a period tale. No mannered Victorian melodrama can survive the heroine uttering the immortal words: "*Leave it out, will you*", or "*Give me a break*".

It's not just the lyrical feel of a story that can be damaged by a bad choice of language. You can make readers feel uneasy and disgusted if you use expressions which are uncouth or offensively earthy.

The biggest danger area is how the writer describes his characters' sexual behaviour and the various parts of their bodies. Be too graphic or use playground slang and the piece will seem seedy. Be too polite in your choice of expressions and the story will be twee and risks being unintentionally amusing.

You have to strike a balance. Read your work aloud. Do the descriptions of love-making sound coarse, clinical or strait-laced? If they sound odd or ugly, experiment with different expressions. See if you can alter the tone and feel until you're happy with it. Read erotic magazines and books to get an idea of what words are acceptable and which are frowned on. Study how different writers cope with the problem. If you like the language one author uses, see if you can emulate it – but not slavishly.

Sexual swear words are a particularly difficult problem. Years ago the use of a four-letter word would have had great impact and shock value but repeated overuse has dulled the effect. Sometimes it seems that writers feel they must litter their work with expletives to give it a spurious street cred.

My advice is to leave swearing and sexual insults out of your writing. A good erotic tale can survive quite happily without it. There's no need to dot obscenities in your narration or to have characters who are foul mouthed. Erotica – like love making – should be beautiful.

Plot

The last main element of a good sexy read is a gripping plot. Even though the purpose of an erotic story is to be arousing, it must hold together as an entertaining narrative. Descriptions of sweaty sheets and naked bodies are not enough. An exciting, fast-paced, incident-packed plot is essential. And that plot has to be brimming over with conflict.

Perhaps your protagonists initially hate each other but can't quite resist the chemistry that attracts them on a sexual level. They could be rivals for promotion, a policewoman and the criminal she has vowed to bring to justice, the master of the hunt and the girl protestor who clash in a country lane or two ruthless cut-throat negotiators staring at each other over a boardroom table.

Perhaps they come from differing backgrounds or ages and society would be scandalised by their relationship – the rich older woman and the poor teenager who looks after her garden. The respectable middle aged businessman and the young lap dancer determined to break out of her seedy life. Perhaps their intimacy will hurt others they care about – the lovers may both be married but unable to fight against the attraction they feel. The scope for gripping plots is huge – there are countless variations on these *love/hate* and *forbidden love* storylines, and lots of other dramatic themes to explore.

The most important point to remember is that the sex must be crucial to the plot. It must be at the heart of the narrative, acting as the engine that powers the central conflict. It can't just be an extra ingredient bolted on to an otherwise ordinary story to give it some spurious titillation factor.

Desire, sexual obsession and forbidden passion must be what motivates your characters to act as they do. It must make them live beyond a mundane, everyday existence. Lust makes them surrender to their deepest, most hidden fantasies – betraying their friends or abandoning their responsibilities or acting in a self-destructive, reckless or extreme way. If the plot isn't about the effects of a sexual encounter or attraction then it really isn't an erotic story.

Be plausible

Fantasy and escapism are at the heart of this genre, but stories must still be credible. Readers must be able to think: *Yes, in certain circumstances that could have happened.*

There is no point in having an acne-faced, bad-breathed, computer geek who lives on pot noodles being pestered day and night by sex-starved international supermodels. It's just not believable. (Sorry, computer geeks!) Neither is the idea of someone who is overweight, middle-aged and balding having an inexplicable, lust-inducing power over the opposite sex. He might like to dream that he has but it isn't likely.

Don't ask us to accept the improbable. If you are telling us that your character is an irresistible love god or has hair-singeing romantic encounters, he or she must be physically attractive. They must be the kind of glamorous or charismatic person we believe could have earth-shattering sex.

And they must have sexual incidents that seem possible. They must end up in bed (or anywhere else) in a plausible way. The manager of a supermarket might take a fancy to one of the check-out girls and she might be similarly attracted to him. After the store has closed they might cement their new-found friendship between the freezer cabinets. I'm sure it's happened somewhere at some time. But the reader will find it difficult to accept it if he simply grabs the woman in the middle of the supermarket's Saturday morning rush. Without a word, they start rolling around the floor grunting and tearing off each other's clothes while hundreds of shoppers step over them. No-one in real life would act like this ... at least, sadly, no-one I know.

Use your imagination to the full, but keep within the bounds of possibility. And avoid the more obvious hackneyed set-ups. As one erotic magazine advises: *Try hard to avoid The Norm wherein the narrator, who typically 'never used to believe those stories in magazines' suddenly, and implausibly, meets their dream sexual partner at the door saying they have come to borrow a cup of sugar/mend the video/ask directions; and promptly bonks their lights out.*

How much sex?

Most mainstream film-makers know that a little sex can do wonders to spice up an otherwise routine movie, but they also know that unrelenting scenes of sexual escapades soon become a turn-off. That's why they carefully calculate just how many raunchy scenes to include, and how long and explicit these scenes should be.

The writer of erotic stories has to exercise the same amount of judgement on how much sex to include. Too little and the piece won't sizzle, too much and it becomes static, repetitive and boring.

A good rule to use is: aim for the maximum titillation from the minimum amount of sex. Don't devalue the currency. Make the reader wait for the action. Develop the mood. Build up the suspense and tension.

Beware of taboos

Many erotic magazines have a fairly liberal idea of what you can put into a short story. But even they have their own taboos and it's important that you know just where they draw the line.

That's why doing market research is so vital. Find out what sexual practices are acceptable and which aren't. Read erotic magazines and study the type of stories they print. Send off for contributor's guidelines, then read and digest these thoroughly. They set out in clearly understood terms how explicit you can be without descending into depravity. Here are a few examples:

The guidelines for one magazine state: *Please note that although there are few restrictions on content, we do not publish material involving incest, under-age sex, bestiality, necrophilia or non-consensual sex.*

Another says: *We are not allowed to print stories which deal with anything illegal, including under-age sex, anal sex, incest, bestiality and anything which features extreme violence or appears to glorify rape or the use of force. Stories with a gay or lesbian theme and those which deal with mild bondage or SM are acceptable, as long as it is made clear that both partners are willing participants.*

Erotica should be sexy, not scandalous or puriently salacious. Stories should fizz, not sicken or shock. Perhaps one of the greatest differences between pornography and erotica is the attitude of writers towards women. In pornography females are objects of lust to be used and abused. In erotica they are empowered – fully equal partners in sexual acts who enjoy themselves, indulge their own desires and make their own decisions. No women should ever be afraid, injured or coerced.

Viewpoint

Erotic tales offer many choices of viewpoint. You can tell the story through the eyes of either sexual partner (or from the perspective of any of the three or more partners if it's a very raunchy read indeed!)

In a seduction yarn you can create totally different effects according to whether you have the seducer as the narrator or his or her victim. For instance, you might find it an enjoyable "twist" to start off the story with the man boasting of how he cleverly set about trapping the gorgeous girl he desired. Later on, you could switch viewpoints to have the female character reveal that not only did she know that she was being trapped, she'd been secretly waiting for the man to make his move and was getting bored that he took so long. Remember that there's scope in erotica for humour, as long as the comedy doesn't ruin the sexy mood.

A great deal of adult material is written especially for women, so you may decide that it's a good idea to always make the woman the main character. This would help get round any feelings that the sex scenes being described are purely for male pleasure.

First person stories written in a confessional style are popular. These have the main character saying: "*I can hardly believe it. I never thought I could be so wild and abandoned.*" Magazines are very keen on first person yarns, but that's no excuse for being crass. One editor warns: *Please note that any story that begins 'Hi readers, my name's Mandy, I'm 19 years old with blonde hair, big boobs and full luscious lips just made for sin' will be returned without exception.*

Ideas

Okay, so you think you'll have a bash at penning an adult tale. Great – but where can you go to get ideas? You can hardly ask your friends and work-mates for suggestions.

Don't worry, there are plenty of places where you can look for inspiration. Newspapers, especially Sunday newspapers, are always packed with real life tales of sleaze and shame. Change a few details and hey presto!

There's also plenty of material to be found in the readers' letters and problem pages of racier women's magazines. Then there's the real life confession tales to plunder. Two minutes watching a Jerry Springer-style TV talk show (*My stripper girlfriend ran off with my transvestite cousin*) will give you enough material to last a lifetime. That's if you don't end up with terminal depression about the sorry state some people get their lives into.

Exercises

Take a romantic story from a women's magazine and spice it up by including two short sex scenes of about 300 words each.

Look through a racier tabloid Sunday paper and make a note of any item in the news or features section that could be turned into an erotic tale. Then write it up as a 1,000-word short story.

Make a list of twelve unusual and sensuous locations where you could set a sexy yarn. Think up a basic dramatic set-up for each, with characters. Write up one of these into a 1,500-word tale.

Write a story (approx 1,000 words) where two strangers are immensely attracted to each other but although they want to, they don't actually have sex. Make it sizzle.

Summary

- ✓ Skilful erotic writers are in demand. If you can turn out a slick, raunchy tale you'll never be out of work.
- ✓ This is one market where women writers equal and often outshine the men – in numbers, profile and success.
- ✓ Erotica celebrates sexual thoughts and feelings. Stories deal with the magic of passion, not just the mechanics of love-making.
- ✓ Fantasy is the key. It isn't about sex as it is – it's about sex as we'd dream it could be.
- ✓ You can find out about publishing opportunities or competitions by joining *The Erotic Readers Association*.
- ✓ Make sure you are comfortable writing erotica, because any embarrassment or prudishness will show through.
- ✓ If you are worried what people will think, use a pen-name to conceal your identity.
- ✓ Some authors imagine that they can produce shoddy, badly constructed work, as long as it has lots of sex. In fact, erotica is very demanding.
- ✓ It's about creating atmosphere, tension and sexual frisson. This needs a light, subtle touch, balancing fantasy and credibility.
- ✓ There are only a few basic plots so the writer has to be very imaginative to keep devising fresh, lively settings and conflicts.
- ✓ Choose locations where there's a feeling of lust, desire and danger in the air. The more exotic, intriguing or glamorous the better.

- ✓ The most sexually charged settings are stories involving rich, famous or influential people.
- ✓ Any situation where one person has command over another has sexual sub-text. Any story which is set in a place of confinement has carnal overtones.
- ✓ Avoid the squalid and the seedy.
- ✓ A historical setting lets your female characters dress in enticing garments and costumes.
- ✓ Don't break the mood with inappropriate language. You can make readers uneasy by being uncouth or offensively earthy.
- ✓ An erotic story is arousing, but it must hold together as an entertaining narrative. An exciting, fast-paced, incident-packed plot is essential.
- ✓ Characters must be glamorous or charismatic and they must have sexual incidents that seem possible.
- ✓ Strike a balance on how much sex to include. Too little and the piece won't sizzle, too much and it will become static, repetitive and boring.
- ✓ Know what topics are taboo. Read guidelines and study erotic magazines. Violence and illegal sexual acts won't be permissible.
- ✓ Always make the woman the main character. First person stories written in a "confessional" style are always popular.
- ✓ Look for ideas and inspiration on TV, in Sunday newspapers and in the readers' letters and problem pages of racier women's magazines.

20

SCI-FI AND FANTASY

Science fiction has always had a cult following but suddenly it's gone mainstream and it's taking off like a rocket.

No longer is sci-fi seen as the realm of a few adolescent *Doctor Who* fans and spaced out *Trekkies*. It's bold, exciting, headline grabbing big business. Publishers, movie-makers and TV companies have discovered that there's a huge demand for intergalactic drama and are going all-out to satisfy it.

This is great news for short story writers. With hundreds of small press magazines here and in America, plus a plethora of e-zines on the web, the sci-fi market is vast. And not only do these magazines hungrily gobble up floods of stories but the editors actively seek out new writers to nurture.

As many well-known science fiction novelists have already proved, these small press publications can provide an ideal launching pad for a full-time career. And as they move on, there's always room for new talent.

So if you have a vivid imagination, a willingness to try new ideas and a sense of wonder and awe about the future, this is the genre to be in.

Dispelling the myths

Sci-fi offers you the chance to let your imagination run free. There are no limits to where you can take readers in space and time. There are no restrictions on what wild characters you can create or what amazing adventures they can have. It's the ultimate dream playground for authors with flair, verve and daring.

But sadly, not all new writers see sci-fi as being the thing for them. Some are put off because of silly misconceptions. The one most often voiced by women is that the genre is the sole preserve of male writers. It's a remark I frequently hear at writer's circles, but believe me – it's just not true.

Have a look in your local bookshop. You will see that a sizeable number of the authors in the sci-fi section are female. They fill the best-seller lists. For example, Anne McCaffrey, author of the popular *Dragon-riders of Pern* series, has penned 75 blockbusters. Fantasy writer Wendy Pini, author of the *Elf Quest series*, has had 41 chart-toppers, and *Star Trek* writer Diane L. Carey has written 29 best-sellers. Many other women authors have more than ten top-selling sci-fi books to their credit.

And it's the same in the magazine world. Women regularly write for science fiction publications and several edit them. So much for male domination!

Another comment I hear is that science fiction is trite and childish. Admittedly, some small press publications seem to feature lurid covers and quirky names but look beyond the comic book exteriors and you'd be surprised. They contain a lot of serious, highly polished writing dealing with contemporary issues in a thoughtful and challenging way. Their authors ask searching questions about how we live and the values we uphold.

What about the notion that sci-fi is read only by the sad and friendless; by people who can't cope in relationships or get along in the real world?

Well, do your homework and you'll find it's read – and written – by normal, everyday people from a variety of ages and backgrounds. It's even read by glamorous, sexy people, whose preoccupation with heavenly bodies goes no further than eyeing up the talent in their local nightclub.

As for the dismissive remark that it's only about little green men and space rockets – that couldn't be more wrong. Sci-fi has always been about people: how we are, how we ought to live and our relationships with each other. Far from being obsessed with strange, unworldly beings, it's the story-telling genre most preoccupied with our humanity.

The stories may be set in far-off galaxies or in the distant future but the themes and emotions are the same mix you'd find in any thriller, romance story or kitchen sink drama. Tales deal with love, hate, fear, pride, vanity, deceit, ambition, betrayal, idealism, corruption ... death and despair, birth and hope.

After all, people will always be people – even in 300 years time. They'll laugh and cry, strive for a better life, fall prey to temptation, be swept away by passion, tell lies and bear bitter grudges. Human nature will always provide plenty of story-telling opportunities – without a robot, a ray-gun or a warp drive in sight.

So if you want to write "serious" stories about "real" people you've found just the market to target.

Hidden meanings

One of the great things about science fiction is that it dares to ask questions that society isn't ready to face head on. That makes writing in this genre so stimulating.

Back in the 1950s science fiction echoed mankind's fear of nuclear power and the spectre of the Cold War igniting into global atomic conflict. This was best illustrated in the 1951 film *The Day The Earth Stood Still* when a messenger from another cosmos came to warn mankind that unless we learnt to live in peace we'd be destroyed as a danger to other planets.

And in the 1960s, *Star Trek* stunned audiences by tackling the American race issue. The episode *Let That Be Your Final Battlefield* had two aliens determined to destroy each other for no other reason than their skin colouring differed. (One was black down his left side and white down his right. His enemy was the mirror image.) This powerful episode showed the stupidity and futility of black/white hostility and was a blow against prejudice at a time when no-one could go on television and openly discuss racial issues.

It's in this coded, hidden way that science fiction can be so influential. When authors pen a story in a futuristic or alien setting, they can actually be describing life on earth – looking at our lives and how we behave. You don't need to look far below the surface to see the sub-text and social comment.

Sci-fi has always done this. It has an honourable tradition of opening up debate about pollution, technology, the role of women, crime and punishment, the openness of government, the inequality between rich and poor nations, the rights of the individual, the perils of medical research and some of the more disturbing aspects of food experimentation.

Now, this all sounds very noble and grand and I'd be the first to admit that not every piece of space opera nonsense is a deep and meaningful examination of the human experience.

But science fiction is the genre of ideas and questions. It dares to challenge. If you feel strongly about social issues it offers you the perfect vehicle to make people look at what's going on around them and ask: *Is this how I really want to live*?

You don't need to be Einstein

Don't be frightened off by the "boffin" image of some science fiction writers. Anyone can have a go, even if you didn't study science at school and wouldn't recognise a test tube if it crept up behind you and said "boo".

Granted, knowing something about science certainly helps. But most authors write great sci-fi yarns without a single mention of quarks, quasars or ionised particle trails. In fact, it's possible to have great futuristic stories that contain no real science at all.

If you go back to chapter thirteen and read *Rat Pack* again you'll find that despite having all the traditional trappings associated with science fiction – secret experiments, super rats, scientists, quarantine suits and high-tech security systems – it doesn't explain a single scientific theory.

The nearest I get to it is the section that says:

Project Alpha, he explained, was an MoD-funded experiment to artificially boost the intelligence of animals using genetic engineering techniques. The idea was that they could be used in battlefield conditions where it was dangerous for humans.

Well, that has the thinnest of scientific-sounding veneers but that description wouldn't exactly get me a PhD. I haven't a clue what genetic engineering techniques really are – it just sounded good. And that's the secret of science fiction. It has been called the home of plausible lies. As long as your scientific explanations sound impressive – and the reader is prepared to go along with them – then you've cracked it.

Don't go into detail

The safest approach is to always be vague about exactly how anything works. If a reader is prepared to believe that the *USS Enterprise* is somehow magically powered by delithium crystals (which sound suspiciously like bath salts) then they will be equally happy to believe that the imperial battleship in your story runs on energy created by harnessing the enormous gravitational pull of black holes.

No-one but the most annoying geek will ever ask you to sit down and show mathematically how the gravitational drive would operate. No-one wants blueprints and a test drive.

Take time travel as another example. We all accept it as a fictional plausibility but how many people apart from Stephen Hawking really understand how time works? Who's to say what a time machine would look like or exactly how it would operate? Who's to say that using a machine wouldn't be like this?

The time-tunnel sparked into life. Christine felt herself being pulled – tugged from the present. Blinding lights flashed around her. Needles of noise skewered her brain. Her body screamed as it was broken down, sub-divided, ripped apart. With a numbing, skull-rattling temporal jolt her atoms twisted and writhed, and she was hurtling away – thrown back into the past.

It sounds plausible, but it's just a lot of smoke and mirrors. There's no science in this description – no details to get tripped up on – just good old story-telling magic.

Ironically, scientists have no way of accurately predicting what the future will be like. They make educated guesses about what the next few centuries may bring. But their guesses are still just hunches – pure speculation. This means that your ideas of how life might be are every bit as valid as the experts' opinions. The new technologies, social orders and communities you imagine in space are just as likely to become a reality as anything dreamt up by NASA.

So don't feel that your lack of hard scientific background is a hurdle to your writing. If you want to give your stories a feel of authenticity you can pick up a few buzz words from the science sections in newspapers and magazines. But you only need a very superficial and general grasp of the topics being discussed.

Think of it this way: you don't need to know how to clone a sheep to be able to write a cautionary tale about the dangers of cloning and where it could lead. Nor do you need to understand the detailed biological and medical implications of an existence in a sealed dome on Pluto to be able to write a smashing tale about how trapped or claustrophobic you'd feel living there.

Be unashamedly popularist. Write about the trends and news stories that have caught the public's attention, the topics which get them talking – and arguing. Keep a keen interest in the impact and implications of new discoveries and advances in technology. Write about the issues – not the nuts and bolts.

Concentrate on the heartbreaks of the future – not the hardware. Tell us what it will be like to live on another planet, in another time. Make the reader experience what it's like to pilot a star cruiser on the far reaches of the solar system.

Story ideas

Science fiction is a thriving market, and you couldn't be blamed for thinking that with so many writers churning out sci-fi stories that it's all been done before.

Well, it's true there are certainly no new grand themes to discover. Everything is inevitably a variation on the motifs of:

Exploration

Man becoming dehumanised or enslaved by machines

Fear of the unknown

First contact with aliens

War between races

The aftermath of natural or man-made disasters

Totalitarian regimes and Big Brother computers

Infection by extra-terrestrial diseases

Good versus evil

Pollution and environmental damage

Time travel and its paradoxes

Alternative or parallel worlds

Altered histories

Paranormal or psychic powers

But there's still loads of life, excitement and story-telling variety left in these traditional themes – more than enough to keep readers glued to the page. The trick is in how you rework the mixture; the freshness, originality and quirkiness that you bring to your tale.

A subtle change of setting, era or viewpoint can completely alter even the most familiar storyline beyond recognition. Let's take that old romantic story formula: *boy meets girl/loses girl/wins girl back* as an example.

How about boy meets girl and then loses her when she is accidentally killed? He sets about trying to win her back by inventing a time machine and going into the past to save her. Or what if he uses an untried medical procedure to bring her back from the grave?

These set-ups would work in their own right but we can take them a stage further. What happens if he goes back into the past and causes her never to have been born? What if the revolutionary medical treatment re-animates her but now she's a zombie ... or has sinister psychic powers?

We're already going some distance from our starting point. Any tale we construct will be radically different from any other romantic plotline – even one that kicks off from the very same beginning.

Let's try an "inter-species" plotline. A human boy falls in love with an alien girl but cultural pressures force them apart. After a while he realises what he's lost and sets out to win her back. But for the love affair to work he must become an alien, he must abandon everything human about his life – and his body. Is the sacrifice worth it? Is being human all that great anyway?

How about looking at the comic side of things. How would our romantic formula storyline work in a world where beings had no gender at all? And so on ...

There are countless ways of dreaming up good story ideas but you could do worse than re-make westerns by giving them an alien or futuristic setting.

There will be great similarities between the hardships the American pioneer families experienced and those any space settlers would face. The new colonies could well be as lawless and dangerous as the old Wild West – especially if gold was found on a new planet.

Then there are parallels you could easily draw between the conflict between the Red Indians and the European settlers, and the way aliens might resent human settlers who suddenly arrive on their planet. There are any number of storylines to be written on the theme of slavery and the demand for *human* rights.

If westerns aren't your thing, then the *What If?* principle will give you more stories than anyone could possibly write in a lifetime. Just let your imagination run wild. Take the world as you know it and give it a quirky twist or two. Turn reality on its head. Ask yourself what if ...

- One day, without warning, we could all read each other's thoughts? Just think of the problems that would cause.
- Aliens landed on earth and began worshipping us as Gods? How would most people behave? What would the leaders of organised religions have to say about it?
- Someone invented a "virus" that actually ate computers from the inside, gobbling down the circuit boards?
- You could tell in advance not just the sex of your baby but his or her expected life span?
- An Egyptian mummy's tomb was opened and it contained 3,000-year-old stone carvings of cars, planes and helicopters?
- A spiritualist could record the voices of the dead on to CD disks but no-one would believe him?

The possibilities are boundless, and the more fanciful or outrageous you are, the more entertaining and intriguing your stories will be.

Still looking for inspiration? Another way of devising a sci-fi story is to invent a gadget that might exist in the future. Maybe it will be a transport beam that will magically move you from one side of the world to the other. Maybe it's a machine that can turn water into energy to fuel cars. Perhaps it's an automatic teacher that puts all the schooling you'll ever need into your head in just five minutes.

See what story-telling ideas the innovations suggest. What benefits would they bring? What drawbacks would they cause? There's plenty of scope for conflict if the machines have a flaw or don't quite work the way their makers intended.

There must be conflict

See how many possible plots there are? In some ways science fiction is the easiest market to dream up stories for.

But don't fall into the trap of making your twist on history or new invention all there is in the yarn. A clever scientific idea is great, but it's only the start. Your tale stills needs a hero, facing up to a dilemma or a conflict. It still needs likeable characters involved in a drama.

Show the impact that new inventions have on ordinary life. Show us people struggling to adapt and cope – fighting change or technology which they believe is harmful. Give your story an emotional lure – a hook to grab the reader. Give it action. Make the narrative move.

Too many stories flop because the author gets bogged down explaining dollops of unnecessary background detail:

"*Warning, captain, sensors have picked up an expository lump heading right for us ...*" or characters just sit around debating the ethical and moral implications of new scientific developments: "*so what you're saying in actual fact, professor, is that man has no right meddling with the processes of life and death. It isn't his role to play God ...*"

And please avoid the *story-with-a-message* trap. This is particularly dangerous in sci-fi because it deals so much with dire predictions. It's great if your yarn makes people think about the future or the plight of mankind in the present, but don't lecture. You are supposed to be entertaining so don't load the story with preaching or a moral. It'll kill the drama.

Characters

I've already said that in the future people will still have flaws, motivations and attractions. So you should find the same variety of personalities and individuals in science fiction as you would in any other type of story.

But it's a good idea to think about what characters would be appropriate for the particular landscape or environment you're dropping them into. Rough, tough mining operations aren't likely to be home to flower-arranging vegetarians and idyllic Eden planets will better suit poets and thinkers rather than beer-swilling, curry-guzzling space marines.

To milk the maximum drama from your stories always devise characters who are shaped and challenged by their environment. Life for them should be a struggle – not a dawdle. If they have it cushy we won't care what happens to them.

What about aliens? Who's to say what they will look like or how they will behave? It's anyone's guess so you've got a fairly free run there – they could be two-headed reptiles, blobs of jelly, giant insects ... or whatever. But always try to think *why* they are like they are. Is there some logical reason for their form and does this give them a survival advantage in their own environment? If you do this you will probably make them more acceptable to your reader. An alien can be as way-out and bizarre as you want but he still has to be believable – that means he must have a recognisable personality. He must be an individual. And the more human he is in his attitudes and behaviour, the more your readers will warm to him. We're a conceited species and we like to think that most beings in the cosmos are either very like us or want to be very like us.

Personally, I've always thought of Mr Spock as merely an undertaker with half mast trousers and pointed ears ...

Settings

With all of time and space to play with, as well as the wildest flights of your imagination, you shouldn't have any problems dreaming up settings which are fascinating, breath-takingly beautiful and serene or extreme and frightening.

They can be elsewhere in the universe, in another time, on a parallel dimension, even shrunk down into a submarine popped inside a human body.

The choice is yours but make sure that you describe your location in enough depth that the reader can picture it fully and that the setting – no matter how fantastic or unusual – is plausible. And don't get so wound up telling us about this new world that you forget to have a proper story, packed with adventure.

Sometimes the most powerful stories feature a world that varies from our own in only the smallest detail. The more readers feel familiar with a landscape, and the more they can identify with its inhabitants, the stronger the empathy with the characters and their conflicts.

If you are making a political or sociological point, the closer to "real" earth your setting is the more likely readers are to take on board your message.

Conjuring up an entire planet together with the societies and countries that cover it is a daunting task, but there is a huge compensation for all your efforts. Because you are dealing with the future – and exotic, imaginary locations – you are producing stories which aren't obviously British. This lack of cultural specificness means they can be published anywhere in the English-speaking world – in particular they can be sold to the vast, lucrative American market.

A quick sweep through the Internet will show you just what a mind-boggling array of outlets this opens up!

An excellent page to investigate is *The Market List* on *www.marketlist.com*. This bills itself as a resource for writers of science fiction, fantasy and horror and has detailed editorial information on more than a hundred small press magazines and E-zines.

You might also like to consult *The Novel and Short Story Writers' Market* published by *Writers' Digest* and updated annually. This is an American publication and lists a good variety of both Sci-Fi and Fantasy outlets. Here in Britain, we have the *Small Press Guide* and the *Small Press Guide USA* published by *Writers' Bookshop* – again updated annually.

Join the family

A big attraction of writing for small press sci-fi magazines is their informality and friendliness. They are a bit of a social club and you can feel like you've joined a new family.

Often you will get feedback from other writers and fans on a story you have had published. If a story you've submitted is unsuccessful, many editors will take time out to explain why the piece has been rejected and suggest changes to it or a new approach for you to adopt. You really can feel that The Force is with you ...

Well, I hope that I have encouraged you to look at science fiction with an open mind. It really is worth a try.

In this next section we will look at the cousin of science fiction, the sub-genre of fantasy stories.

Section Two: Fantasy

People are often confused about what differentiates a science fiction story from a fantasy yarn. The line between these two genres isn't always clear. Sometimes – as with Anne McCaffrey books – they overlap. Even magazine editors can't agree.

It's a fairly esoteric debate, but I always go on the idea that science fiction is about the future while fantasy deals with a mystical past. Your hero wears a space suit and pilots a rocket ship in one, and wears tights and rides a flying horse in the other.

Now I know this definition will upset a few purists in the small press world but it's at least a good starting point to work from.

To take it a step further you could say that science fiction is essentially prophetic – it guesses at possible events that may happen either in the future or on some other world or parallel universe. Fantasy stories are like folklore legends. They are accounts of titanic struggles in an enchanted *Never-Never Land*; a constant battle between good and evil.

Spellbinding

I've used the words *enchanted* and *mystical* quite deliberately. This is because the realm of fantasy is a place of witchcraft and spells. Whereas the the main driving force of science fiction is hardware and technology, the narrative engine of fantasy is myth and magic.

In this magical world we encounter all the characters and settings of ballad and folklore. It's a place full of dragons and unicorns, wizards and kings, elves and fairies. But it's also a place of dark and terrible forces – scheming sorcerers, witches, wolves and hobgoblins.

Beautiful princesses send suitors on impossible quests, heroes with magical weapons battle man-eating monsters, and enchantresses brew exotic and enticing potions to steal the heart or courage of an unwary traveller.

Sounds a bit familiar? Even if you've never read a fantasy magazine, you'll recognise the conventions, the conflicts and the main protagonists. We heard about them in our childhood. The stories all began: *Once upon a time ...*

A blast from the past

Fantasy has been called story-telling with the three Ms – magical, mythical and medieval.

The last "m" comes from the fact that most fantasy tales tend to take place in settings which are pre-industrial. They recreate a medieval world of wooden and stone buildings, feudal overlords, craft guilds, simple woollen clothing, water powered mills, monks and manuscripts.

Characters use simple weapons and transport – a trusty horse and an even trustier sword. Justice is rough and swift, forests are the lair of beasts and robbers; cities are dark and mysterious places full of danger and excitement.

But this romantic, rustic, wattle and daub world has more wonders than just the delights of Middle Ages history – there are systems of magic, imaginary creatures and supernatural forces to make this fantastic land crackle with story-telling opportunities.

A world of pure imagination

The biggest buzz of writing fantasy is being able to create a new world – stark, unusual landscapes and exotic societies in which to explore your dramatic themes. You can devise a world where customs, religions and social orders are all radically different from those in real life.

You can even alter traditional fairy-tale gender roles. It can be a serious, noble, feminist land where women are in charge and have outlawed pointless wars and male bickering. Or it can be a comical place where Queen Guinevere and her female knights of the Round Table do battle with dragons while

Arthur and the menfolk make Camelot look pretty and ensure dinner is on the table at the end of a heroic day.

It's up to you. You are the ultimate architect. But whatever backdrop you decide on, your world will only come alive if you truly believe in it and can describe every facet. It's the small details of clothing, dress, customs and speech that will bring the lifestyle of the period alive; that will ensnare the reader.

Remember your audience has no frame of reference to fall back on. This world is a place they have never seen. Readers depend on you for all the information about how this mythical society operates, what rules it has, what people are like and how they act towards each other.

You must convince the reader that this is a place where magic can – and does – happen.

Magical mystery tour

You can have any amount of black arts in a story, but it is important to explain what form the magic takes, who has the power to wield it and why. You must have rules and they must be consistent and believable.

This means setting limits on magic. If every character has the ability to conjure up demons and weave spells, then this enchantment rapidly loses its magic – it's a debased currency. Likewise, there's little to hold a reader to a character who can do literally anything with a wave of his fingers. Where's the interest? Where's the challenge? He'll never really be put to the test or risk failure.

Just like the machines in science fiction, fantasy magic must be flawed, it must be fallible or at least have limitations. That's what creates the conflict.

There's great dramatic tension in an elderly wizard who might forget his spells in moments of crisis or a half-trained sorcerer's apprentice who finds himself pitted against an overwhelmingly powerful opponent. The reader will be on the edge of his seat, wondering if it is all going to end tragically. Is this the one time hexes and potions aren't going to come to the rescue?

Always make sure you set out your stall right at the beginning of the yarn. This is a place where magic exists – it takes this form and this is how it works. Don't suddenly invent magic half-way through the story as a way of getting yourself out of a plotting difficulty or to rescue your hero from danger. The reader will rightly feel cheated by this.

Plots

Because fantasy deals with sweeping, heroic themes, storylines don't have to be complex. In fact they can be very simple – as simple as: a quest, the struggles it throws up and the delight of the final homecoming.

The essential element is the conflict between good and evil – a dramatic struggle as old as story-telling itself. This is the warring world of heroes and monsters, villains and victims, the victor and the vanquished. This battleground of enemies and ideals forms the framework within which your drama unfolds, but this doesn't have to be restrictive or limiting. It doesn't mean your stories have to be predictable or hackneyed.

Conflict can come from the characters, from the forbidding and inhospitable geography or from culture clashes. There's room for a multitude of different narrative lines ... love lost and won back; young men finding manhood through battle or ordeal or quest; redemption for those thought lost; betrayal; greed; cowardice; the search for knowledge; revenge; rescue; sacrifice and hardship; the weak becoming the strong.

It's all gripping stuff! Themes to stir the heart. Themes to pull at the emotions. And most importantly for the short story writer, themes capable of endless reworking.

You don't even have to go for a classic fantasy theme. You can have a story like *The Lion, The Witch and The Wardrobe* where ordinary people from our world find themselves suddenly transported to a mystical fantasy world. How do they cope? How do they adjust? Do they unwittingly play a crucial part in winning a colossal struggle? Does the mythical conflict give them answers to problems in their own lives back home? There's no end to the possibilities.

Anything you say, sire

In the chapter on erotica I said that you can destroy the mood of a sexy tale by using inappropriate or crass language. Well, the same holds true for fantasy. You're creating an *Olde Worlde* atmosphere of chivalry, honour, duty and heroism. The genre works because the writing is ethereal, mystical, lyrical. The moment you introduce even a single modern word or have any slang or jargon the mood is shattered. Take this example:

He looked at the sword with awe. It was all he'd ever dreamt of – keen edged, perfectly balanced, light and swift in his hand. He knew that the blacksmith's toil had not been in vain.

See how the word *toil* gives it an old-fashioned feel? But look what happens when a little bit of modern street slang intrudes.

He looked at the sword with awe. It was all he'd ever dreamt of – keen edged, perfectly balanced, light and swift in his hand. He knew that the blacksmith's toil had not been in vain. This is a well wicked blade, he told himself.

Ouch! All the good work destroyed by just two incongruous words.

Don't get me wrong, I'm not suggesting that you have to do intensive research and dig out eleventh century manuscripts to study. But try to give your language a period feel. In those days speech was more polite and more mannered. People didn't use many contractions (like didn't!) Everything was a little more formal. You would be deferential to those higher up in society's pecking order.

A character would say something like: *I know I have not pleased you master, but if you give me a second chance I will strive my utmost to do better.*

Not: *Look I'm really sorry. It's all my fault. Give me another chance, boss and I'll come good. You can count on it.*

It's important that your characters don't sound modern, but avoid making them sound like extras from a second-rate Shakespeare production. Steer well clear of:

thou, thee, thine, doth,
she's a spirited wench
a flagon of your best ale, inn-keeper
be off, you varlet

scurvy knave
prithee
sire
forsooth
flaxen-haired maiden

... and all the other embarrassing little medieval clichés we've come to know and hate.

Everyone's Tolkien at me

It's impossible to look at this genre without mentioning the most famous fantasy story of all time: JRR Tolkien's *Lord of the Rings*. If you're serious about tackling this market then I'd definitely recommend reading it.

It has every classic ingredient – magic rings, ghostly horsemen, goblins, dark lords, mountains of fire, giant spiders, trolls, dwarves, beautiful princesses, elves. You name it, it's in there. Tolkien's land of *Middle Earth* is an archetypal fantasy world packed with sorcery and evil deeds.

Another author well worth catching is humourist Terry Pratchett. Although his *Discworld* books are comedies (and very funny ones, too) he creates a vivid and highly believable medieval landscape populated by magical – but absurd – people and creatures.

You might also like to read Bernard Cornwell's Arthurian trilogy. It's an excellent example of an ironic story told in the first person and has all the right elements – heroic battles, plenty of gore plus a cast of round-table knights that are anything but chivalrous. It gives a new twist to a very familiar tale.

To get a good feel for authentic Middle Ages language and speech patterns you can't do better than the whodunnit novels of Ellis Peters. Her detective monk, Brother Cadfael, speaks in ways that are readily understandable to a modern audience but have more than a whiff of the ancient about them.

To give you an example from *The Devil's Novice*:

"A pleasant day for your ride," he said, "though I should be better pleased if you would take meat with us."

"I would and thank you," said Cadfael, "but I am pledged to return and deliver your answer to my abbot. It is an easy journey."

Study pays off

Read as much as you can by other fantasy writers. Study how they tackle language and descriptions. And don't forget to do your own research in the library. Most fantasy societies are hierarchical and military and you'll need to swat up if you want to get the details of kinship, aristocracy and weapons just right. Put in some time. You'll find it not only useful for your writing but fascinating in its own right.

Exercises

Pick an important event in history – perhaps a famous battle. Devise three storylines showing what could have happened if history had been altered. Write up one of these into a 1,350-word short story.

Look in the paper and pick a scientific development that is causing controversy. Devise a storyline based on the fears of those who oppose it. Write it up as a 1,350-word short story.

Write an 800-word piece on the chaos caused by a domestic robot "maid" going out of control.

Take a famous fairy story and rework it to turn it into a fantasy tale of 1,500 words. Give the hero (or heroine) magic powers which he/she uses to overcome an evil opponent. Have a twist in the ending.

Summary

- ✓ Science fiction is big business. There are hundreds of small press science fiction magazines offering huge opportunities for newcomers.
- ✓ All you need is a vivid imagination, a willingness to try new ideas and a sense of wonder and awe about the future.
- ✓ Don't think it's only for men. Many women write for sci-fi magazines and some edit them.
- ✓ And don't think it's trite and childish. Magazines contain serious and polished writing dealing with issues in a thoughtful, challenging way.
- ✓ It's read – and written – by normal, everyday people from a wide variety of ages and backgrounds.
- ✓ The genre is very much about people: how we are, how we ought to live and our relationships with each other.
- ✓ It has an honourable tradition of opening debate on a range of controversial topics. It dares to challenge.
- ✓ You don't need to know any hard science. You can write about how people deal with new technology rather than dwell on the hardware.
- ✓ The safest way round the problem is to always be vague about exactly how any gadget or innovation works.
- ✓ Scientists have no way of accurately predicting what the future will be like, so your predictions are as valid as anyone else's.
- ✓ If you want to give your stories a feel of authenticity you can pick up buzz words from the science sections in newspapers and magazines.

- ✓ Most science fiction stories deal with the same small number of themes. They are well-worked areas but they still offer great story-telling opportunities. The trick is in how you rework the mixture.

- ✓ A subtle change of setting, era or viewpoint can completely alter even the most familiar storyline beyond recognition.

- ✓ Try a western plot in an alien or futuristic setting or turn a well-known story on its head by using the *What If?* principle. Invent gadgets that don't perform the way their makers intended. All these techniques can create great storylines.

- ✓ Don't make your twist on history or new invention all there is in the yarn. Your tale still needs drama and conflict.

- ✓ And don't get bogged down in the explanation of scientific detail.

- ✓ Avoid the "story-with-a-message" trap. Don't lecture or moralise.

- ✓ Think what type of characters would be appropriate for the particular landscape or environment you're dropping them into.

- ✓ Alien characters should have recognisable and individual personalities. The more "human" an alien is the more readers will warm to him.

- ✓ Describe your setting in enough depth for your reader to be able to picture it fully and decide that it is plausible.

- ✓ Because sci-fi stories deal with imaginary cultures and places they have a lack of Britishness which means they can sell in the huge US market.

- ✓ Fantasy stories are like folklore legends. They tell of titanic struggles in a mythical medieval land where magic reigns.

- ✓ The biggest buzz in writing fantasy is being able to create stark, unusual landscapes and exotic societies.

- ✓ It's important to explain what form magic takes, who has the power to wield it and why.

- ✓ Because fantasy has such sweeping, heroic themes, the storylines can be very simple. All deal with the conflict between good and evil.

- ✓ Make sure you use traditional speech patterns – avoid modern words and slang.

21

HORROR

It's frightening but true – we just love to be scared. We can't get enough terror in our tales. The more hair-raising a story, the more we like it.

Authors such as Stephen King, James Herbert and Clive Barker sell books by the million. Publishers produce thrillers charting the murderous orgies of serial killers and Hollywood churns out a conveyor belt of menacing movies guaranteed to keep us petrified. But still we clamour for more.

Now it may be sheer escapism – the thrill of peering into darkness and terror secure in the knowledge that we can step back into our safe and cosy world – or horror may serve some deeper need within ourselves. But whatever the reason, our fascination with things that go bump in the night offers a rich vein of opportunity and profit.

The horror market is huge. Next to science fiction, it makes up the bulk of all small press titles. So go on, sell your soul – if you dare to delve into the occult, or dice with the devil, a monster market awaits you.

Broad church

People tend to think of horror as tales of rampaging zombies and supernatural terrors. They remember the Hammer films packed with ghouls and ghosts, werewolves and vampires. But although the more traditional *creatures of the night* make up a sizeable slice of much horror magazine fare, it's not the whole story.

These days a scary yarn is just as likely to feature the aftermath of an ecological disaster, the panic of a killer plague, the infestation of ravenous rodents or the murderous "slasher" tendencies of a knife-wielding madman. Psychological terror is particularly popular at the moment with characters being menaced by stalkers or facing secret fears and phobias – so much so that the fiends inhabiting our nightmares are more likely to be flesh and blood murderers than decaying mummies rising from their tombs.

This wide-ranging medley of mayhem, madmen and manias means that no-matter what your tastes in terror, there should be a magazine out there with an editor eager to print your type of horror. So there's no excuse for not grabbing your keyboard, firing up your imagination and letting the demons out of the darkness.

Checking out the market

Because there are so many sub-genres of horror and the term can mean so many different things, it is vital that you know exactly which macabre magazine you are targeting. Content varies dramatically from one title to the next. In some, the accent is on sheer terror. In others, there's a barely suppressed sense of mockery and black humour.

It's up to you to get hold of several copies of a publication and study the stories thoroughly. Read them several times, taking note of how the writer builds atmosphere, suspense and the feeling of creepiness. See how much actual horror they contain. Do they feature graphic descriptions of gore or do they prefer that you only hint at the terrors? These stories are your yardstick – they're the best clue to what the editor is looking for.

So how do you get hold of copies to study? The chances are that if you go into your local newsagents you won't find a single horror magazine on the shelves. Most titles are subscription only. Many are E-zines which appear solely on the Internet. So you have to do a bit of detective work to track them down.

Many stores which sell computer games also carry horror comics and magazines, and can give you details of local clubs and publications. Second-hand magazine shops which handle science fiction books and memorabilia are also worth trying – as are small independent record shops. If you live in or near a university town you should have no problem finding hordes of young horror fans thumbing through old magazines on market stalls.

If you have a computer, the Internet is an ideal place to look. It is simply sagging under the weight of pages devoted to horror titles. A quick skim through will point you towards more publications than you could read in a vampire's lifetime!

All are seeking quirky, imaginative work with a disturbing slant. Many take ghost stories and science fiction/fantasy that is dark and horrifying. And the big plus of this approach is that most have their guidelines on the web site. These let you see at a glance what the magazines want. Here are some typical comments:

One editor writes: *Our needs are for soft, extreme, cutting-edge, supernatural stories – if it's horror we can use it. Plot and characterisation are key, with an underlying element of dread throughout.*

Another says: *We are looking for thoughtful, extravagant stories that will grab a casual browser. We like intelligent and unconventional stories that shock with a point. Twisted, angry, frightening, wild, excessive – but always still readable. We're sick of the outdated horror clichés. So, sorry, no vampire stories or stories with traditional monsters. We've read it all before. We're looking for stories to scare jaded poseurs like ourselves.*

In addition to E-zines, the web has several sites set up by successful horror writers which, in addition to giving you an insight into their work and thought processes, often have links connecting straight to horror publications.

One web site worth visiting is run by horror author Carol Ann Davies at *www.tellitlikeitis.demon.co*. This has a large number of useful links.

If the Internet isn't your thing then *Freelance Market News, Sevendale House, 7 Dale Street, Manchester, M1 1JB* often contains details of horror magazines looking for new stories. You can also get excellent advice and contacts from the following horror/sci-fi organisations:

- The British Fantasy Society, 2 Harwood Street, Heaton Norris, Stockport SK4 IJJ
- The New SF Alliance, c/o BBR magazines, PO Box 625, Sheffield, South Yorkshire S1 3GY
- The Ghost Story Society, PO Box 1360, Ashcroft, British Columbia, Canada VOK 1AO
- The Gothic Society, Chatham House, Gosshill Road, Chislehurst, Kent BR7 5NS
- The Horror Writers Association, PO Box 418, Annapolis Junction, MD 20701, USA

New scares for old

Now, it's only fair to point out that really effective horror and ghost stories are difficult to create. That's not because they involve more skill than any other type of short story, but because so many of the obvious themes have been covered. If you'll forgive the pun, they've been done to death.

Editors groan when they see yet one more reworking of Dracula or Frankenstein, or read through another dark, foggy Victorian melodrama knowing that the inevitable punchline will be the narrator's unveiling as Jack the Ripper.

Vampire tales are particularly predictable – why does that boy she's met only ever see her at night and why does he scuttle off home before dawn? And why does he never eat or drink? The reader is usually pages ahead of the author and can predict the exact moment that the stakes come out and the batty boyfriend gets an impromptu heart op.

Ghost stories follow the same well-trodden paths. In the final paragraph the heroine walks through a wall or the hero is greeted with the words: *but it couldn't have been her you spoke to ... she's been dead for weeks.*

It's a similar situation for every horror magazine editor. His slush pile will be overflowing with stories that are virtually identical, yet his readers cry out for originality and surprise. The genre is about shock but often the only startling thing about the stories is their staleness.

So how do you get round this headache when the creatures and conventions of horror are already so well known? That is the terrifying challenge.

The answer is to clear your mind of all the scary films you've seen and books you've read, and then aim for a unique, inventive approach. That might not involve re-inventing the horror story, but it does mean giving it a new lick of paint. Go for modern settings, unusual characterisations, unexpected locations. Take the reader's assumptions and turn them on their head.

Who says that all horror tales have to take place in the last century? Why must the action always be centred on an eerie mid-European castle next to a village of cowering peasants?

Why do possessed people always spin their heads and vomit pea soup? Where does it say that haunted houses always have to be crumbling country mansions? Why can't they be modern estate homes?

Be radical. Give your horror yarns a modern make-over. Make the blood-sucking vampires a group of bank managers! Show ghosts in a futuristic setting ... perhaps a haunted space station. Have an unsuspecting victim download a curse from the Internet. Show your hero turn into a werewolf because he's eaten genetically modified food.

Tap into people's technological worries. Topics like cloning, medical experimentation, high-tech surveillance, food being tampered with and mind control all offer immense potential for paranoia.

Dare to be different. Break the mould by using your talent and quirkiness. If you can come up with revolutionary ideas or exciting new takes on the old favourites then editors will love you.

Monstrous metaphors

One way to help the process is to think of horror stories as being "coded" – as having hidden meanings. They say more than is immediately apparent to the casual reader.

Take *Little Red Riding Hood* for example. At face value this is a scary children's tale of what happens to a little girl when she encounters a ravenous wolf. But think of it as a parable about sexuality and suddenly the story takes on whole new depth. Now it's a fable about how a girl copes with her transformation into a young woman and how she will deal with the men who will desire and chase her.

Using this technique, take a fresh look at fairy tales and folk stories. Re-interpret them to produce powerful new horror plots.

The Pied Piper of Hamlyn, for instance, is a famous fable of a medieval musician who takes his revenge on an ungrateful community by luring away all their children. But what if that musician were a modern day pop star with an unhealthy hold over teenagers? What if he were turning them against society?

Then there's the story of *Hansel and Gretel*. You don't need to peer deeply to see the darker elements in this cosy story. It may seem at first to be a wholesome children's yarn about two babes lost in a wood who find a yummy gingerbread cottage. But just take another look at the ingredients ... cruelty, abandonment by parents, cannibalism, murder. This sounds more like *Silence of the Lambs* than a bedtime story! Imagine how much more frightening this would be if it was given a gritty inner city setting.

Have a think about other famous stories you could use as a template for terror. I'm sure you could devise something horrible for *The Three Pigs*. What if Aladdin's lamp produced not a helpful genie but a malevolent demon? How could he get it to go back into the lamp?

While we're at it, let's look again at horror creatures. What if they aren't meant to be taken literally as monsters but as a metaphor for man's inner beast?

Or what if the ghouls and bogeymen aren't supernatural beings but just a way of us examining our own dark and violent side? Robert Louis Stevenson's horror classic *Dr Jekyll and Mr Hyde* explores this psychological theme to terrifying effect. The mild mannered doctor turns into an aggressive, hedonistic brute when he drinks a magic potion. In coded terms, Dr Jekyll is surrendering to his primal desires, stripping away the thin pretense of civilization.

Perhaps the werewolves and vampires of legend are not meant to be seen as real monsters but merely a guise for those whom society fears – the outsider, the maverick, the displaced, the under-class.

Re-examine the classic vampire myth from this viewpoint and there's no end to the way you can give gothic tales a chillingly contemporary feel.

Spooky settings and characters

Go for locations which immediately create feelings of dread in the reader. These don't have to be as obvious as a graveyard, a mortuary or a haunted house. A dentist's surgery can be frightening. A natural history museum or a waxworks is creepy after dark. Even a lonely, remote railway station has the ability to chill.

Always exploit the eeriness of ordinary surroundings. If a reader is familiar with the settings you describe, he'll be more frightened when you take his world and make it menacing. It's one thing to read about bloodsucking demons skulking in a Transylvanian castle – it's quite another to have them riding the underground.

And use the same powerful approach for your characters. The ordinary-seeming man who steals babies and boils them into broth is much more terrifying than a cloven hoofed hell creature who appears in a big puff of sulphur during a supernatural fireworks display.

The reader can easily shrug off a ghoulish devil as the fevered imaginings of a horror story writer. But when the fiend tends a rose garden and wears a suit, when he could be real, living just next door ... that's not so easy to dismiss.

Plausible plotlines

Always aim to make your tale as believable as possible. It doesn't matter how extraordinary or supernatural your writing is, readers will become more involved if you show the blood-chilling events happening in a plausible way.

Explain *why* your main character is facing the wrath of the Undead, tell us *how* he came to be in this terrifying plight. Make his predicament the direct result of a logical chain of events ... on holiday in an exotic land he steals a jewel from a religious artifact ... or he goes to a back-street sex club with an unusually dark reputation ... or he is a boss who bullies an employee so much she commits suicide – then her troubled spirit returns for vengeance. Perhaps you are going for a futuristic storyline. It could be an ecological disaster tale where the mutant survivors hunt down the man responsible for the pollution which killed millions ... or an arrogant surgeon could go against nature with an experiment which tries to cross a man and an animal. The abomination he creates comes to destroy him.

You'll find the readers more willing to go along with your tale if the motivations are clear, and if the main character has brought the terrors on himself and isn't just an innocent victim.

They'll feel sucked into the narrative if there's a coherent storyline, packed with conflict and drama and it's not just an excuse for a gore-fest or an exercise in monster mumbo-jumbo. So make sure the plot still works even if you remove all the trappings of the paranormal and the frightening.

Always have a strong emotional element to your fiction and try not to make it so dark that it alienates your audience. We want readers scared but not scared off – so don't be unrelenting in the horror. There must be a ray of hope. Don't put your fans into a terminal depression.

Build up the terror

Descriptions play an important part in creating an atmosphere of dread and unease. The storm brewing overhead, the long shadows cast by the candle, the noise outside that could be the wind or a howling scream all add to the feeling of suspense.

So always make sure you use your descriptive talents to the full but don't fall into the trap of creating overblown and unnecessary purple passages. You want the pulse to quicken, the breath to come in gasps. Pages full of slow, plodding, baroque images just won't do the trick.

Keep descriptions exciting, pacy and short – no more than three of four sentences long. For example:

The ghostly whispering grew louder; each word hissing and howling, mocking him. Douglas held his hands over his ears, fighting the pain; fighting the overpowering urge to scream. The voices swirled nearer – so close he could feel them worming into his brain. A thousand demon tongues assaulted him – insistent, demanding ... threatening.

Also, don't let the reader know he is being manipulated. Use a deft touch. Build up the terror little by little. Quietly hint at the nightmare to come – don't advertise it in huge neon letters. The longer you hold off the real horror, the more scary it'll be. Take it one small step at a time:

Doug frowned. He knew he'd locked the study door. So why was it open now? And who had switched on the light? Maria was asleep upstairs. He was certain she hadn't come down. There was no-one else in the house.

Swallowing hard, he pushed the door ajar. The room was quiet, still, empty. He scanned the corners nervously but there was no-one there. His eyes swept over to the desk. The computer was switched on, its screen glowing an eerie green.

Now, I turned that off. I know I did, he told himself, with a growing sense of unease. I remember it as clearly as anything. Someone's been in here.

He gazed at the machine, transfixed for a moment. If someone has broken in why would they have touched the computer? A burglar would just have stolen it. Why switch it on? It didn't make sense.

His thoughts were shattered as the machine beeped at him. He had an E-mail. Touching the keyboard gingerly, he called it up. There was no address, no name for the sender – just one word written large in the centre of the screen ... "soon".

Don't be unnecessarily gory or graphic

Many new writers make the mistake of trying to go for a hit-them-with-a-sledgehammer approach and then wonder why it doesn't really work.

The reason is quite simply that explicit horror – although sickening and disturbing – just isn't that scary. Graphic scenes of mutilation and gore – what Americans call the "gross-out" – can turn your stomach, but they won't frighten. This is why many editor's guidelines say: *Gratuitous violence just isn't necessary and is really best avoided unless you have something to say.*

The secret of a good horror tale is suspense, nail-chewing tension. And for that you need the subtle power of suggestion, not crude exploitation. It's your reader's own imagination that makes a story sizzle. A good writer knows how to let the subconscious terrors and fears of his audience work for him.

You don't need to draw a graphic sketch of a monster, down to its drooling fangs, for the reader to get the picture. Just a short description of the heavy breathing in the distance or the sound of claws scraping across a tiled floor will do. It'll have your readers dreaming up all sorts of hideous images in their minds – much more terrifying than you could possible conjure up.

Remember, something unseen and threatening is always more scary than the reality. It's the mystery, the not knowing, that makes us afraid. Don't have a howling demonic poltergeist tearing a house apart if you can create more tingling fear by having an empty rocking chair slowly moving backwards and forwards.

Is that it?

Try to hold off the moment you show readers what the monster or demon looks like, because no matter how good a writer you are or how vivid a description you give, it's bound to be an anti-climax. Your creature of the night is never as terrifying or bloodcurdling as the reader has already imagined. It's the moment in the film when the audience realise that they're not looking at a bone-crunching creature from Hell but just an extra in a latex monster suit.

That's why I always say the most potent monster is one that's never seen. The invisible hand of evil. The force that could be behind you, watching, waiting ... the demon seen only by the prints that its feet leave in the sand. Only show your monster if you have to.

Likewise, think twice about having a ghost or bogeyman actually speak. In your mind its tones may sound like an eerie echo from the crypt, its whisper may suggest malevolence in every syllable, but this is very difficult to create on the page. The line: *There's no use running. You are mine. You cannot escape*, may suggest to you great menace, but a reader may take it as just petulant.

No need to sicken

Many chiller tales rely on a twist-ending for their effect. Just as you thought it was safe, the beast comes back for another bite ... the policeman who rescues you from the madman turns out to be a fiend himself; you realise with a scream that the Halloween visitor isn't wearing a mask after all!

A sting-in-the-tale climax is great but its purpose is to shock – not to sicken or disgust. Don't feel you need to be gory or gratuitous at the end just to make a big impact.

If you've managed to surprise the reader by coming up with a denouement that he wasn't expecting, then you've succeeded. That's all you have to do. Don't leave him nauseated or make him regret having read the piece. After all, you want him to come back for more – and tell his friends.

Dead on target

Loud, Technicolor horror extravaganzas are great fun to pen but they aren't necessarily the biggest profit makers – so don't feel you have to go down the vampire and mad axeman route.

Gentle ghost stories are an acceptable alternative and sell phenomenally well – both here and in the States. They are just as popular now as they were a hundred years ago. Readers of all ages love them. There's an eager audience of adults and children who yearn to be chilled and thrilled with creepy tales from beyond the grave.

Small press magazines are often packed with ghostly shenanigans and even normally staid women's publications will take a supernatural spine-tingler to break up the mixture of romance and twist-enders. Radio stations love them and most editors look eagerly for a *spirited* yarn with a Christmas theme.

So, don't worry if you find traditional gothic horror a little too robust for your liking. A well-told ghost story that gives the reader a mild tingle is still a lucrative and worthwhile yarn to write.

Just be careful that you avoid the worst clichéd plotlines – stories about haunted mirrors and portraits, demon cars and people buying hexed houses unwittingly built on ancient burial or execution sites.

Always bring a new dramatic twist to the genre. Try to rework the mixture.Trick the reader into making the wrong assumptions.

... the old woman is worried when she encounters an odd-looking young man begging on a street corner. He has a strange manner and unearthly pallor. He's been out all night in sub-zero temperatures yet doesn't seem to feel the cold. No-one else seems to see him ...

Is he a spirit? A wraith? Did he die of neglect and hunger? Maybe, but what if he is alive and his unearthly pallor is because he's just seen the narrator – who *is* a ghost!

See how easy it is to bring a freshness to the genre – and be topical at the same time. This modern ghost story deals with homelessness. There are countless other topics and settings you could choose and be just as relevant and spooky.

Get into the spirit

I hope this chapter has provided you with plenty of creepy and disturbing things to think about!

One thing's for sure – whether you think the legions of the damned are coming for our souls, or reckon that it's all a lot of nonsense and there's nothing more terrifying on the face of the earth than a tax inspector – horror is a genre you can't afford to ignore. It just gets bigger and bigger – scarier and scarier – and more profitable!

Go on, give it a try and see what you can do. Who knows? Maybe you'll enjoy working the graveyard shift.

Exercises

Write a 400-word scene where a woman is running away from an unseen terror. Don't mention the weather.

Now rewrite the scene in 600 words and set it during a storm. Compare the two. Your second piece should be much more atmospheric.

Try a 500-word scene where a silent monster enters a man's bedroom at midnight waking him. Make it as terrifying as possible. Now rework the scene to make the monster speak.

Did you find the second version more difficult? Did you succeed in keeping the scariness or did the monster speaking actually detract from it?

Write a 1,000-word ghost story set in either the Millennium Dome or on board a train going through the Channel Tunnel.

Summary

✓ Horror is huge. After science fiction, it makes up the bulk of all small press titles.

✓ There are more than just monsters and vampires. Yarns feature ecological disasters, plagues, killer animals and knife-wielding madmen.

✓ Psychological terror is "in" with characters being menaced by stalkers or facing inner fears and phobias.

✓ Because the term horror can mean many different things, it's vital that you know exactly which magazine you are targeting.

✓ Get hold of several copies and study the stories throughly; they're the best clue to what the editor is looking for.

✓ Most horror titles are subscription only. Many are E-zines which appear solely on the Internet, so it's a good place to look.

✓ Many stores which sell computer games also carry horror comics and magazines, and can give you details of local clubs and publications.

✓ All seek quirky, imaginative work with a disturbing slant. Many take ghost stories and "dark" science fiction/fantasy.

✓ Really effective horror and ghost stories are difficult to create because so many of the obvious themes have been covered comprehensively.

✓ Go for modern settings, unusual characterisations and unexpected locations. Tap into our technological worries.

✓ Look for hidden meanings in traditional fairy tales. Re-interpret them to produce powerful new horror plots.

- ✓ Think of monsters as a metaphor for man's darker and more violent side.
- ✓ Go for locations which immediately create feelings of dread. Always exploit the eeriness of ordinary surroundings.
- ✓ Have characters who seem ordinary but who hide a horrific secret.
- ✓ Aim to make your tale as believable as possible. Show the blood-chilling events happening in a plausible way.
- ✓ Make sure the plot still works even if you remove all the trappings of the paranormal and the frightening.
- ✓ Use your descriptive talents, but don't create overblown and purple passages. Build up the terror slowly, hinting gently at the horror to come.
- ✓ Let readers use their own imaginations to create tension and suspense.
- ✓ Something unseen and menacing is always more scary. So hold off the moment when you show what the demon looks like. The most potent monster is one that's never seen.
- ✓ Think twice about having a ghost or bogeyman actually speak.
- ✓ A sting-in-the-tale should shock – not sicken or disgust. Don't be gory or gratuitous at the end just to make a big impact.
- ✓ Gentle ghost stories sell phenomenally well – both here and in the States. Readers of all ages love them.
- ✓ Avoid clichéd plotlines – haunted mirrors and portraits, demon cars and people buying hexed houses.
- ✓ Choose topics and settings that are modern and relevant, as well as spooky.

22

WRITING FOR CHILDREN

Nothing is more satisfying – or demanding – than writing for children. No other audience can be swept into a tale so deeply, feel so committed to the characters, and their adventures, and view the fantastic worlds you create with such awe and wonder.

No other readers dive into a story with such passion and excitement, eager to find out what happens next and whether good will triumph over evil. And no other audience demands so much from its authors.

If you want to write for children, you'll find it an immensely rewarding experience – in terms of story-telling pleasure as well as hard cash. You'll know that you've helped to shape a child's reading habits – introducing him to the magic of words, and widening his imagination, knowledge and curiosity about the world.

You'll also know that you've made it as a writer, for this genre asks more of you in terms of brevity, characterisation and narrative drive than any other. For one thing, some short stories for children are 600 words or less. For another, there is no margin for error. Get it right and a young reader will be kept spellbound in your fantasy world. Get the mixture wrong or have a voice that is too adult, fussy or insincere and he'll abandon you for something more relevant and punchy, for something more fun to read.

So are you up to it? Have you got what it takes to keep the most critical audience in the world amused?

Still a big market

It is amazing how many people don't bother to write short stories for youngsters because they wrongly believe that no-one publishes them anymore. They simply assume that authors must either go for full-length books or turn out cartoon strips for comics.

Well, it's true that the market isn't as big as the women's magazine or science fiction genres, but it's vibrant and exciting with new story-based publications being launched all the time.

And there are great opportunities for authors who apply a little lateral thinking in their marketing.

You'd be surprised at some of the magazines which often print "junior" short fiction. Among them are pet magazines, travel mags, newspapers and magazines read by the over 50s. In addition, many publishers bring out Christmas annuals and anthologies of ghost stories or adventures for the young.

It's all a question of keeping your ears and eyes open, looking beyond the obvious and considering overseas markets. The Internet – as always – provides access to an enticing array of possible outlets.

But don't be fooled into thinking that writing for youngsters is child's play. You'll find it more difficult than tackling the adult market. Just because stories are shorter it doesn't mean they require less thought or care. In many ways it means being more concise and precise in what you write.

Plots have to be mean, lean and bubbling with enthusiasm. Writing has to be upbeat, pacy and exciting. And you need to stimulate, inspire and entertain. Children don't take prisoners and won't think twice about giving you a metaphorical raspberry if they think your tale is old-fashioned, inaccurate or boring.

Don't kid yourself

Sincerity is crucial. If you try to be false or lie to children they will spot it straightaway. You must believe implicitly in what you're writing. You can't afford to be tongue-in-cheek.

You have to be truthful with yourself as well. Ask yourself why you want to write for children. If it's because you have children of your own and want to enthral them with stories that will spark their imaginations, then great.

If you are a teacher or librarian or anyone else who has regular contact with youngsters and know what excites and interests them, then get cracking on some super yarns.

However, if you are looking at this market because you want to provide something *improving* for modern kids to read, then forget it. This is the worst possible motivation you could have.

Children hate being lectured – even by someone who has their best interests at heart – and will run a mile from your stories. That's if you find an editor who is prepared to print fiction which preaches. The best children's stories may be packed with meaning but this should always take second place to entertainment and be hidden so that a young reader finds it for himself.

Another equally bad motivation is thinking that everything printed for kids these days is rubbish and it's time we all got back to proper story-telling – like it used to be when you were a child. This attitude will guarantee failure. Times and tastes have moved on and there is no going back to the jolly Enid Blyton days of holiday adventures, crooks who wear striped jerseys and picnics with lashings and lashings of home-made lemonade.

Children are great fans of soap operas and want drama that is grown-up in tone and content. They look for stories that mirror adult themes, although in a more safe and sanitised way. Editors know best how to please this audience and won't suddenly change direction. So you must write the kind of material that children want – not what you'd like them to read.

Like it or not, children's writing these days takes its lead from television. As the editor of a recently launched magazine says: *We want our stories to capture the spirit and vibrancy of children's TV.*

So what do children want?

That's a really difficult one! Whoever managed to unlock that secret would be a multi-millionaire.

But it's safe to say that children want more than just competent story-telling and clever dialogue. They expect their short stories to absorb them totally. A child doesn't read a tale – he enters it, becoming part of the drama.

Excitement, plenty of action and conflict are essential. So are characters that a child can easily recognise and identify with. They don't all need to be children, but must include someone of roughly the same age as, or slightly older than, the reader. Alternatively, you need a heroic figure that the child can identify with.

Other necessary elements are settings that a child can recognise – school, home, youth club, disco, shopping mall – or backdrops set in fantasy worlds where magic and monsters lurk around every corner. Children are fascinated by the supernatural and the beasts and darkness of folk tales. They love to be scared – the success of the *Goosebumps* series of horror chillers proves that.

Ghost stories are hugely popular, as long as they aren't too scary, and anything with aliens or space travel is a guaranteed winner. The love affair with dinosaurs continues undiminished and most kids would love to own a T-Rex.

Girls are still mad about ponies and want to be ballerinas. Boys dream of racing cars, planes and trains. Animals are a big draw for both sexes. But the biggest attraction is humour. Children love to laugh. So if you can pack a tale full of (bad) jokes, silly names, slapstick antics and groan-making puns you'll be a firm favourite.

Market snapshot

Perhaps the best way of getting a feel for what kids like is to sample a typical week's magazines. A glance round the shelves in my local newsagents provided four publications aimed at the under-12s featuring short stories.

The yarns ranged from a 600-word tale for six-year-olds where two girls were trying to find a new mother for a litter of orphaned kittens, to a fairly grown-up ghost story running to 1,500 words where a young teenager helped the troubled spirit of a boy to finally find peace.

The other two tales – falling in the middle in terms of length and tone – featured two sisters finding a magic board game that transported them to a TV studio, and a yarn for ten-year-olds about a girl being teased at school because her family was poor. But she gets the last laugh when her mum wins the lottery.

The stories were all different, but had a jaunty air, likeable characters, up-beat endings and fast-paced action. And they had loads of dialogue. This extract is typical:

Billie Piper was also on the stage, and she turned to them and shouted: "Superstar sisters, are you ready?"

"Sam, we're on Top of the Pops. We're Billie's backing singers!" called Danielle, above all the noise.

Samantha started to panic. "What? I can't sing in front of all these people, besides I'm only eight years old and you're ten!"

"It doesn't matter. Remember, it's just a game and the instructions said that if we believe, we would succeed. Let's just enjoy ourselves."

Pop stars, glamour, being on television, magical games ... it's what modern youngsters dream about. See if you can make your fiction reflect these themes and you'll be well on your way.

Do your homework

Talking to kids is essential – find out what they like. If you spend a fortune every Christmas buying presents for all your nieces and nephews, now's the time to get something back.

Gain an up-to-date knowledge of what the latest fads and fashions are – what TV programmes children like, what clothes and toys they buy and what films they go to see. Ask them to show you what magazines they read, and get them to tell you what appeals about the stories.

It's important that you decide what age group you want to target. Youngsters' tastes and interests vary dramatically as they grow older. What captures the imagination of a nine-year-old may seem too babyish for a child just two years older. So you need to work out what age group is likely to be most receptive to your work.

Detailed market research is crucial. Get hold of as many children's magazines as you can. Study the stories until the print wears thin. See what elements make the stories work. See how they are pitched at different ages; how the dialogue and plots become more complex, and the stories become longer (up to 1,500 words) as you go up towards the early teens.

Consult the experts. Make sure you get hold of magazine guidelines before attempting any tale. These tip sheets will tell you exactly what's in and what's a sin.

One thing editors definitely don't want these days are twee stories about the antics of fluffy Beatrix Potter-style animals. They're also not keen on cheery talking household appliances who pass witty observational comments about the people who own them: *Hi, I'm Vic the vacuum cleaner. I live under the stairs. You wouldn't believe the things the family I live with get up to!*

Perfect pitch

Putting the right ingredients into your story will get you off to a great start but all your good work will be destroyed if the tone – the narrator's voice – jars. Children should believe in the story and not think it was concocted by an adult at a word-processor.

That means keeping the sentence structure, ideas and expressions simple and straightforward, but not patronising or under-estimating your audience. It's best to think of yourself as writing not for children but for adults who have a limited vocabulary. They want fairly complicated concepts and plots, but told in a basic and uncluttered way.

You should know the correct vocabulary level for the age-group you are targeting (a brief talk with your local school or children's librarian should help there) and never include any hard or unusual word that will mean the reader stopping the story to go away and find a dictionary. You wouldn't do this to an adult, so why inflict it on a youngster?

It's good to make your style as relaxed and chatty as possible but beware of using slang unless you are absolutely sure that children use the expression, you have understood exactly what it means and that it won't date or be applicable in only one part of the country.

This last point is particularly important if you hope to sell your work to American magazines. Never has the adage: *two countries separated by a common language* been more true than in talking about children's slang. It doesn't travel well and can give your story a Britishness which makes it unsuitable for a US audience. It also makes a story difficult to sell on the Continent – translating slang into foreign languages is a nightmare.

Second childhood

Perhaps the most difficult part of writing children's fiction is becoming a youngster again in your mind. It's no good looking at life through cynical adult eyes.

You must be able to see the world as your nine-year-old reader sees it; feeling the same awe and curiosity. You must be amused by the same things, and just as easily bored and turned-off by subjects that appear irrelevant or too adult. Never forget that youngsters read for fun and have a short attention span.

And you must be idealistic. Many children feel passionately about issues like the environment, poverty and famine so you must understand and share their conviction.

All this is more difficult than it sounds. Becoming a youngster again is more akin to acting than writing. But all the most successful children's writers do it. They tap into "the child within".

They've got the power

It's fine to have adults in your stories – they are, after all, a part of any child's life. But it's important that you don't paint them as all-knowing authority figures who constantly tell the kids what to do.

There's no attraction in a story where kids are bossed around by grown-ups. They get enough of that at home and at school. Kids want to feel that the young characters in their stories have control over their destiny. They must be able to affect events and be capable of making their own decisions. They must be important.

In real life children are subjected to rules and regulations. They are constantly told how to dress, how to behave and what they can and can't say. They look to fiction as a means of escape – of being "grown-up". Free your characters from these bans and restrictions and your readers will warm to them.

That doesn't mean that everything a young character does is automatically right or that he won't get himself into a scrape that he can't handle. But even if an adult has to come in at the end and sort it all out, let the kids in your tale have a bit of slack to play with.

No more Mr Nice Guy

While we're talking about the portrayal of kids, don't feel that any story aimed at them must always have kids who are too good to be true.

You can have children who are liars or cowards or who are stupid, vain, bullying or conceited. Remember, this genre is as dramatic, as hard-hitting as any other. It deals with tough narrative themes. And your task, as well as entertaining, is to prepare youngsters for the life ahead.

So resist the temptation to wrap kids in cotton wool, or tell them life is all bunny rabbits, sandcastles and ice creams.

Plots

The average child's world is quite narrow and confined. And, apart from holidays, follows basically the same daily routine of school, home, playing with friends and studying. So from a plotting point of view that may seem extremely limiting but don't worry. You'd be surprised what lively storylines you can still construct within this rigidly defined range of settings.

Take schools, for example. As *Grange Hill* demonstrated, classrooms are a hotbed of conflict and dilemmas. Life can be tough for the pupil who is too fat, struggles with lessons, is bullied or is too poor to afford the CDs, computer games and trainers his classmates have.

School sports can provide lots of potential plotlines. Maybe (as I did) your pupil hates PE and will get up to any dodge to avoid it. Maybe Colin is hopeless at games and fears being humiliated in front of the others.

Perhaps it's the other side of the coin and he is desperate to make it on to the school football team. He'd give anything to be picked ... even bribing another kid to pretend to be ill so he can take his place. Or maybe Colin is the centre-forward picked to play in a vital inter-school cup and frets whether his busy businessman father will come to see him or make yet another excuse.

Individual sports like track events offer huge story-telling scope. In the finals of the 100 metres Debbie finds herself lined up against the gang who have bullied her for years. She must win but fears what will happen if she does. Or maybe she is picked for the England under-15s netball team but knows her single-parent mother can't afford the expense of sending her to London for weekend training sessions. Debbie is too proud to ask for help and instead sets out to make some cash.

And then there are extra-curricular activities. Colin and Debbie are involved in a campaign to save a wood from being bulldozed, or discover a spooky mystery as they research a school project in the library. Perhaps on the way home they find themselves witnesses to a robbery.

There can be powerful dilemmas to deal with. Our heroes can try to save a friend who is in trouble but won't admit it; fight the temptations of *bunking off*; be unsure whether or not to tell tales on older kids who've been shoplifting; be invited to a party at a mate's house when his parents are away ...

The plotting possibilities from just this one basic setting are enormous. Just think how many plots you can have when you look at the other backdrops.

Another way around the problem is to have a fantasy story in a wild and exotic setting, or maybe a historical adventure taking place in an exciting period of the past. You aren't tied down to mundane surroundings or kitchen sink dramas – you can let your imagination explode.

History is packed with story-telling opportunities. Children have been eye-witnesses to many of the most important events on record. In Napoleonic times, for instance, a ten-year-old drummer boy would have gone into battle with the troops.

Just think about it ... when families settle in outer space they will have children helping to forge these communities on strange and challenging new planets. These youngsters will encounter bizarre aliens and unexpected dangers.

Maybe they live in a medieval fantasy world where their father is a knight fighting a dark and evil overlord. Perhaps they find the lost book of spells which can make the difference between victory and doom.

On the terror front, children are just as likely as adults to attract the unwanted attention of ghoulish demons. In fact, most monsters are reputed to have quite a taste for youngsters (although personally I never think there's enough meat on them).

Why not mix realism and fantasy? A child moves into a house and finds it is haunted or there are evil goblins living in a derelict factory nearby. There's something not right about the way the new teacher never blinks, never seems to laugh, never eats or drinks. Is he a robot – or even worse?

Start using the *What If?* principle and you will find the problem won't be a shortage of plots, but not having enough time to write them all.

One last word on plotting: obviously for younger children – those under nine – your storylines must be very simple. There isn't the space in a 600-word story to go much beyond the basic set-up so don't make the events you describe too involved. Also avoid any conflict that might take too long to be resolved.

Young children love animal stories so plots where a family pet goes missing, a child has to nag his father to let him have a rabbit, or a dog misbehaves and causes upsets are likely to be big hits. Any tale set in a zoo, stables, pet shop or vet's practice will charm this age group.

Teen scene

In many ways teenagers are the toughest young audience to write for. This is because they live in a constantly changing world. They use hip words and expressions, follow the latest crazes and fashions and view anything that's gone before – even by a few months – as embarrassing and boring.

That means that if you aren't right up to the second with your topical references you'll miss by a mile. If you have a teenage character listening to a boy band and that band has slipped from favour, you'll come across as being totally out of touch – and readers won't identify with your *cool* heroine. Instead they'll see her as a bit of a drip.

As if that isn't difficult enough, you have to write in an authentic teenage voice. You have to reflect the speech patterns of this age group. Teens are quick to spot a fake, an outsider, and will know if you use language or dialogue that isn't spot-on.

Getting the narrator's voice right is vital as so much material for this audience is written in the first person – much of it "confession" tales.

But it's not all negative. Writing for teens offers a greater chance for plotting and dealing with serious issues. All the major choices, conflicts and dilemmas which face adults are mirrored in the world of teenagers. But they also face the insecurities that come with adolescence. All this is a rich vein of material.

And teenagers love spooky tales and ghost stories. If you write science fiction or horror, this market offers you a wealth of additional outlets.

Love's young dream

When they reach their middle teens, boys tend to stop reading, lured away by the delights of football, computer games and girls. Those who do continue to read either go for books or sneak a look at *laddish* lifestyle magazines meant for young adults.

For this reason, most teenage magazines are aimed at girls, and echo the content and concerns of the more trendy women's magazines. This means the major theme in their fiction is romance. After all, this is an age when adolescents experience crushes, first kisses and broken hearts.

It's important that you have stories which mirror the pre-occupation with boys and dating, but which don't go too far towards the physical side of relationships. Girls of 16 may have sex as a routine these days but editors prefer their stories don't dwell on it. Instead your narrative should deal with the emotional aspects – the heartaches and joys of relationships – not what happens behind teenage bedroom doors. Heavy kissing is okay, but nothing stronger.

This is a tricky area so it's useful to get guidelines and study them well. They will tell just how far your dating couple can go.

From a purely dramatic point of view, a happy, steady relationship is a bit dull. Intriguing stories come from a girl wondering if the handsome hunk she sees each day on the bus secretly fancies her. Maybe he's already going out with a girl whom the heroine (and the readers) knows is unsuitable and the tale charts how she convinces him that he's made the wrong choice.

Disappointment, dashed hopes, feelings of betrayal, and resentment, are all emotions which give teenage romance stories their punch. But not all the feelings need be negative. Your heroine may be floating on air when she receives her first Valentine Card and she just knows it's from Rick!

Why can't I be like everyone else?

One over-riding feeling that teenagers have is insecurity. They are anxious to fit in, to be one of the crowd, and often secretly think of themselves as being odd or freakish.

This desire for conformity, and fear of being different, is a recurring theme in magazine problem pages. Tap into this for your fiction. It's a strong motivation for an otherwise well-behaved teenager to act in an irresponsible and stupid manner.

Your main character may steal from her parents to buy the designer trainers that all her friends have because she feels humiliated wearing cheap ones. She may accept a dare to shoplift or be rude to teachers. She may join in with bullying someone helpless and terrified just because the "in" crowd do it. She might stay out late to go to a concert ...

None of these things makes the girl a bad person – just someone who is confused and unhappy and struggling to fit in. This makes her sympathetic to readers. They'll care about her and want her to learn from her mistakes and realise what she should do to make amends.

Confessional pieces

I'm sorry if I'm about to shatter anyone's illusions but the first person confessional pieces you see in teen mags: *I dumped my best mate; I stole my sister's boyfriend; The secret I can never reveal* ... are rarely genuine.

Although they may read like pieces of factual journalism – a reader's true story – they are made up. They are pieces of fiction, written by adults. It stands to reason if you think about it. The most common factor that links teenagers is their inability to communicate in anything more than a grunt. When pressed to give an opinion on something, most shrug their shoulders and say: *I dunno. It's all right, I suppose.*

Isn't it strange that they can miraculously become wildly articulate in the pages of magazines and can produce long and emotive pieces about the anguish and angst of teenage life?

Some editors will vehemently deny that their confession tales are fakes – but trust me, these "tell-all" tales are as genuine as a politician's smile. The storyline may have been suggested by a genuine three-sentence letter to the magazine's problem page – but that's as far as it goes.

This revelation opens up huge opportunities for short story writers. Suddenly, instead of viewing teen mags as a small outlet taking the occasional yarn, recognise them as a huge market for material.

So why the pretense? The answer is simple. A teenager will be unwilling to sit and be lectured by an adult on the perils and pitfalls of life. She won't want to know what's best for her or take advice – all adults are stupid, remember? But a teenager will listen to the experiences and warnings of another youngster.

Stories either deal with temptations – the lure of drugs, drink, cigarettes, crime, or under-age sex – or brief teenagers how to act when they confront an adult dilemma. What should they do about the unwelcome advances of an adult or a best-mate's fella? Should they abandon or betray a friend, or lie to protect someone else?

Stories centre on one dramatic incident that has thrown the girl's life into chaos and confusion. This excerpt from *My Dad's Having A Fling*! is fairly typical. According to the byline it was written by *Trisha, 14, from Devon.*

I don't know what to do. I know something awful but I can't tell anyone. Not my friends. Not my sister. Not my teacher. Most of all not my mum!

You see dad's been having an affair with our next door neighbour. No-one's supposed to know but I saw him with her at the barbecue last week when he thought no-one was looking.

I didn't mean to spy on him. Mum sent me back into the house to get more orange juice and they were there in the hallway, him and Brenda, kissing! I couldn't believe it. I nearly screamed – but luckily I didn't. I just stood there, stunned, feeling sick.

How could he? How could he do that to mum – and with our neighbour? I remember running back into the garden, crying.

Mum wanted to know what had happened but I made up some lie about hurting my hand. I couldn't tell her.

Now I don't know what to do. Should I tell? Should I keep quiet? I can't look dad in the eyes now. I'm sure he suspects.

We've always been so close. I've always looked up to my dad. He's always been great to me – not like some dads you hear about. But I can't bear to be near him now ...

Not all "true" stories are so harrowing but they all have the same theme – a teenager facing a tough decision and being emotionally troubled. The more emotive the tale, the more gripping it is.

Now I know that some writers feel this true confession format is dishonest and are uncomfortable pretending to be a teenager, but I would say that just because a piece of writing is made-up doesn't mean that it's reprehensible. Good fiction tells us truths about ourselves and our experiences. And if young readers are helped to face up to a crisis in their own lives by reading a confession piece then I think a little subterfuge is acceptable.

End note

Writing fiction for youngsters is as demanding as it gets but it's well worth the time, the effort and the research. Crack this market and any other should be a doddle.

If you want to ensure that your work is on target always read it to some children of the appropriate age. Most schools are very obliging about giving you access to a class of "guinea pigs". But you must have a thick skin and be prepared to listen and learn from the feedback you get. When it comes to writing for children – they do all the teaching.

Exercises

Buy three different children's magazines and analyse their contents and fiction as shown in chapter two. Complete a *research form* for each. Say what age group you think each publication is aimed at and what you think the specific major interests are of the readers. Now write a short story for each of between 500 and 700 words.

Pick one of the sporting plot set-ups mentioned earlier in the chapter and write it up as an 800-word short story.

Write a 1,000-word first person confession tale for teenagers. If you find it difficult to think of an idea, look at the problem page of a teen magazine and expand one of the letters.

Describe, in 100 words, a hero for a children's story. Next, define the age you are writing for and explain the appeal of the character to that group.

Summary

- ✓ Nothing is more satisfying – or demanding – than writing for children. You need great brevity, characterisation skills and narrative drive.

- ✓ Writing for youngsters is more difficult than tackling the adult market. Because stories are shorter you need to be more concise and precise.

- ✓ Children won't think twice about giving you a raspberry if they think your tale is boring, old-fashioned or inaccurate.

- ✓ Sincerity is crucial. If you try to be false or lie children will spot it. You must believe in what you're writing.

- ✓ Don't attempt children's stories because you are keen to tell them how to behave or think. They don't like being lectured.

- ✓ Don't think that all modern stories are rubbish and you can write the type of tales you enjoyed as a child. Times and tastes have changed.

- ✓ Children's writing takes its lead from television, especially soap operas.

- ✓ Young people expect their short stories to absorb them totally. Excitement plus plenty of action and conflict are essential.

- ✓ So are characters that a child can easily recognise and identify with. They must include someone of roughly the same age as the reader.

- ✓ Children are fascinated by the supernatural and monsters. They love to be scared. Ghost stories are popular, as is anything with aliens, space travel or dinosaurs. Animals are a big draw and humour is a sure-fire hit.

- ✓ Talking to kids is essential – find out what they like. Know what the latest fads and fashions are, especially what TV programmes children like.
- ✓ It's important that you decide what age group you want to target.
- ✓ Make sure that you get hold of magazine guidelines before attempting any tale.
- ✓ Keep your sentence structure, ideas and expressions simple and straightforward. Think of a child as an adult with a limited vocabulary.
- ✓ Know the correct vocabulary level for the age-group you are targeting and never include any hard or unusual words.
- ✓ Beware of using slang – it can date, and make your story difficult to sell abroad.
- ✓ You must be able to see the world through a youngster's eyes and still have a sense of awe and wonder.
- ✓ Your child characters must be able to influence events and be capable of making their own decisions.
- ✓ Don't feel that you must have young characters who are too good to be true – make them realistic. Deal with tough narrative themes.
- ✓ Even mundane school settings can offer a wealth of plotting possibilities if you give characters important dilemmas to cope with.
- ✓ Fantasy, horror and science fiction offer great scope for escapist drama. So do historical stories.
- ✓ You have to be bang up to date to write for teenagers. You must know what's "trendy".

✓ Most teenage fiction is aimed at girls, and a major theme is romance. But stick to flirting and emotions – no sex.

✓ One over-riding feeling that teenagers have is insecurity. They are anxious to fit in – use this theme in your stories.

✓ First person confessional pieces aren't written by teenagers they're concocted by adults. But they all have the same theme – a teenager facing a tough decision and being emotionally troubled.

✓ No matter what age group you write for, try your stories on a target audience, but be prepared for some forthright feedback.

23

WRITING ON THE WEB

A few years ago it sounded like science fiction, a quirky plaything for computer geeks, librarians and high-tech researchers. But the Internet is now part of our everyday lives and if you aren't already hooked up to *The World Wide Web* it's time you thought about switching on.

There's a whole cyber world out there just waiting to be explored and with powerful computers starting at only a few hundred pounds, there's never been a better time to go on-line.

The Internet offers a wealth of exciting opportunities for writers, and has opened up an enormous, hungry market for short stories. E-zines – special electronic magazines published solely on the Internet – have sprung up by the thousand, all desperate for material.

Even if writing for the more traditional paper-based magazines is your preference, the Internet can still help. It's now easier than ever to contribute to magazines abroad, submitting your stories by E-mail at the touch of a mouse button.

And for writers who have their own unique fiction vision or who can't be bothered trying to fit in with the demands of editors, there's the thrill of becoming your own publisher. You can display your short stories on your own web page – making them available to an audience of millions across the globe.

Heady stuff – and a little scary sounding at first – but don't be frightened. This technological revolution is easy to join, simple to understand and within the grasp of virtually anyone with a little curiosity and a willingness to experiment.

In this last chapter we'll have a look at this *brave new world*. Don't worry if you have no experience of computers – this book is about writing short stories, not keyboard wizardry. So there'll be no jargon, techno-babble or mention of baffling things like RAMs and ROMs, micro-processors or circuit boards. We'll stick to looking at how you can take advantage of the new opportunities to be better informed, make new friends and sell more stories.

How the net works

So what exactly is the Internet? We hear people talk about it all the time and the papers seem to be packed with information about *surfing the net*. Well, in its simplest form, the Internet is a huge link-up of millions of computers and data bases around the world. It's a cross between a gigantic telephone exchange and a vast international library.

You can use it to send information to computers on the other side of the planet. Or you can call up web sites – pages of text and pictures – that individuals or companies have set up for others to view and use.

You can think of it as the largest notice-board in the world or as a book with an infinite number of pages covering a multitude of topics and interests. Another way of looking at it is as a means of travelling without leaving your seat. It's a way of inter-acting with strangers without ever actually meeting them face to face.

Some people like to think of the Internet as a world of its own – a land with no national or cultural borders – a place that exists in its own *cyberspace*. It has its own clubs, magazines and meeting places.

Whatever way you choose to think of it, the Internet is a huge new market for material and one that you can't afford to ignore if you want to be part of the future. Membership is free and open to everyone. All you need is access to a computer.

Advantages for authors

It's been said that the Internet could have been especially invented just for writers and it's easy to see why. Apart from the luxury of having access to an enormous information resource 24 hours a day, the Web offers you a chance to submit work instantaneously to editors and find out the same day whether it has been rejected or accepted.

It makes dealing with editors abroad as effortless as submitting work to a UK outlet. It allows you to react instantly to changing world events and write a story that is topical.

Market research becomes easier, quicker and cheaper as you call up a magazine's web page and study its guidelines, editorial policy and read sample stories. Many small press magazines now operate their own web sites.

E-zines, magazines of the Net, actively encourage work by newcomers and give you the chance to receive quick and detailed feedback from readers – something few paper-based publications can do. No other medium can offer access to such a large readership and such a close relationship between the writer and his audience.

But one of the biggest attractions is the camaraderie and friendship the Web can offer. Through E-mail you can get round the loneliness of writing by exchanging ideas and carrying on correspondence with fellow authors. This is a fantastic boon to those who live in remote areas or who are housebound. You can participate in group discussions through *Usenet Newsgroups* – electronic writer's circles – where you can pick up all the gossip and current advice on various markets, competitions and editors.

And because your E-mail address is a nominal *mailbox* on the Internet, and not a real geographical location, your on-line friends need only know as much about you as you choose to tell them. You can be known only by your pen-name if that's what you want. So you can have the world at your fingertips, but not on your doorstep.

Self publishing

Perhaps the most exciting aspect of being on the Internet is having your own web page – a site where you can publicise yourself and your work, sell any books you may have written, offer your services as a speaker for writer's groups or air your opinions generally.

Many successful authors are turning to this as a way of keeping their fans in touch with new projects, offering intriguing inside biographical information about themselves and showcasing previous works. This saves them having to do interviews, speak to groups and end up answering the same popular questions *(Where do you get your ideas?)* over and over.

But you don't need to be famous or a professional to have your own web site. Lots of people are turning to the Internet as a way of self publishing. They use their *home page* to publish their latest short story or poem. Anyone who wants to read the story can just call it up. This can be exciting because you never know just who might be reading your work at any point – maybe an agent or an editor looking for new talent!

If seeing your work in print and knowing that people are enjoying it is enough for you then this is the ideal solution. You can write about whatever you like, in whatever style appeals, making the tale whatever length you feel it deserves to be. There's no-one waving guidelines at you or saying: *You must follow this formula.*

That's real freedom – but remember that it isn't a licence to be crude or offensive. Nor is it a licence to produce poor writing. Readers, even electronic readers, will expect your work to be well constructed, lively, polished and engaging.

Now, I know that a few people will think: why should I give away my hard work for free? I'm not a charity.

Well, there's no reason why you can't be enterprising and bring in some money. There is nothing stopping you selling advertising space on your page. That's how newspapers and magazines make their money.

Or you could sell subscriptions in the same way that a small press publication does: *If you liked this story I can send you hard copies of a dozen more just like it. Contact me at my E-mail address to subscribe.*

There are even some enterprising E-zines out there who print the opening few paragraphs of a story and then they sell access to the remainder of the tale for a small fee. Doesn't that just confirm everything I said in chapter ten about the need to grab readers with your intro? Alternatively, they give access to a few pages free but you have to subscribe if you want to see the rest of the contents.

Okay, so none of this will make you rich but it could well cover your costs. And who's to say what the future will bring as more and more people connect up to the Net and treat it as their main source of reading material? In a few years' time paying for a short story on the Net might be as common as walking into a newsagents today and buying a copy of your favourite magazine.

Getting started

Okay, so now you're intrigued. The next question is how do *you* get on to the Internet.

If you really want to know all the nuts and bolts of buying a machine and connecting up there are several excellent computer magazines available on the subject from newsagents. They frequently carry information about setting up a personal computer, what models are best for certain tasks and what operating systems are most efficient. These are usually written in simple, easy-to-follow terms and explain all you need to know.

If, however, you're like me and can't really be bothered researching all the technical guff and just want to get on with it, then all you need to do is walk into your local computer shop. Tell them: *I want to buy a computer so that I can get on to the Internet and I don't want it to cost me a fortune. What should I buy?*

If you want to run sophisticated business programmes and play high-speed computer games it's probably a good idea to go for a slightly more expensive and powerful model. But if all you really want to do is use the machine for writing, keeping a few household accounts and surfing the Net then a basic model should be fine.

Larger warehouse-type shops have competitively priced packages – usually with free software, printers and scanners thrown in. If you are wary about the advice you're given, try two or three different stores before signing on the dotted line.

The great thing about buying such a package is that the store will offer – for a price – to send someone to your home to set up the computer for you. You don't need to touch a plug or a cable.

Once you're set-up, going on-line is easy. Many companies offer you free access to the Net. Some shops will give you the necessary CD disk when you buy the machine. Others advertise their free CDs in newspapers.

Simply put the CD into the slot in your computer and the instructions for installing the software will come up on the screen. Go through each stage as instructed (it's easier than making a cup of tea), click on the "Okay" button at the end and Bob's your electronic uncle.

Once you've got this software installed, you'll always be able to log on to the Internet with one click of a button. When you want to come back out of the Internet, you merely click a "close-down" button and the connection is severed until the next time you activate it.

I've just said that access can be free but don't forget that you connect to the Internet over the telephone, and will be charged on your phone bill for the time you spend surfing. The good news is that all calls are charged at local rates – no matter where in the world you are connected to on the Net.

Using the Internet

When you log on to the Net you will have the opportunity to search for a web page you want either by asking the machine to search for all the pages on a certain topic (a generic search) or by typing in the exact address of a particular site you want.

The generic search method is great if you are researching a market or want information on a topic. The search is likely to throw up more web sites to look at than you'll have time to read. It takes a lot of self-discipline not to become sidetracked and go off to look at sites which – although they have no direct bearing on what you're researching – look intriguing.

It's a fair thing to say that although the Internet does offer a number of exciting sites, about 90 per cent of what's on the Net is irrelevant. Much of it is just plain rubbish. So to avoid having to wade through hours of waffle and weirdness, always be precise in what you ask the machine to search for.

If you type the keywords "magazines" or "short stories" the search will throw up thousands of pages from around the globe. If you are looking purely for UK science fiction small press magazines, typing "UK sci-fi magazines" or "UK sci-fi short stories" will dramatically reduce the number of pages offered.

Always look for sites where someone has already done your homework for you. There are a number of "gateway" sites which can point you towards dozens, if not hundreds, of on-line literary magazines.

Two of the best of these "portal" sites are:
www.ezine-universe.com
and
www.google.com./top/arts/onlinewriting/ezines

These sites have columns of e-zines categorised by genre or type. By clicking on any of the headings you find there – science fiction, horror, teen, prose etc – you will be "linked" (transferred) to the web site of the e-zine you have selected. Many magazine sites also have "reciprocal" links to other e-zines and sites with similar material.

I said e-zines were a huge market and a quick scan through these lists will quickly show the full extent of the opportunities. And the number of new sites and magazines increases by the week.

Even if only a few of these publish short stories it still gives you more targets than you could ever possibly look at. It's a startling comparison to the limited number of magazines in newsagents which publish fiction.

E-zines are great but there are a few points to remember when you deal with them:

1. Just like small press magazines they have a tendency to spring up out of nowhere, last a few issues and disappear. So always keep a copy of anything you send so it doesn't vanish forever into the ether.

2. Like most small press magazines they often don't have a budget for contributors. That means that they'll expect you to offer material for free – the only payment being the joy of seeing yourself in "print". It's probably more lucrative to target large conventional magazines before looking to the Internet.

3. Those people who have been using the Internet for years tend to have a maverick, freewheeling attitude – especially to copyright – and look upon the Web as a huge resource centre where everything published can be lifted for free. Even if you put a copyright notice on your work it's unlikely to stop it being distributed without your knowledge or permission.

If you weren't paid in the first place by the E-zine, you may think it's hardly worth getting steamed up about the story being passed around on the Web – but it is something to consider if you feel your stories are your babies and you don't want them falling into the hands of strangers.

Don't let me worry you. These are fairly minor drawbacks and you may well feel that the attractions of E-zines hugely outweigh any potential snags.

Setting up E-mail and web pages

Getting an E-mail address is simple. In fact when you use your Internet installation CD you should automatically get an E-mail address as well. All you have to do is tell people what it is and you'll soon be receiving and sending lots of messages. There's no charge for this beyond the normal Internet phone rate.

Creating your own web page is slightly more complex. I won't go into the details here – except to say that you can buy inexpensive software programmes from large computer shops which show you how to set up a page step by step. Once again, as most service providers offer you free web space cost isn't a problem.

End note

If all this cyberspace talk has captured your interest and you want to know more about the wonders of the Web then there is a wide range of books devoted to the subject. The best I've found is *The Internet for Writers* by Nick Daws published by *Internet Handbooks Ltd.*

Exercises

Connect to the Internet and search for four E-zines. Study their guideline pages for contributors. Choose one E-zine and write a short story to fit. Submit it – electronically, if that is what is asked for.

If you don't have a computer visit a *cyber* café where you can have a go at connecting to the Internet for half an hour. Also, ask if your local reference library has facilities for visitors to use computers for research.

E-mail me at Iain@writersbureau.com and say hello! Tell me how you are getting on and what you think of the book. I look forward to hearing from you!

Summary

- ✓ The Internet – a global link-up of computers – is now part of our everyday lives.
- ✓ Powerful computers start at only a few hundred pounds, so it's easy to go on-line.
- ✓ The Web offers a wealth of opportunities for writers. It has opened up an enormous hungry market for short stories.
- ✓ E-zines – special electronic magazines published on the Internet – have sprung up by the thousand, all desperate for material.
- ✓ It's now easy to contribute to magazines abroad submitting stories by E-mail.
- ✓ As well as having access to information round the clock, you can submit work instantaneously to editors and receive a response the same day.
- ✓ Dealing with editors abroad becomes simple and market research is easier – just call up a magazine's web page and study its guidelines.
- ✓ Many small press magazines now operate their own web sites.
- ✓ Through E-mail you can exchange ideas and correspond with fellow authors.
- ✓ You can also participate in group discussions through Usenet Newsgroups – electronic writer's circles.
- ✓ Your on-line friends know as much or as little about you as you choose to tell them.
- ✓ You can display your short stories on your own web page – available to an audience of millions across the globe.

- ✓ You can write about whatever you like, in whatever style, making the tale whatever length you feel it deserves to be. But your work should still be well constructed, lively, polished and engaging.
- ✓ There's no reason why you can't be enterprising and bring in some money through your web page.
- ✓ In a few years paying to read a short story on the Net might become commonplace.
- ✓ Computer magazines offer good advice on how to buy a machine and get started. So do computer stores.
- ✓ A basic model should be fine if all you really want to do is use the machine for writing and surfing the Net.
- ✓ Going on-line is easy. Many Internet access providers now offer a free service. All you pay for is the cost of the phone call. You'll be charged at local rate.
- ✓ Looking for material on the Net is straightforward. Ask the computer to search for all the pages it has on a topic or give it the exact address to take you to a specific page.
- ✓ You can buy an inexpensive programme that shows you how to set up your own web page.
- ✓ You'll get your own free E-mail address when you sign-up with an Internet access provider.
- ✓ There are a wide range of books devoted to the subject if you want to find out more wonders of the Web.

AND FINALLY ...

Well, this is it – the sign off; the edifying ending to our look at the secrets of writing cracking short stories. Has it been twenty three chapters already?

I've tried to pack as much information and useful tips as I can into this book. I hope it's helped you to look at the short story world with a more professional eye and given you the push to give it a go at the keyboard. The market is still wide open.

Even with the many thousands of people regularly sending off short stories, fiction editors are *always* looking for bright new writing talent. So the next yarn you send off might be the one that starts you on the road to fame and fortune.

I've had a lot of fun writing these chapters and I hope you've had fun reading them – because fun is what it's all about. Writing should always be a good laugh, a wonderful way of relaxing and letting go.

I'm hoping that you'll see your next story in print, but even if you don't – as long as you enjoyed dreaming up the plot, the characters and the twist-in-the-tail, I'll be happy ... and I think you will be too.

Good luck and happy writing. Who knows? Maybe the next competition winner I pick will be you!

Other Useful Titles

The Writers' and Artists' Yearbook
Pub: A & C Black

The Writer's Handbook
Pub: Macmillan

The Writer's Market
Pub: Writer's Digest Books

Novel and Short Story Writer's Market
Pub: Writer's Digest Books

Small Press Guide/Small Press Guide USA
Pub: Writers' Bookshop

How Grammar Works
by Patricia Osborn
Pub: John Wiley & Sons, Inc

The Penguin Guide to Punctuation
by R L Trask

Improving your Written English
by Marion Field
Pub: How to Books

Writing Science Fiction, Fantasy and Horror
by Chris Kenworthy
Pub: How to Books

Creating a Twist in the Tale
(How to write winning stories for women's magazines)
by Adèle Ramet
Pub: How to Books

An Author's Guide to Literary Agents
by Michael Legat
Pub: Robert Hale

Writing Dialogue
by Tom Chiarella
Pub: Writer's Digest Books

How to Write Realistic Dialogue
by Jean Saunders
Pub: a & b Writers' Guides

Building Believable Characters
by Marc McCutcheon
Pub: Reader's Digest Books

Writing Erotic Fiction
and getting it published
by Mike Bailey
Hodder & Stoughton

NOTES